In this book, Dr Ali provides an intelligent and compelling sociological narrative of the nature of Islam and the cultural character of Muslims in Australia. In doing so, he examines key topics under broad headings of settlement, integration, sharia, education and terrorism and looks at how these phenomena operate in the broader structure of Australian society. His deep understanding of the Australian Muslim community, coupled with the skills of an astute academic, makes this book accessible to all Australians—academics and the general public alike. It is a must-read for anyone wanting a concise, clear and articulate account of Islam and Muslims in the Australian context, with a deep awareness of contemporary realities, and will go a long way towards providing a platform for constructive discussion on the issues raised within it.

PROFESSOR MOHAMAD ABDALLA AM

Jan Ali has masterfully crafted tapestry of the Muslim story in Australia. As an artisan, he skillfully weaves information on Muslim immigration into Australia, their assertion of identity within the multicultural context of the country, de-ethnicisation of Islam among the second generation of Muslims, organizational structures, legal and educational landscape and experiences of social exclusion against the backdrop of the focus on terrorism in a globalized world. A picture emerges of a community that has been a part of the Australian history predating European settlement, but one that can also be best understood as a set of communities with differing ethnicities, interpretational preferences, and sense of inclusion as citizens. Drawing upon shades of experiences in other western liberal democracies, he reminds us that the Muslim story in Australia is both similar and different to what is happening elsewhere. A great source of information for academics, students and policy makers.

PROFESSOR SAMINA YASMEEN AM

Islam and Muslims in Australia

Settlement, Integration, Sharia, Education and Terrorism

Jan A Ali

MELBOURNE UNIVERSITY PRESS
An imprint of Melbourne University Publishing Limited
Level 1, 715 Swanston Street, Carlton, Victoria 3053, Australia
mup-contact@unimelb.edu.au
www.mup.com.au

First published 2020
Text © Jan A Ali, 2020
Design and typography © Melbourne University Publishing Limited, 2020

This book is copyright. Apart from any use permitted under the *Copyright Act 1968* and subsequent amendments, no part may be reproduced, stored in a retrieval system or transmitted by any means or process whatsoever without the prior written permission of the publishers.
Every attempt has been made to locate the copyright holders for material quoted in this book. Any person or organisation that may have been overlooked or misattributed may contact the publisher.

Series: Islamic Studies Series
Series Editor: Shahram Akbarzadeh

Text design and typesetting by J & M Typesetting
Cover design by Phil Campbell
Printed in Australia by McPherson's Printing Group

 A catalogue record for this book is available from the National Library of Australia

9780522877304 (hardback)
9780522877076 (paperback)
9780522877083 (ebook)

For my beloved family:
Amirah Ali, Amaan Ali, Aneeqah Ali and Aqilah Ali

Contents

Foreword by Michael Humphrey	ix
Abbreviations	xii
Introduction	1

Part 1: Muslim settlement, immigration, and the emergence of Islam in Australia

1 History of Muslim settlement in Australia	11
2 Immigration, multiculturalism and Muslim migrants	28
3 Muslim community and organisational development and the institutionalisation of Islam	43

Part 2: Muslim exclusion and inclusion in Australia

4 Muslim experience of social exclusion in Australia	65
5 The need for Muslim social inclusion	81

Part 3: Sharia and Muslim clergy in Australia

6 The formal accommodation of sharia in Australia	95
7 The role of Muslim clergy in Australia	114

Part 4: Islamic education in Australia

8 Origins and development of Muslim schools	133
9 Islamic studies in Australia	145

Part 5: Australia in the era of global terrorism

10 Radicalised Muslim 'Other' and countering violent extremism	163
11 Securitised Muslims and Islam in Australia	178
Conclusion	185
Acknowledgements	193
Notes	194
Glossary	217
Bibliography	220
Index	236

Foreword

Islam and Muslims in Australia combines a sociological account of Muslim immigration, settlement and community development in Australia with an account of the Muslim lived experience of the migration process. The book aims to educate people about Islam as a religion and its social and cultural presence in Australia, and about the Muslim experience of migration and the conditionality of citizenship.

The author, Dr Jan Ali, is uniquely placed to write this book as a well regarded sociologist working at Western Sydney University teaching Islamic Studies, as a respected and very engaged member of the Muslim community contributing to welfare and education, as a consultant to different government agencies on the needs of the community, and as a Muslim migrant himself, originally from Fiji.

I first met Jan as a young undergraduate when I taught at the University of Western Sydney in the 1980s. I later got to know him much better as his PhD supervisor at the University of New South Wales when he worked on the Tablighi Jama'at movement. This book is very much a synthesis of his different roles and experiences and knowledge gained as an academic sociologist, an educator of Islam and Islamic Studies, a religious person deeply concerned with the wellbeing of his community, and a citizen concerned about social justice and equality in Australia. A major theme running through the book is for social inclusion to allow Muslims in Australia to realise their full potential as citizens in a multicultural society.

The importance and enduring value of this book is as a historical document that reflects on the life of Muslim communities in Australia and the debates and issues that are shaping them in the early twenty-first century.

Jan provides the essential 'Introduction to Islam' with a brief summary of Islam's main tenets of faith, its historical origins and the evolution of its main sects. These are not just matters of cultural and historical interest but bear directly upon the everyday lives of Muslims today, especially those living in the West, with their concerns about the continuity—if not cultural survival—of social and cultural traditions in non-Muslim secular societies. While all Muslims collectively belong to the one *ummah* (community of believers) in Australia, they constitute a small community (representing less than 3 per cent of the Australian population) whose members come from diverse religious, cultural and linguistic backgrounds generated by international migration.

Their diversity presents practical problems for them to be able to reach a consensus on how to live as a religiously observant Muslim in Australia. Who has religious authority in Australia? What credentials are necessary to become an imam and who should accredit them? Who has the religious authority to interpret Islamic law in Australia, and what does such a diverse group of Muslims understand as sharia?

Jan engages in polemical debate about the logic of secular society that accepts cultural pluralism but in practice puts limits on cultural autonomy. He reasons that if sharia provides a code for a proper Islamic life, then why can't it be recognised in law? But, as Charles Taylor notes, there are (at least) three different kinds of secularism: a French version of *laicité*, where religion is strictly a private matter removed from the public sphere; the secularism produced by a population increasingly disinterested in religion even though the state may support religion; and the secularism where religion enters the public sphere but is just one voice among many—the Australian model. Jan's examination of Islamic education and Islamic schools highlights the Australian approach to religious pluralism. Independent schools, including Muslim schools, can be established but only under strict guidelines and curriculum requirements laid down by the state.

A major theme running through the book is the issue of discrimination against Muslims in Australia based on misinformed perspectives about the cultural incompatibility of Islamic beliefs and practices, or about the political transformation of all Muslims into a suspect category as a result of the international politicisation of Islam and Islamic terrorism that has turned Muslims into a suspect category. Jan's response to discrimination against Muslims in Australia is that the construction of Islam as culturally incompatible and the complaint that Muslims don't integrate are, from the Muslim perspective, expressions of their experience of social exclusion. He argues that Muslims are already integrated: they just need to be recognised as belonging. Over the past twenty years, the issue that has impacted so negatively on Muslim immigrant communities is radicalisation and the security threat of political violence in Australia. Jan explores in depth the impact of the state's counterterrorism policies, the impact of securitisation and the collective stigmatisation of Muslims, and the problems arising from framing terrorist acts as being attributable to individual vulnerability to radicalisation. Instead of reassuring Muslim communities about their status as valued members of society who are also shocked at the idea of such violence, state securitisation has produced further alienation and social exclusion.

Jan seeks to enter into a dialogue about many issues facing Islam and Australian Muslims from many different constituencies. He invites all Australians to think critically about the nature of our secular society and the acceptance of cultural difference that it implies, and to recognise the injustice of state policies that essentialise ethnicity and stigmatise the whole Muslim community. He addresses government agencies and politicians, asking them to understand the national implications of securitisation and counter-radicalisation as governance strategies for multiculturalism and citizenship. He invites Australian Muslims to reflect sociologically on the challenges of their predicament as a culturally and religiously diverse community created by international migration and to search for ways to achieve greater unity to become more active and influential voices in twenty-first century Australia. He encourages the Muslim clergy to play a more active and engaged leadership role in representing their communities in mainstream Australian political and social life.

Jan concludes his book by observing that Muslim communities are now an integral part of multicultural Australian society: they are here to stay. He argues that Australians must embrace the reality of our multicultural diversity and work at making sure everyone has the opportunity to fulfil their potential. I fully endorse his vision.

Michael Humphrey
Professor Emeritus in Sociology
The University of Sydney
14 September 2020

Abbreviations

ABC	Australian Broadcasting Corporation
ABS	Australian Bureau of Statistics
AFIC	Australian Federation of Islamic Councils
ANIC	Australian National Imams Council
ASIO	Australian Security and Intelligence Organisation
CSO	civic society organisation
CT	counterterrorism
CVE	countering violent extremism
DIMIA	Department of Immigration and Multicultural and Indigenous Affairs
EU	European Union
GIS	geographical information system
ISIL	Islamic State of Iraq and the Levant
ISIS	Islamic State of Iraq and Syria
JI	Jemaah Islamiah
LGA	local government authority

Introduction

Despite the long—if disjointed—history of Muslims in Australia, there is still a lack of sophistication in the mainstream understanding of both Islam and Muslims, leading to superficial and often harmful representations in the largely non-Muslim media. This book explores the nature of Islam and the cultural character of Muslims in Australia, and examines how certain processes, institutions and phenomena operate in the broader structure of Australian society.

Viewed in the context of the 'problem' of multiculturalism for nation-state sovereignty in a post–September 11 world, Islam has come to exist as a diasporic culture and Muslims as an immigrant community that has to cope with various secular sociopolitical environments of Australian multiculturalism. In Australian multiculturalism, which promotes cultural assimilation as the long-term objective of nation-building, Muslims find themselves to be a minority group. Challenged by this, they are forced to negotiate and innovate to sustain their religious identity in the context of modernisation and assimilation in liberal Australian multiculturalism. I examine these in the context of settlement challenges Muslims face, and look at whether these challenges have been met by the state. Muslims, like any migrant group, have various needs—some short-term, such as settlement assistance and services upon arrival; and some long-term, such as job security so they can be included in Australia's project of nation-building and cultural diversity. An understanding of the fundamentals of Islam and its value system for adherents in the Australian media and the education system, for instance, would also prove beneficial for this Australian project.

In this book, selected aspects of Islam and Muslims in Australia are considered under the broad headings of settlement, integration, sharia, education and terrorism. I open with a brief account of the earliest recorded Muslim presence in Australia: the contacts between Macassan Muslim fishers and Indigenous Australians dating back to the fourteenth century, when the two groups were engaged in a trade of trepang (sea cucumbers), followed by the cameleers commonly called the 'Ghans' (shortened from Afghans) who were instrumental in the exploration of the Australian deserts, establishment of trade and communication routes, and industrialisation of Australia's interior in the late nineteenth and early twentieth centuries. Following this came the post–World War II waves of migration, when the Muslim population started to show real signs of growth and the institutionalisation of Islam in Australia began to occur.

Although there was clear evidence of permanency of Muslim presence in Australia in the Afghan settlements in the nineteenth century when some camel drivers married Indigenous women, started families and built mosques, it was only after the end of World War II that more formal Muslim institutions and a visible Muslim presence started to occur. This history allows us to interpret and analyse the early Muslim presence and compare it with contemporary Muslim reality, including relations or lack thereof between Muslims and non-Muslims in Australia.

Islam is a monotheistic, prophetic, egalitarian, salvational and universal religion teaching that there is only one god, called in Arabic 'Allah'. For theologians, Islam is a religion and social system and a complete way of life. Etymologically speaking, Islam is a verbal noun originating from the triliteral root S-L-M, or in Arabic *Seen, Laam, Meem*. This forms a large group of words mainly relating to concepts of wholeness, safeness and peace. In Arabic, Islam means 'complete surrender or submission to Allah'. Those who submit to Allah are called Muslim.

Established by the Prophet Mohammed in 610 CE in the Arabian Peninsula, Islam quickly spread to Iberia in the west and the Indus River in the east. Within a century of the death of the Prophet in 632 CE, Muslims had brought a large part of the world, from Spain across Central Asia to India, under a new Arab Muslim empire. The period of Islamic conquests and empire-building marks the initial phase of the expansion of the religion of Islam. Due to the vast range of racial and cultural backgrounds of the people who embraced Islam, not only in the early periods of expansion but even as recently as the last century, important internal differences resulted.

Despite the idea of a unified and consolidated community as taught by the Prophet Mohammed, deep differences arose within the Muslim community shortly after his death. The first major schism in Islam, between the Sunnis, or 'people of traditions', and the Shi'ites, or 'followers of Ali' (the Prophet's cousin and son-in-law), was initially politically motivated over the question of leadership, but over time theological differences developed. Rebellion broke out during the reign of Ali and some of his supporters split, forming a separate group that became known as the Kharijites. In response the Murjites ('those who postpone') emerged, advocating the idea of deferring judgement of other people's beliefs. As a result of translations of Greek philosophical and scientific works into Arabic during the eighth and ninth centuries, a movement of rational theology emerged whose representatives are called the Mu'tazilites (literally 'those who stand apart'). They were countered by Ash'arites, who developed a system of Islamic religious thought based on both reason and revelation.

Withstanding these internal differences, Islamic practices based on the scripture remained prominent among Muslims. Wherever Islam went, the process of Islamisation of culture followed. Islamisation entailed bringing rituals and practices under the influence of Islam and its law, or reforming them according to Islamic creed. Despite this process, Islam was never the sole source of Muslim identity: other forms of community and community practices continued in the Muslim world. Naturalisation of some aspects of Islam and Islamisation of local culture proceeded simultaneously to conform to local customs.

All these and many other sociocultural and political factors have made Islam an extremely heterogeneous religion. However, the rise of Islamism and simplistic media depictions of Islam and Muslims in the past several decades have distorted the understanding of Islamic history and culture in the West, including Australia. At worst, stereotypes portray Islam as a homogeneous, backward, hyper-patriarchal and fanatical religion and Muslim people as uncivilised, intolerant, uncooperative and violent. But the fact is that Islam encompasses a long history of intellectual tradition and a great diversity of theological, jurisprudential and puritanical practices, and Muslims embody a great deal of variation within and between cultural traditions.

If this is the case—that is, heterogeneity is the nature of Islam and Muslims in Australia—then what is Islam, and who is a Muslim exactly? If Islamic identity can be eclipsed by other types of group allegiance, is it a valuable entity for investigation?

In this book, Islam is understood to be a way of life in which all human energy and focus is directed at a single God—Allah—and anyone who subscribes to this doctrine and attests in some form to sociocultural and spiritual affiliation with Islam is considered to be Muslim. Whether the individual practises their faith or not, insofar as they unequivocally accept the fundamental tenets of Islam no matter how differently they are interpreted, they are Muslim. A Muslim who selectively practises their faith or doesn't practise it at all but still believes in the unity of God and identifies with Islam as a part of their cultural heritage is a 'faithful'. There exists a bond between Muslims who selectively practise their faith or don't practise it, and those who practise Islam regularly. This makes Muslim identity a valuable basis for analysis regarding the needs and concerns of over 600,000 Muslim people who call Australia home.

The contention of this book is that Islam in different parts of the world, including in Australia, is more than just a religion, a cultural system or a social structure: it is existentially a complex composite of diverse institutional processes and functions, social routines and norms, and sacred rituals and practices responsible for shaping the lives of Muslims. Furthermore, Muslims are more than a product of their religion. While there are some cultural norms common to most Muslim societies and periods that originate from religion and common historical locus, to assume that the ideas and practices embodied in these norms—such as the clergy class—are sociopolitically constant is far from correct. In fact, they are assigned diverse meanings and roles by sociopolitical context. The large variety of social and political forms to be found historically and in the present time cannot be explained as differences in a common model of an ideal Muslim society. They are explicable only in terms of the normal practice of social and political examination that considers change as a constant in all societies.

Thus, Islam is not a unified or monolithic religion. This has been abundantly demonstrated in numerous sociological studies of Islam and Muslims.[1] Discussing Islam particularly in the contemporary context, Gabriele Marranci states that 'Hence, since interpretations are multiple, the personal embodiments of Islam are likewise multiple. It is not Islam that shapes Muslims, but rather Muslims who, through discourses, practices, beliefs and actions, shape Islam in different times and spaces.'[2]

Language, culture, tradition, and the political and social contexts in different geographical locations certainly play an important role in making Islam eclectic. Also important are the numerous sectarian groups, theological clusters and legal schools and their interpretations, which add to Islam's further eclecticism. Islam is a religion based on sharia (Islamic law) but variations in interpretation of the law abound, contributing to both local and regional differences in what constitutes 'Islamic' practices.

It is not practically possible to discuss all the very complex aspects of Islam and Muslims in a single volume, and this certainly also holds true for *Islam and Muslims in Australia*. In this book, five broad aspects of Islam and Muslims in Australia are discussed: settlement, integration, sharia, education and terrorism. These subject areas have been chosen because they are the ones in which Muslims struggle the most and the ones that have been under some academic investigation.[3] This volume adds to that investigation, but from a rarely used sociological perspective.

Islam and Muslims in Australia are not being adequately sociologically studied, although they have become permanent features of the society. This book is an attempt to make a contribution to such a gap in the literature about Islam and Muslims in Australia. Thus, the overarching focus of the book is to explore the nature of Islam and the cultural character of Muslims and examine how certain processes, institutions and phenomena operate in conjunction with or in isolation from one another in the broader structure of Australian society.

Settling in a new country is never an easy process. Settlement in Australia for Muslims has been an ongoing critical problem, raising questions about state support during the settlement process. Like any ethnocultural group, Muslims require both short-term and long-term state support during their initial settlement so they can easily integrate into the society and start making contributions to Australia's project of nation-building and cultural diversity. For the government, the media and the Australian community at large to gain awareness of the basic creed of Islam and its value system can be particularly productive in terms of developing greater levels of tolerance towards Muslims, in turn showing Australia's embrace of cultural diversity.

Integration or inclusion faced by Australian Muslims is another ongoing major issue. In Australian immigration history, the question of who should be permitted to settle here has been directly associated with the idea of successful assimilation or integration. Australian immigration until the 1970s was essentially about maintaining the white monocultural national identity through a practice of selective immigration. This, however, changed in 1972 with the official abandonment of the 'White Australia policy', which had its origins in the Immigration Restriction Act of 1901. It was replaced with multiculturalism as the dominant force in immigration and settlement policy.

Despite Australia being a multicultural and multi-faith society and Muslims having a long historical presence in the country, Muslim inclusion in mainstream society remains dubious. Often Muslims are labelled as the 'Other' with allusions to them not being part of the broader society. The focus on Muslims since the events of 11 September 2001 has intensified, with counter-terrorism legislation increasing the tendency of 'othering' Muslims. Research[4] shows that Australian Muslims experience unequal access to the economy and that their participation in it is often restricted directly or indirectly, and that this has the potential to extend to future generations of Muslims. In light of this, a question arises: what is the place of Islam and Muslims in Australia? Muslim experiences need to be understood in the context of the dynamics and complexities of Muslim and non-Muslim relations.

Islam is a complete way of life with its own sharia (legal system). Some minor Australian political parties, often with conservative views, and shock jocks, journalists with biases, and even academics with certain agendas, have argued that Muslim experience of social exclusion or lack of integration is a direct or indirect consequence of Muslims following sharia, which is purported to be incompatible with Australia's common law system. There is evidence in

Australia of a movement towards right-wing politics that demands limits on the implementation of sharia, advocating restrictions on public veiling by Muslim women, curbing of mosque-building and private Muslim schools, halting halal certification, and imposing firmer restrictions on Muslim immigration. These political attitudes have been prevalent for some time; however, the debate about sharia has only recently surfaced in the public arena. It has centred on attempts to control the spread of sharia. Muslims in Australia are faced with the challenging task of proving the compatibility of sharia with the Australian way of life.

These developments raise another important question: has Australia been successful in accepting Muslims as valuable citizens and an important and integral part of the civil society? The popular responses suggest the existence of fear and resentment towards Islam and Muslims. Muslim practice of sharia and calls for formalisation of sharia in Australia are not a call for legislating sharia but a call for official recognition of it, and should not be a basis for fear or a threat.

Like Muslims elsewhere, Muslim religious experience and spirituality in Australia are a product of Islamic education. Islamic education influences the formation of Muslims' spirituality, prepares them for better understanding of knowledge, guides them in the provision of religious services and teaching, and trains them in preserving religious heritage. In a country like Australia, which is characteristically secular, this can be a real challenge for Muslims. Muslim schools are venues where these principles are cultivated. Although other Muslim teaching organisations exist in Australia, Muslim schools are important spaces with which the state and the broader Muslim community closely interact. The schools foster dynamic intellectual engagement with modern living, but can also become places of corporate and entrepreneurial activities. In addition, Islamic education is becoming popular in Australian universities. Unlike Muslim schools, organisations, colleges and institutes that take an essentially theological approach to religious education, Islamic education in Australian academia is taught according to the principles of social science, and students are immersed in a dynamic intellectual engagement with modern education. This is worthy of investigation.

Responses to global terrorism pose a major challenge to Muslims, particularly those living in the West. Research reveals that in the post-9/11 era, prejudice and discrimination against Muslims have increased dramatically and are pervasive in Western societies.[5] In response to global terrorism, almost all Western countries, including Australia, have developed counterterrorism strategies, policies and laws, and it is important to understand the impact of these on community cohesion, equality and human rights. Research shows that these measures are increasingly and indiscriminately targeting Muslims and alienating them.[6] The inability of the internal mechanisms of these measures to clearly differentiate violent extremist Muslims from ordinary Muslims results in the construction of all Australian Muslims as violent extremists, and exacerbates their experiences of social exclusion. Radical fundamentalism, Islam and terrorism are often lumped together and equated with political Islam in Australian political discussion, journalism and mainstream discourse. Consequently, Muslim communities encounter xenophobia and racism and come under intense official scrutiny by government agencies.

In many Muslim societies a counterculture exists alongside cultural traditions, focused on replacing culturally specific practices with those based on Islamic scripture. This dichotomy distinguishes accretional Islam from pristine or scriptural Islam. The latter is claimed to be timeless Islam, which is puritanical and transnational, transcending ethno-parochial and national boundaries and forming the foundation for an ideal *ummah* (community of believers).

The distinction between the two forms of Islam has important implications. Accretional Islam concentrates on reproducing prevailing social relations and practices, while pristine or scriptural Islam has a rigid quality instructing Muslims on the 'proper' (in line with Qur'anic teachings) way of conducting themselves. Take, for instance, Australia, where Muslims largely live in urban centres and the majority are concentrated in Sydney and Melbourne, where they have established mosques, youth facilities, schools, charity organisations, community centres and cemeteries. Given this, is the Australian experience making way for pristine or scriptural Islam and the development of a Muslim ummah or an Australian Islam? In this book I endeavour to address certain aspects of this question. However, it is critical to note that accretional Islam and pristine or scriptural Islam are sociological typologies and that in reality the boundary that divides the two groups is porous, making the task of placing Muslims into one or the other category extremely difficult and complicated.

The ideal Muslim community, or its semblance, was seriously damaged in the late nineteenth century and the twentieth century by the European colonial powers. The abolition of the Ottoman caliphate by Kemal Ataturk in 1924 was the major turning point for Islam in the Muslim world. Generally speaking, the West became directly involved in the Muslim heartland at the end of World War I, with significant and ongoing consequences. The focus of the new rulers of many Muslim countries turned to nationalism, which led to a weakening of the line that differentiated Islam and the nation-state and further complication of the concept of Muslim identity. The experience of ethno-nationalism was complemented by Islam in many Muslim countries, and therefore there was a clear mixing of Islamic and national identities and Muslims were given added layers of identity.

Before the abolition of the caliphate, those who studied Islam—particularly the Orientalists—described Islam as the Other, existing on the outside.

However, after the abolition of the caliphate and the subsequent world wars, Muslims moved westwards in more significant numbers and new Muslim communities developed in Western countries. Muslims in the West have come from many different parts of the world, including other Western countries. This has created new relationships between Muslim communities and other religious communities but at the same time has produced new conflicts and complicated experiences centring on citizenship and faith. In Australia, Muslim communities have very complex relationships among themselves and with other faith communities such as Christians and Jews, and their status as a minority community leads to many faith-based challenges and complex socio-economic and political challenges, including their membership of Australian society as second-class citizens.

In this volume only selected aspects have been covered. It is worth noting that although for many sociologists the nation-state is considered to be declining due to globalisation,[7] nation-state sovereignty is in fact on the rise in the age of the 'war on terrorism'. Since state formation inevitably renders people either citizens or aliens, the modern nation-state creates the problem of multiculturalism instead of solving it. One of the tasks of the state is to produce formal identities for its citizens. In the process, it creates membership categories where those with formal identities fall in one category and those without them fall in another, resulting in a binary division between the in-group and the out-group—in other words, between citizens and aliens.

This and other social changes raise very important questions about how migrant religious communities, such as the Muslim community, and their faith can survive in modern secular societies, particularly societies such as Australia that are characterised by religious diversity. Is there a clash of civilisations that is failing or has failed multiculturalism? Is Australia one of these cases?

For Australian Muslim communities and their leaders, the question arises of whether is it possible to live with sociocultural diversity without compromising or losing orthodox belief and practice in a setting where it is impractical to impose religious authority. Such diversity raises concerns around the implementation of religious law alongside secular law and secular lifestyle. For Muslims in Australia it raises the question of the implementation of sharia and the establishment of Muslim schools, Islamic studies, and the authority of Muslim leadership alongside secular law and secular lifestyle. The state's focus on terrorism and countering violent extremism raises further concerns about Muslim integration into mainstream Australian society and how Muslims can manage this when, for many Muslims, they and their faith are not openly welcomed into Australia's multicultural and multi-faith mosaic.

Part 1

Muslim settlement, immigration, and the emergence of Islam in Australia

Chapter 1

History of Muslim settlement in Australia

Muslim presence in modern Australia cannot be denied. Muslims form a significant part of the wider mix of Australia's diverse multicultural society.

The latter part of the twentieth century saw a new kind of Muslim movement to Australia, one in which citizens of Muslim countries arrived in growing numbers in search of business prosperity, employment, refuge and, in some instances, religious freedom. However, they were often seen as a foreign people and were kept on the margins of society away from public visibility. It is only recently, perhaps within a few short decades, that Muslims have emerged as the second-largest religious group in Australia.

Awareness and appreciation of this new Australian reality has materialised slowly. Some difficult adjustments, for both Muslims and non-Muslims, have had to be made and much work is still in progress. It is important to note, though, that it is no longer sustainable to deem Muslims and their faith as 'foreign', and the long-held view of them as the 'Other' is no longer defensible, if it ever was. They must now be accepted as part of the fabric of Australian society. Muslims are fellow citizens and equal members of society and have a rightful place as part of Australia's Judeo-Christian tradition.

Like many immigrants and ethnic and religious communities before them, Muslims have encountered serious difficulties in defining and determining their place in Australian society. They have been confronted with issues of identity, loyalty, worship, education, religious law and civil rights. Despite the commonalities of experience among Muslims who have made Australia home, there are also distinct differences. Demographically, Islam is the fastest-growing religion in the world as well as in Australia. Relatively invisible in

Australia only a few decades ago, Muslims today have significantly contributed to reconfiguring the geographical landscapes of many cities and towns through building mosques, Islamic centres and Muslim schools; the donning of Muslim attire; and introducing *halal* (permissible) commodities in places such as halal restaurants and Muslim nursing homes. Increasingly, we are seeing that the major Muslim communities and cities of the world of Islam are not only Jakarta, Cairo and Karachi but also Sydney, Melbourne and Brisbane.

Prominent and permanent Muslim settlement in Australia has its origins in the post–World War II national mass immigration program initiated by the federal government to recruit immigrants for national economic development and advancement. Muslims have arrived from diverse social, cultural and national backgrounds, making them the most diverse religious group in Australia.[1] Thus, it is more fitting to say that Muslims in Australia are numerous communities rather than a single community. These communities have emerged from places within Australia where large concentrations of Muslims live. They have developed around different languages, nationalities, ethnicities and community origins. For instance, large populations of Lebanese Muslims are found in Lakemba, a suburb in south-western Sydney, and of Pakistani Muslims in Rooty Hill, in Sydney's west.

In this chapter I look at Muslim settlement patterns over a period stretching from the fourteenth century to now and provide an opportunity to learn how Muslims were introduced to Australia and the processes through which they gradually grew in number and achieved permanency. An understanding of the past is helpful for understanding the present as it gives us a clear perspective on contemporary Muslim reality. A deeper understanding of the origins and growth of Muslim communities in Australia, which I discuss in depth in Chapter 2, is only possible with a coherent narrative of the period, which this chapter provides.

Early Muslims

The pluralistic nature of Islam in Australia belongs to an immigrant culture, and for this reason Islam is a fairly new religious tradition here. Gary Bouma confirms that 'Islam in Australia is represented by relatively recently arrived immigrant communities'.[2] It is true that Muslims have been linked with Australia since before European settlement. Andrew Jakubowicz says, 'It is feasible that ships from the fleet of Chinese Muslim eunuch admiral Zheng He reached Australia's north coast in the fifteenth century CE.'[3] Nahid Kabir notes that Islam has been documented to have had links with Australia before this time period, perhaps as early as the fourteenth century.[4] Macassan fishers from the south-western corner of the Indonesian island of Sulawesi made seasonal trips to *Marege* (literally 'wild country') on the north and north-west coastlines of the Australian continent in search of trepang, the sea slugs commonly known as *bêche-de-mer*.[5] This contact definitely predates European interest in the Australian continent, and Regina Ganter asserts 'That Macassan contact predates the arrival of the British on the Australian continent is not disputed.'[6]

Trepang are marine invertebrates well known in Chinese markets for their culinary and medicinal value and supposed aphrodisiacal qualities. Remnants of the influence of Indonesian Muslim trepangers are evident in the cultural traditions of some northern Aboriginal peoples. Ganter notes that the trepangers 'left profound imprints on the cultures and languages of the far north shores'.[7] Referring to Macassan visiting fleets, she says, 'The crews and captains were predominantly Muslim, and Muslim prayer references still survive in some secret/sacred incantations on the northern Australian shores, alluding to "Allah".'[8] Archaeologists John Mulvaney and Johan Kamminga documented that the Macassan fishers left their mark on several Indigenous communities, evidence of which can be found in the practice of intermarriage and the Macassan influence evident in various local art practices and rituals.[9] Annie Clarke, another archaeologist, found in her fieldwork on Groote Eylandt in the Gulf of Carpentaria that due to the frequent exchange between Indonesian Muslim trepangers and the Indigenous people, the latter became more strongly engaged with coast and marine resources.[10] Anthropologist Ian McIntosh similarly notes that contact between the two peoples led to Aboriginal people adapting various aspects of Islam.[11]

Due to their small numbers and temporary residency, and the absence of a fully-formed community structure, these Muslims made unsystematic and only localised impact on Australian social and cultural life.[12] The arrival of British colonists in 1788 dashed all possibility of Macassan Muslim growth in Australia. Cross-culturalist Peta Stephenson writes that:

> Indigenous and Muslim people [Macassans] traded, socialised and intermarried in this country decades before its white 'discovery' and settlement … Above all, Indigenous engagement with Islam has bequeathed to Australia a largely unknown human heritage in the form of memories, precious belongings, bicultural or multicultural identities and spiritual identifications that continue to be proudly invoked by descendants across the country.[13]

Then came the cameleers, commonly called the 'Ghans' (shortened from Afghans). Jakubowicz writes that 'Muslim Afghans, Pushtu and Dari speakers from the northwestern provinces of British India had been brought to

Australia in the mid-nineteenth century as cameleers in support of European exploration and communication.'[14] As the Ghan community grew, Durranie Afghans, Tareen Afghans, Pishorie Afghans, Punjabi Indians and Bengali Indians joined gradually.[15] These Ghans were pivotal in helping explore the Australian deserts, establish trade and communication routes,[16] and industrialise Australia's interior,[17] and in the process formed small Muslim communities called 'Ghantowns'.[18]

Compared to the Macassans, the Ghans made a more lasting impact on Australia religiously as they were the first Muslims to institutionalise Islam. The first mosque was built in Marree in northern South Australia in 1882, followed by a 'Ghantown' mosque built in 1889 in Broken Hill in outback New South Wales; the latter survives as a museum occupied by the Broken Hill Historic Society.[19] The Afghans also built mosques in Adelaide in 1890, Perth in 1904, and 1907 in Brisbane—all of which continue to function as mosques to this day.[20]

These early mosques symbolised the initial establishment of Islam in Australia. However, the introduction of the railway in the remote interior and the utility truck made camel cartage redundant and hastened the demise of the industry.[21] The situation was compounded in the early twentieth century by the malevolent 'White Australia policy', which saw a gradual public disappearance of Islam in the country.

Post–World War II Muslim migration to Australia

Muslim settlement proper started after World War II, when the Muslim population began to increase again in Australia. By now, Australian governments and businesses realised that in order for the country to be a part of postwar development, it had to grow demographically and economically. The sourcing of large numbers of migrants as workers, therefore, was related to the dynamics of the global economic position of developed capitalist societies.[22] The need for large numbers of migrant workers was not just a national issue but directly related to the nature of Australia's economy and its positioning in the global capitalist world. At the end of World War II, Australia was a developing capitalist society that had the necessary preconditions, financial structure, political will and natural resources to develop industrially. It did not, however, have adequate labour resources or capital to achieve such development.[23]

While the mass migration program initiated in 1947 sought immigrants of British origin, the ambitious targets gradually saw the net expand and become more global and culturally diverse. As a result, Australia started receiving immigrants from other overseas countries and Muslim immigration was part of the process.

Although Albanians—former citizens of the Ottoman Empire—had arrived in Australia in the 1920s and 30s, their numbers were too minute to make much difference to the national landscape.[24] Aside from the largely Muslim (Malay) inhabitants of the Indian Ocean's Cocos (or Keeling) Islands who transferred to Australia in 1955,[25] Turkish Cypriots were the first Muslim immigrants to start arriving in significant numbers in the 1950s and 60s, followed by more Turkish immigrants between 1968 and 1972.[26] Lebanese Muslims followed; they constituted the largest Muslim community in Australia by early 1970 and their numbers continued to grow, particularly after the outbreak of the Lebanese Civil War in 1975.[27,28] The period from 1950 to 1975 saw an increase not only in the Muslim population as such, but also in the number of Muslim professionals and skilled personnel who arrived in Australia, including 'teachers and engineers from Egypt, doctors from the Indo-Pakistan subcontinent, and tertiary students from Malaysia, Indonesia, Bangladesh, India and Pakistan'.[29]

It was between 1947 and 1971 that the Muslim population showed real signs of growth, increasing from 2704 to 22,311.[30] Then the last quarter of the twentieth century and the first decade of the twenty-first century saw a steep increase. For instance, in 1991 there were 148,096 Muslims, constituting 0.9 per cent of the total Australian population;[31] in 1996 there were 200,902 (1.1 per cent);[32] in 2001 there were 281,578 (1.5 per cent);[33] in 2006 there were 340,392 (1.7 per cent);[34] in 2011 there were 476,291 (2.2 per cent);[35] and in 2016 there were 604,200 (2.6 per cent).[36]

Table 1 shows the growth in Muslim population over the course of six censuses: it grew on average by 1.7 per cent of the total Australian population, or 341,910 people, from census 1991 to census 2016. This steady increase has been mainly attributed to immigration, although high birthrates have also contributed. The steady increase in Muslim birthrate in Australia is a significant factor in Muslim population growth: if this trend continues, it is possible that the number of second- and third-generation Muslims could gradually grow over the years and then become an important factor in Australia's social, economic and political reality.[37] Notwithstanding this, it is worth noting that compared to the total Australian population, Muslims are significantly more likely to be 'first-generation' Australians, meaning people living in Australia who were born overseas.[38]

Table 1: Growth change in Muslim population in Australia, 1991–2016

	1991	1996	2001	2006	2011	2016
No. of Muslims	148,096	200,902	281,578	340,392	476,291	604,240
% of total population	0.9	1.1	1.5	1.7	2.2	2.6

Source: Australian Bureau of Statistics, Censuses 1991–2016

Though Muslims live across the Australian continent, they are mainly concentrated in New South Wales and Victoria (see Table 2) and mainly live in the capital cities.[39]

Table 2: Australian Muslim population by state/territory

State / Territory	Total population	Muslims	% of all Muslims in Australia	Muslim % of total population
New South Wales	7,480,228	267,659	44.30	3.6
Victoria	5,926,624	197,030	32.61	3.3
Queensland	4,703,193	44,885	7.43	1.0
Western Australia	2,474,410	50,649	8.38	2.0
South Australia	1,676,653	28,547	4.72	1.7
Tasmania	509,965	2498	0.41	0.5
Australian Capital Territory	397,397	9883	1.64	2.5
Northern Territory	228,833	2335	0.39	1.0
Other Territories	4589	754	0.12	16.6
Total	23,401,892	604,240	100	2.6

Source: Australian Bureau of Statistics, Census 2016

From Table 2 we can ascertain that Australia's largest Muslim population lives in New South Wales—44.30 per cent of all Muslims in the country. Within New South Wales, over 50 per cent of the Muslim population lives almost entirely within a radius of 50 kilometres of Sydney, making it the city with the greatest concentration of Muslims in Australia.[40] Since the 2016 census there have been some natural demographic changes and these have probably had some impact on the configuration of the radius, leading to an expansion to over 50 kilometres.

To gain further understanding of the demographic characteristics of Australian Muslims and an insight into where the vast majority of the Muslim population resides, the information in Table 3 is invaluable. It provides an overarching picture of Muslim population in each of the top twenty local government areas (LGAs), relating to the number of residents identifying as 'Muslim' in the 2016 census.

Table 3: Top 20 LGAs in terms of number of Muslim residents, 2016

Rank	LGA	State	No. of Muslims
1	Bankstown-Canterbury	New South Wales	71,892
2	Cumberland	New South Wales	47,290
3	Hume	Victoria	32,490
4	Liverpool	New South Wales	24,551
5	Blacktown	New South Wales	22,645
6	Brisbane	Queensland	22,500
7	Casey	Victoria	22,200
8	Greater Dandenong	Victoria	18,940
9	Wyndham	Victoria	15,903
10	Moreland	Victoria	15,849
11	Whittlesea	Victoria	14,525
12	Campbelltown	New South Wales	12,438
13	Fairfield	New South Wales	11,791
14	Brimbank	Victoria	11,321
15	Rockdale	New South Wales	10,598
16	Parramatta	New South Wales	9660
17	Gosnells	Western Australia	9083
18	Logan	Queensland	8600
19	Stirling	Western Australia	7123
20	Darebin	Victoria	6643

Source: Australian Bureau of Statistics, Census 2016

Furthermore, data drawn from the 2016 census shows the breakdown of place of birth for each of the top twenty LGAs, as well as a breakdown at state and federal levels (see Table 4). Much can be learnt from this data, including the ethnic diversity of Australian Muslims, particularly in relation to the ethnic mix of each council area. One most interesting and important finding is that Australian-born second-generation Muslims are the largest group of Muslims in the country, constituting 36.4 per cent or 219,936 people of the total Australian Muslim population.

Table 4: Top 20 source countries of birth of Australian Muslim population, 2016

No.	Country of birth	Muslims	% of Muslim population
1	Australia	219,936	36.4
2	Pakistan	54,728	9.1
3	Afghanistan	42,705	7.1
4	Lebanon	34,192	5.7
5	Bangladesh	33,506	5.6
6	Iraq	21,137	3.5
7	Turkey	20,605	3.4
8	Iran	18,106	3.0
9	India	15,650	2.6
10	Indonesia	13,848	2.3
11	Saudi Arabia	9,841	1.6
12	Somalia	7,161	1.2
13	Malaysia	7,159	1.2
14	Fiji	7,023	1.2
15	Egypt	6,191	1.0
16	Syria	5,701	0.9
17	Bosnia and Herzegovina	5,561	0.9
18	Sudan	4,066	0.7
19	Singapore	3751	0.6
20	Kuwait	3577	0.6

Source: Australian Bureau of Statistics, Census 2016

The Geographical Information System (GIS) map in Figure 1 provides further insights into the demographic characteristics of Australian Muslims who live in the top twenty LGAs. The shaded areas show the geographic spread of these LGAs. It can be seen that Muslims are concentrated primarily in four major cities, namely Sydney, Melbourne, Brisbane and Perth. In the context of Sydney as a global city, the map shows that the vast majority of Muslims reside in the lower-socioeconomic area of Greater Western Sydney, which is a large region of the metropolitan area comprising the north-west, south-west, central west and far western subregions and which contains thirteen LGAs: Blacktown, Canterbury-Bankstown, Camden, Campbelltown, Cumberland, Fairfield, Hawkesbury, Hills Shire, Liverpool, Parramatta, Penrith, Wollondilly, and the western portion of the City of Parramatta Council. Following this is Melbourne, where Muslims generally tend to live away from the central city in various outer suburbs. In Brisbane they mostly live on the south side, and in Perth they reside mainly in and around the large outer suburb of Thornlie and in Mirrabooka and Beechboro, which have predominantly Bosnian communities.

Figure 1: Map of top 20 Australian LGAs in terms of number of Muslim residents

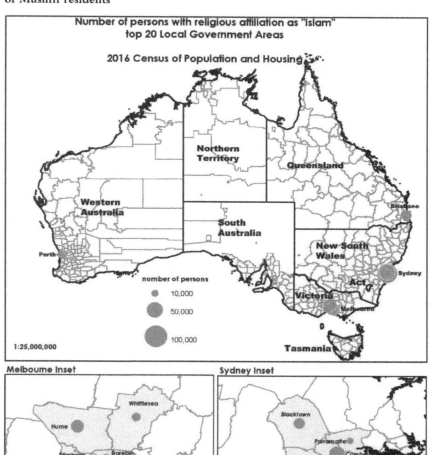

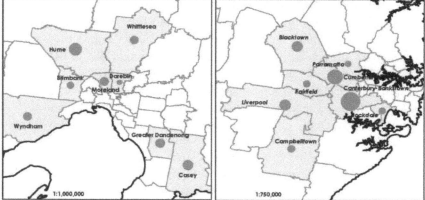

Based on data from 2016 census.

From this data, an important conclusion can be drawn that debunks the claim that Australia's suburbs are 'swamped' by Muslims. As James Forrest writes:

> The geography of Muslims is very different, and much less segregated [than Asian populations in Australia]. They are a much smaller proportion of Australia's 11 metropolitan and major urban areas. But they are almost entirely absent from many neighbourhoods and suburbs.
>
> In only 82 of the 33,337 neighbourhoods and in just one suburb—all in Sydney and Melbourne—do Muslims constitute half the local population. This amounts to 0.025%.
>
> In only four Sydney neighbourhoods and one in Melbourne (0.015% combined) is the Muslim population as high as 70%.[41]

Like other world religions such as Christianity and Judaism, Islam has various groups and subgroups. They are divided along ideological, theological, sectarian and jurisprudential lines, immensely complicating Islamic diversity. Some Muslims attach themselves to a particular theological or legal school, some belong to particular groups that seek to align religious teachings with contemporary issues or vice versa, and some belong to groups that focus on how one should interpret religious texts. Some divisions are politically based; others are theologically or spiritually based. This division is further compounded by separation along cultural, denominational/sectarian, linguistic, parochial and national lines. As such, Muslims in most parts of the world, including Australia, are not a homogeneous people. Australia's Muslim population is very diverse and the tables above provide a glimpse into this diversity.

The world's Muslim population of 1.8 billion[42] is essentially divided into two major denominations. The majority are Sunnis (87–90 per cent, or approximately 1.6 billion Muslims),[43] with Sunnism considered to be the mainstream Islam. The minority are Shi'ahs (10–13 per cent, or approximately 200 million).[44] 'Sunni' means 'tradition', and Sunnis regard themselves as followers of the traditions of the Prophet Mohammed and of the first two generations of the community of Muslims. Shi'ahs are the 'party of Ali' who believe that the Prophet's son-in-law Ali was his chosen successor (imam) and that the Muslim community should be led by a nominated descendant from the Ahl al-Bayt (family of Prophet Mohammed). There are numerous forms of Shi'ism, the largest being the Imami or Twelver (Ithna-Asharis) subgroup; it is followed by the majority of Muslims in Iran, southern Iraq, Azerbaijan and Lebanon.[45] There are two other main subgroups: the Seveners (Isma'ilis) and the Fivers (Zaydis). The two major denominations are further split into different madhabs (schools of jurisprudential thought). The Sunni–Shi'ah

Figure 2: A snapshot of Muslim diversity in Australia

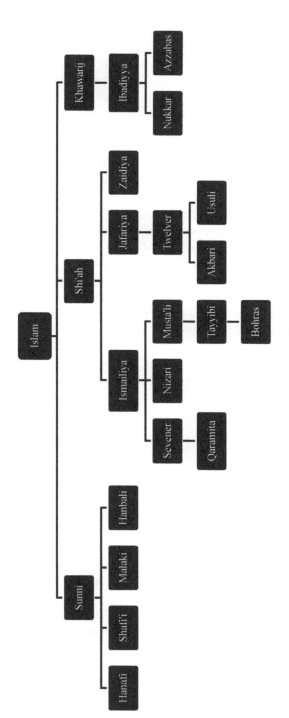

- Sufi Orders (*Tariqahs*) - The Mystic
- Bhai and Ahmadiyya Groups are considered non-Muslims by mainstream Sunnis and Shi'ahs
- Druze, Alawi, and Alevi are considered non-Muslims by mainstream Sunnis and Shi'ahs

divide is in essence more a political and sociological category than a theologically based distinction, and becomes significant only in political debates and during social and political turmoil.[46]

Islam and Muslims are further complicated by Islamic mysticism, or Sufism. Practitioners of Sufism are known as Sufis, and they go beyond meeting the external requirements of Islam to discover or reach God in personal experience through spiritual concentration and devotion. Within Sufism a number of Sufi orders, known as tariqahs, exist; they can be from the Sunni sect or the Shi'ah sect. Some Sufi rituals and practices are controversial and are criticised and even rejected by traditional elements in the Sunni and Shi'ah camps.

Druze, Alevis and Alawis are small subgroups often linked to Shi'ism; they are considered to follow a mixture of unorthodox and non-Islamic beliefs and practices. Orthodox Sunni and Shi'ah Muslims consider such beliefs and practices un-Islamic and therefore renounce Druze, Alevis and Alawis as non-Muslims. Similarly, Baha'i and Ahmadiyya are nineteenth-century offshoots of Sunni and Shi'ah Islam and their adherents are considered by most mainstream Muslims—both Sunnis and Shi'ahs—as non-Muslims and heretics because their forms of religious belief and practices are contrary to orthodox Islamic doctrine and tradition.

In Australia the vast majority of Muslims belong to the Sunni denomination, followed by a minority belonging to the Shi'ah denomination. What generally exists in Islam and Muslim populations elsewhere, both in Muslim-majority countries and diasporas, is true in the Australian context (see Figure 2).[47]

Abdullah Saeed notes:

> [Muslims in Australia] come from practically every corner of the world: from the Middle East, Russia, Europe, the Indian Subcontinent, Africa, South East Asia and even China. They speak languages ranging from English, Arabic, Turkish, Persian and Bosnian to Chinese, Tamil, Italian, German, French, Greek, Croatian, Thai, Vietnamese, Serbian, Spanish, Russian, Maltese and Hungarian.[48]

According to Riaz Hassan, Muslim migrants have been arriving in Australia from various parts of the world for many years. Using 2011 census data, he calculated that 'Altogether Australian Muslims came from 183 countries, making them one of the most ethnically and nationally heterogeneous communities in Australia.'[49]

First-generation Muslim immigrants

The experience of first-generation Muslim immigrants, in Australia and other Western countries, has generally been characterised by the fear of losing their culture and faith. This was abundantly evident in the 'Rushdie affair' of the late 1980s. The controversy over Salman Rushdie's 1988 novel *The Satanic Verses* was a significant incident that drove home to many Muslim immigrants in Britain that living in the West posed dangers to their culture and faith. On the one hand, living in the West could represent the fear of losing cultural and religious values; on the other hand, making *hijrah*[50] or the act of travelling to the West could produce a 'heightened sense of being Muslim'[51] and draw '[t]hose Muslims who may not have been active in the mosque in their country of origin ... into a deeper level of participation as they make their place in the new community'.[52] In Islam the tradition of 'travelling'[53] has played an important role in gaining greater religiosity. Hijrah is one example; the practice in Sufism of moving from place to place to preach and promote Islam is another.

As discussed earlier, Muslim immigration and settlement experience in Australia has been one not of cultural assimilation but of an increased awareness of ethnic and religious identity. Furthermore, for a vast majority of Muslim immigrants, social marginality as semiskilled and unskilled workers has rendered them particularly susceptible to unemployment, welfare reliance and racism as a further basis for emphasising their separate identity.[54] Those with professional qualifications and overseas university degrees have even been forced to join the ranks of unskilled workers because their qualifications are devalued and in some cases unrecognised. First-generation Muslim immigrants, not only in Australia but in the West in general, share a common social background: they are overwhelmingly from rural and poor urban backgrounds, and migrate to large cities.[55] This is true of, for example, Turkish and Lebanese Muslim immigrants in Australia,[56] Maghrebians in France,[57] Bangladeshis, Indians and Pakistanis in Britain,[58] and Turks in Germany.[59]

This process of identifying urban ethnic groups has had a diverse impact on Muslim immigrants. Michael Humphrey notes that some Turkish first-generation immigrants in Australia 'put greater emphasis on their ethnic consciousness than on their religious one. Travel in their case permitted greater political and religious freedom than had existed in Turkey.'[60] He also notes that Kurds identified themselves differently (based on their ethnicity) from Turks in an attempt to strengthen their separate sectarian awareness and identity by establishing distinct community associations.[61] The Turkish Government's direct role in establishing mosques in Australia and recruiting imams from Turkey has also helped to intensify internal ethnic and religious segregation among Muslim immigrants from Turkey.[62]

Gary Bouma and his colleagues observe in their work similar developments of ethnic segregation and religious awareness among first-generation Pakistani immigrants in Australia.[63] They note that 'their practice in the homeland was "automatic" or "unreflective", whereas migration brought a new depth to their faith and religious practice became more regular',[64] and found that Pakistani immigrants acknowledged that it was in Australia that they became more conscious of Islamic values and practice. As one respondent said, 'I was not a religious person when I arrived in Australia. As the children grew up and the Pakistani community increased I also experienced an awakening of religious fervour.'[65]

The urban multicultural experience permitted Muslim immigrants to cement their collective Islamic identity and stress their cultural difference by incorporating their social and ritual needs into daily living within the broader structure of the state system. Common key concerns with organising Muslim life-cycle rituals—birth, marriage and death—became important foundations for interacting with state institutions, which then paved the way for the establishment of national organisations to look after the interests of the whole Muslim population in Australia—for example, the development of the Australian Federation of Islamic Councils (AFIC). Importantly for Muslims, official multiculturalism policies established legislation against discrimination and racism.

However, the degree to which multiculturalism promotes equality and 'unity in diversity' has never been unlimited. Limits of multiculturalism, for instance, can be seen in the opposition expressed towards the establishment of places of worship in the suburbs of major cities. The propensity to alienate and marginalise underscores the inbuilt uncertainty in acknowledging cultural diversity within Australian multicultural society.[66] The Muslim immigrant identity becomes essentialised and racialised through viewing Muslims as a homogeneous group. This involves rendering the Muslim identity under the process of immigration and settlement—through the involvement of state institutions in the so-called interest of multicultural principles—traditional, conservative and even problematic.

Second-generation Muslims

Tariq Ramadan[67] argues in his *Islam and Muslims in Europe: A Silent Revolution Toward Rediscovery* that second- and third-generation European-born Muslims have helped reorient the political debate from the temporariness of the Muslim presence in Europe to its permanency. He claims that many Muslims:

> [do not] have a genuine feeling of belonging within the European society. [However, the] mind-set that prevails among some second-

and third-generation Muslims that one should live isolated, ignoring the societal context without even having mastered the language, makes no sense. The community is the place for enlightenment of the spirit and should provide serenity and an intellectual vigour that permit the blossoming of the Muslim individual as a European citizen.[68]

Thus, Ramadan argues, Muslims have been living in Europe for a considerable length of time and the raising of the issue of a permanent Muslim presence there by second- and third-generation Muslims is a serious attempt on their part 'to carve a place for themselves within European intellectual and social spheres'.[69] For second- and third-generation Muslims Europe is not the *dar al-harb* (abode of war, or un-Islam) once seen as such by their immigrant parents, but 'home'—a *dar al-Islam* (abode of Islam) 'where Muslims ... [should be permitted] to live in security and according to [Islamic] law'.[70] Unlike the first-generation immigrants, these younger Muslims demand (with the strength of their European citizenship) the right to express their faith visibly and develop a truly European Islamic culture.

In comparison to the European situation, Australian Muslim immigrants used their citizenship rights to demand recognition of their Islamic identity within Australian multiculturalism from the very beginning, when the first-generation Muslims arrived in the 1970s.[71] In a sense, then, Australian multiculturalism was already a *dar al-Islam* because it permitted the pursuit of a good Muslim life and offered a genuine feeling of belonging. One measure of Muslims feeling a sense of belonging to Australia is their accepting Australian citizenship in very large numbers.[72] This fact is confirmed by David Smith and colleagues, who used 2006 census data and statistics from the Department of Immigration and Citizenship to find that naturalisation rates were particularly high among immigrants from those countries from which Muslims predominantly came.[73]

The second-generation Muslim experience of living in Australia is not homogeneous, as Muslims from different ethnic backgrounds experience life in different ways. However, Turkish and Lebanese Australian Muslims (who constitute the two largest Muslim communities in Australia) have faced racism and marginalisation similar to that faced by minority Muslim groups in other countries of the West. Examples include the Turks in Germany, and Bangladeshis, Indians and Pakistanis in Britain. This is not to suggest, however, that Muslims from other ethnic groups do not experience racism and marginalisation in Australia. In fact, it would not be an exaggeration to state that most Muslims have experienced prejudice at one time or another based upon the socioeconomic position of their ethnicity, and have faced classification as foreigners despite possessing Australian citizenship or being born here. Joshua Roose notes:

> Young Australian Muslim men and women have been forced to make their transitions into adulthood in a decade [2001–10] when they, and those who look like them, have been placed under extreme societal scrutiny and subjected to considerable hostility and everyday acts of racism ... Australian Muslims have been faced with considerable social pressure to conform and subscribe to a generic manufactured rubric of 'Australian values', while simultaneously coming to terms with what it means to be a Muslim in Australia.[74]

Shahram Akbarzadeh claims that:

> In the context of looking for ideas and practices to define their place in society, the constant questioning of Muslim affiliation to Australia has led many impressionable youth to define themselves in opposition to the group that excludes them. This is a counter-identity to what they perceive to be the dominant identity.[75]

Muslims in general and young Muslims in particular often find themselves under great pressure to acclimatise and blend in with a so-called 'Australian way of life' or 'Australian value system'. In the process, many withdraw from society and keep away from the visible elements of Muslim identity.[76] Akbarzadeh writes: 'They feel targeted unfairly by the media and government policies. They feel their belief system and value system to be subjected to ridicule and derision, and labelled "un-Australian".'[77] Discrimination, prejudice, alienation, marginalisation and vilification end in a great sense of fear, anger, disillusionment and stress among young Muslims.[78] As discussed earlier, such discrimination and marginalisation promotes a sympathetic identification among Muslims in the context of Muslim immigration and with Islam. For second-generation Muslims, then, Islam is a source of bona fide identity that is held and expressed with a sense of heightened pride.

Similar to the case in Europe, in Australia second-generation Muslims are becoming increasingly involved with Islam through participating in what Lars Pedersen refers to as 'newer Islamic Movements'.[79] These are movements of non-ethnic tendencies with a focus on making Muslims 'better' Muslims, based on Islamic scripture. Non-ethnic or universalistic revivalist movements such as Hizb ut-Tahrir (Liberation Party) and Tabligh Jama'at (Convey the Message of Islam Group) in Australia fall in the category of newer Islamic movements. While Hizb ut-Tahrir is political in nature, Tabligh Jama'at is apolitical and ascetic. However, both of these de-ethnicised movements engage in proselytisation. In Australia they appeal to Sunni Muslims[80] from all walks of life, including a large section of Muslim youth. Young Muslims who are second-generation Australians are particularly attracted to Tabligh Jama'at as they increasingly deal with challenges on a number of fronts: racial discrimination, high unemployment, rising 'Islamophobia' and intergenerational tension.

The slow de-ethnicisation of Islam in second-generation Muslims and the development of non-ethnic revivalist movements does not necessarily mean that Muslims in Australia (or internationally) have achieved homogeneity. Although globalisation has broken almost all communication barriers and the world has become a borderless and interconnected sphere, Muslim homogeneity or Islamic recentring is far from being achieved and remains an ongoing project for Muslims globally as well as for those residing in Australia.

Muslim connection to Australia predates European contact. For a number of centuries Muslims visited Australia and traded with its original inhabitants. Large-scale Muslim settlement in Australia only began after World War II as a surge of people left their crisis-ridden places of birth in search of a prosperous life. International events such as the 1973 Arab-Israeli War and the oil crisis of the 1970s, the Iranian Revolution and the Bosnian ethnic war added to Muslim afflictions, creating a new wave of settlers. Australia became home to Muslims from very diverse social, cultural, ethnic, economic and political backgrounds. The way Muslims have settled in Australia as their new home is a reflection of this diversity. Their settlement patterns and experiences have been inevitably dissimilar, and despite a notional bond with the *ummah* (community of believers), real cooperation between Muslim settlers has always been inhibited by their sociocultural, ethnic and parochial diversity.

Chapter 2

Immigration, multiculturalism and Muslim migrants

When European settlement began in Australia in 1788, Australia's Aboriginal population was around 400,000. While the Aboriginal population has declined since, the overall population has increased to the point that there are now over 25 million people residing in Australia. Migration has been the chief force behind this demographic change.

Australia has a rich migration history and is a nation of immigrants. The majority of its European settlers—the convicts brought in from Britain, Ireland and, to a lesser extent, other British colonies between 1788 and 1840—were decidedly involuntary migrants. They were joined by small numbers of voluntary migrants between the 1830s and 1850s, again predominantly from Britain and Ireland, who mainly came using their own resources; some received assistance from public or private schemes that existed at the time.

The discovery of gold near Bathurst in New South Wales in 1851 fundamentally changed the nature of Australian migration. People entered the country in substantial numbers from considerably varied sociocultural, economic and national backgrounds. While the vast majority arrived from Britain and Ireland, others came from Continental Europe, China, the United States, New Zealand and the South Pacific.

In 1901, when Australia was federated through the process of bringing together the six separate British self-governing colonies of Queensland, New South Wales, Victoria, Tasmania, South Australia and Western Australia to form the Commonwealth of Australia, control of immigration changed. The new Commonwealth passed the Immigration Restriction Act, often referred to as the 'White Australia policy', which effectively banned people who were known then as 'non-white'. The idea behind the policy was to keep Australia British, white and Anglo-Celtic, and exclude non-whites from immigration because they were racially unqualified for naturalised citizenship.

The legal racialisation of non-whites rendered them as eternal foreigners who were naturally unassimilable to Australian society. Migration never ceased, though, because there was a perceived need for population growth and economic development. The government kept strict control over it, giving priority to British and Irish settlers. From the time the White Australia policy was established until it was legally ended in 1973, migrants continued to arrive but were officially required to assimilate into Australia's Anglo-Celtic culture. A number of displaced white European Muslims from parts of Europe—principally from the Balkans, particularly Bosnia and Herzegovina—were able to enter Australia. Like the Albanian Muslim immigrants before them, the European heritage of these displaced Muslims was seen as being in harmony with the principles of the White Australia policy.

The White Australia policy was terminated in 1973 under the first Labor government since 1948. The racial definitions of the national project were discarded and racial and religious barriers to immigration were removed. Australia was declared a 'multicultural' society and the official immigration policy changed, replacing the migrant quota system, based on country of origin and preservation of racial 'homogeneity', with 'structured selection' based on personal and social attributes and occupational group. Multiculturalism was developed and promoted in an attempt to shape Australia so it could situate itself in a post-racialised space within a globalising world. In the same year the Australian Citizenship Act was established, giving all migrants the right to equal treatment.

With a new outlook, Australia was now open to potential migrants from all nations of the world. Thus, large-scale Muslim migration of non-whites and non-Europeans began in earnest in the 1970s. Since then, Muslims have arrived in gradually increasing numbers to make Australia their permanent home. However, their task has been neither smooth nor simple, and in fact for some it has been quite challenging. Despite Australia's claim to be the most multicultural country in the world with wide-ranging community acceptance of cultural and religious diversity and celebration of cultural inclusion, and the government's rhetoric of commitment to fostering a harmonious and culturally diverse Australia and the elimination of racial discrimination, the Australian Muslim experience has been one of challenge and marginalisation, with far-reaching consequences.

In this chapter I examine Australia's immigration program and policy, including Australian multiculturalism. I argue that although the revised immigration policy paved the way for a rapid increase in the Muslim population, the Muslim influx to a certain degree generated fear and prejudice in a small section of the Australian population, which potentially led to Muslim economic and social disadvantages. Australians who were unfamiliar with Islamic culture viewed Muslim immigrants as a threat to the majority culture and values, and to security. This public ignorance, coupled with recent international events—namely, the Iranian Revolution, the Gulf Wars, and the events of 11 September 2001 and subsequent terrorist bombings in various parts of the world, particularly in the West—has often put Australians on edge and on 'Muslim alert'. An aura of negativity towards Muslims has subtly surfaced in the media and among some politicians, policymakers, social workers and even academics and researchers, which has resulted in Muslim alienation and marginalisation, and Muslims' retraction from mainstream Australian society.

Muslim ethnic diversity

Like migrants in general, Muslims migrate to Australia for various reasons. Economic advantages and educational opportunities, family reunions and escaping political oppression in their homeland are some of the more prominent reasons for making Australia their permanent home.[1] While some migrants have come from Islamic monocultures such as Afghanistan, Pakistan and Iraq, a lot have arrived from culturally and religiously diverse countries such as Albania, Lebanon and Nigeria.[2] As a result, Muslim migrants have different experiences of Australian society and cannot be homogenised. The plurality of Muslims and their experience as migrants contrasts strongly with popular media representations of Islam and Muslims being uniform and homogeneous.

The majority of Muslim migrants have settled in the capital cities, particularly Sydney and Melbourne.[3] These large urban centres provide relatively cheap accommodation, particularly in outer suburbs, and offer employment in the manufacturing and service industries. They are also home to other groups from the same ethnic backgrounds, which meets the sociocultural and emotional needs of new Muslim immigrants.[4] Thus, Muslim immigrants have settled close to each other. Following the dominant pattern of immigrant settlement in Australia, they have gravitated towards their own ethnic circles and concentrated in working-class suburbs of Sydney and Melbourne.[5] In Sydney, Muslim communities are concentrated in four LGAs: Bankstown-Canterbury, Cumberland,[6] Liverpool and Blacktown.[7]

The overwhelming concentration of Muslim immigrants in Melbourne and Sydney corresponds to the settlement patterns of Mediterranean migrants. According to the 1991 Australian census, 50 per cent of Muslim immigrants had settled in Sydney and 23 per cent had settled in Melbourne.[8] This trend continued, with 2011 and 2016 Australian Bureau of Statistics (ABS) data showing that almost 80 per cent of Muslims in Australia lived in the major metropolitan cities of Sydney and Melbourne.[9] Michael Humphrey observes that chain migration—by which individuals immigrate and later bring over families, relatives and friends—and close settlement were pivotal in creating the geographical concentration of Muslim immigrants, emphasising the significance of social relations based on parochial and family ties and ethnicity.[10] He claims that 'Muslim immigrants have entered Australian society through the cultural mediums of family, community and religion which have located them in social spaces shaping their status, employment and residence patterns.'[11]

All this means that the established social relations of the family and village community have become even more firm and indispensable resources of social exchange. Consequently, they have helped to create social microcosms that have been meticulously built through the application of personal efforts in homemaking, family creation, ethnic language maintenance, and selective shopping based on culture. These social microcosms are also maintained and further extended transnationally by recognising the importance of maintaining links with the past, which is done, for instance, by going 'home' for a visit, sponsoring family members to immigrate, and sending money to parents and extended family back home.[12]

Family and community bonds have been of paramount importance for Muslim immigrants, for whom these bonds are a source of support during settlement and a means of re-establishing their traditional social worlds and ultimately obtaining Australian citizenship. Family, in particular, has been the principal resource in reproducing social and religious culture.[13] Chain migration made immigration possible and acted as the vehicle for penetrating broader society. Family and community bonds facilitated residential grouping, from which emerged Muslim community and Islamic life. As Humphrey notes, 'The family and village community was used as the basis for recreating community and re-establishing religious life.'[14]

However, the emergence of Muslim communities and Islamic life is not so autonomous and has involved a complex web of institutional interactions and coming to terms with certain ideological realities—namely, integration, assimilation and multiculturalism. The nature of Muslim communities and Islamic life in Australia, which I discuss in detail in Chapter 3, therefore needs to be understood with these facts and variables in mind.

Immigration and assimilation

In Australian immigration history, the question of who should be permitted to settle here has been directly associated with the idea of successful assimilation.

Immigration during most of the twentieth century was essentially an issue of maintaining the white monocultural national identity through the practice of selective immigration.[15] This was at a time when a large part of the world was under British rule and British civilisation reigned supreme. British people were very patriotic, placing strong stress on the familial ties between themselves and Australians. These ties were underpinned by the shared character of Britons through language, history, heritage and common ancestry.[16] At the centre of Australian national identity was Britishness, with a strong sense of whiteness. Australians saw themselves essentially as 'white' and 'British'. This outlook was seen as a way to develop Australia and assist its participation in the post–World War II global order based on ethnic and cultural 'purity'.

In nineteenth-century Australian colonial society, culture and race were key issues in the creation of the nation-state. Alongside Britishness, whiteness was integral to Australian national identity. The birth of the Australian nation-state and the transition from colonies to a constitutional monarchy in 1901 clearly acknowledged membership in terms of race. The focus on the preservation of Australia's 'racial purity' was so immediate and intense that the newly formed federal parliament wasted no time in passing the Immigration Restriction Act as a priority and its first major piece of legislation. Its legacy was the White Australia policy, which survived beyond the postwar period of Australian mass migration[17] into the 1960s. The policy reinforced British race patriotism and was entwined with the notion of Australia as a British nation, and continued to shape the postwar immigration initiative.[18] It was adopted for the single purpose of preventing non-Europeans from entering Australia, and was born of a racial idea that was supported across Australian society and played a pivotal role in the formation of the Commonwealth's discriminatory immigration policies. As Nahid Kabir writes, 'It was essentially based on an ideology of white racial homogeneity.'[19]

The Australian Government realised as early as 1945 that attitudes towards non-British migrants had to change in order to boost the country's population. Population increase was associated with a plan to encourage migrants to assimilate into the 'Australian way of life' and for Australia not to lose its homogeneous British identity.[20] Non-British migrants were permitted to enter Australia based on their ability and willingness to easily and quickly assimilate.[21] They were expected to assimilate into the Anglo-Celtic British culture and turn into good Australian citizens.[22]

Assimilation was the approach adopted towards difference to ensure cultural uniformity, expressed as Australian national identity. The key aim of the assimilation policy was the preservation of an imagined homogeneous national community founded on British culture and institutions.[23] According to Reginald Appleyard, 'The justification of what has been called a "White

Australia Policy" was the desire on the part of the Government to maintain a predominantly homogenous, European-type population.'[24] Catriona Elder explains that:

> The logic was that white Australia would be created culturally if it could not be created ethnically ... Newly arrived migrants were invited to come and settle in Australia and make it their home. They were asked to live by the laws of the country and in return receive the benefits of life in Australia. Migrants had to assimilate—be the same—and the type they had to assimilate to, or become the same as, was Anglo-Australian. This was the standard that all citizens or potential citizens had to meet.[25]

Assimilation was basically a racist model that expressed the supremacy of the Australian host society in cultural rather than racial terms.[26]

In the first half of the 1960s, Britishness in Australia started to wane due to the sources of migration beginning to change. The program that allowed a large influx of immigrants from different parts of the world began to weaken the palpably racist construction of the Australian nation-state, with the ongoing arrival of non-British immigrants fracturing the formal ties among Britishness, citizenship and nationalism. The official stance on Australian nationalism and citizenship began to change as early as 1958, when for the first time the Immigration Restriction Act was subjected to reform through abolishing the openly racist dictation test.[27] In 1959 further changes were made, allowing Australian citizens from an immigrant background to sponsor their non-European spouses and single young children to immigrate.

By 1964, importantly, the rules governing the entry of people described as 'of mixed descent' had been relaxed further.[28] Then, in 1973, race and culture were removed from official discourse on the recruitment of immigrants, with the Whitlam Government officially abolishing the White Australia policy and replacing it with multiculturalism as the dominant element in immigration and settlement policy. By this time, mass immigration was changing the character of Australian society: it became literally multicultural.

The aim of multiculturalism was to confer equal opportunities on all Australians regardless of their race, colour, ethnic origin or religion, with discrimination based on any of these becoming unlawful. The policy was embodied in the Racial Discrimination Act 1975, which made it unlawful:

> For a person to do any act involving a distinction, exclusion or preference based on race, colour, descent or national or ethnic origin which has the purpose or effect of nullifying or impairing

the recognition, enjoyment or exercise, on an equal footing, of any human right or fundamental freedom in the political, economic, social, cultural or any other field of public life.[29]

This meant that multiculturalism as the official national policy prohibited discrimination on the basis of culture or race in the recruitment process of immigrants and their treatment in Australian society. In this regard, as Kabir writes:

> Multiculturalism legitimised ethnic diversity within the framework of shared Australian core values: the rule of law, the values of tolerance, harmony, free speech and giving others 'a fair go'. It encouraged the sharing of cultural diversity rather than excluding one from another or forcing them into separate enclaves. It sought to make clear that colour, language, style of dress or mode of worship, would no longer be permitted as historical exclusionary policies. It introduced ethnic affairs' commissions, multicultural education, interpreting services, ethnic broadcasting, and adult migrant English language teaching.[30]

Australian multiculturalism and Islam

Multiculturalism became a concept and policy developed to respond to the growing ethnocultural diversity of Australian society as an outcome of mass immigration in the decades following World War II. It effectively became a mechanism for the management of cultural diversity in Australia.

Government policy on immigrant settlement since the 1940s has often been in a state of flux, with the emphasis moving from assimilation and integration to multiculturalism and, in recent years, a return to assimilation and integration—or what might be called 'assimilation-based integration', garbed in the rhetoric of 'social inclusion'[31] in the name of 'security'.[32] Assimilation policies of the 1940s and 1950s forced migrants to learn English, embrace Australian cultural practices, and promptly assume a new identity that was reflective of the Australian-born population. However, as Lisa Irving writes:

> By the mid 1960s, it was becoming apparent that assimilation was not working. Though immigrants were supposed to become like Anglo-Australians, they were poorer, did not have equal access to education, were not as healthy and were more likely to be in a poorly paid job.[33]

The government became aware of the difficulties encountered by new migrants in assimilating, with the official mood changing and the policy softening to move away from assimilation to integration. Other factors were also in play, as Kabir notes:

> in the mid-1960s, under international and domestic pressure, economic labour needs and trade commitments, the Australian government soon rephrased assimilation as integration. Integration allowed for the retention of cultural differences and a less rapid adoption of Australian traits.[34]

It was understood that an integrational approach would be more suitable for new arrivals, who could still keep their ethnic identity but at the same time successfully integrate into Australian society. Emulating progress made in other Western countries such as Canada, by the late 1970s Australia became more tolerant of other cultures and accepting of cultural diversity or 'multiculturalism' within the larger structure of society.

The multicultural policy took a position of reciprocity, projecting a two-dimensional articulation embodying rights and obligations. The rights were linked to cultural maintenance and expression, and freedom from prejudice and discrimination. The obligations entailed showing respect for Australian democratic core values and practices, and a reciprocal expectation that the cultural expressions of members of society would be tolerated. The official Australian position articulated the celebration and facilitation of diversity and that non-Anglo-Celtic and non-Christian religious practices must not be perceived as in breach of 'national norms'. Although Australia's statements on multicultural policy never explicitly mentioned religious diversity, they did, implicitly at least, assure religious freedom.

Multiculturalism meant recognition of the diversity of the Australian population and a form of minority protection, as Kabir explains: 'The emphasis of a multicultural policy was not that everyone should be the same; rather it was an approach that stressed "unity in diversity".'[35] The policy supported the promotion of tolerance and acceptance of the diverse cultures of Australian people, and encouraged and assisted individuals, groups, organisations and institutions to reflect the multicultural character of Australia in their local and overseas dealings. It meant that all members of Australian society had the right to equal access to services, regardless of their ethnic background.

Fiona Nicoll explains that 'Policies of multiculturalism are designed to ensure that, rather than furthering the interests of a particular culture, the state functions as the neutral arbiter of the interests of an array of different, but equal, cultures.'[36] Thus, Australia's official multicultural policy states that:

> Multiculturalism is in Australia's national interest and speaks to fairness and inclusion. It enhances respect and support for cultural, religious and linguistic diversity. It is about Australia's shared experience and the composition of neighbourhoods. It acknowledges the benefits and potential that cultural diversity brings. Australia's multicultural policy embraces our shared values and cultural traditions. It also allows those who choose to call Australia home the right to practise and share in their cultural traditions and languages within the law and free from discrimination.[37]

Within the broader multicultural framework ethnic and cultural diversity is encouraged, but only to the extent that it does not undermine the values, customs and institutions of the dominant Anglo-Saxon and Anglo-Celtic society. Conformity is required. Basically, it is assumed that immigrants arriving in Australia will automatically adapt to the dominant white 'Australian way of life' and simply abandon their own customs and habits.[38] This becomes the distinctive means to full citizenship. Integration in essence, then, entails participation in the key areas of society—namely, labour, education and housing—as a pathway to a fruitful existence. Failure to integrate will result in deprivation—in other words, immigrants might be cut off from the many benefits and privileges available and offered to other citizens. Equality[39] does not mean similarity or 'sameness' but equal rights for all Australians. The idea of a monocultural society has been abandoned and difference is celebrated, promoted and made the basis of integration.

If Australia is a multicultural society in which cultural diversity is celebrated, pluralism is promoted and difference is accepted, why is it that some cultures are valued over others and belong to a particular sociocultural identity group privileged by multiculturalism? As Humphrey writes, 'The lexicon of multiculturalism differentiates and values cultures differently according to undeclared criteria.'[40] Why, for example, does the Islamic presence produced through immigration represent—or why is it perceived to represent—a threat to Australia's national mosaic? Why are Islamic beliefs and practices considered to be in discord with the patterns of public life in the principal Australian urban centres and public spaces? Why are practices such as Muslim women wearing the hijab (veil), or prayer and fasting, seen to challenge the 'normative patterns' of the modern public sphere and its ideals? These examples bring out the limitations of multiculturalism, particularly as a purported form of minority protection. They raise concerns about group inequalities that relate less to cultural disadvantages and more to socioeconomic deprivations. They also raise questions about the notion of socioeconomic equality in the public sphere, and the kind of cultural equality envisaged and privileged in the multicultural framework that the framework purports to provide to minority groups in the public domain.

Attitudes towards Islam and Muslims in Australia show that despite the formulation of multiculturalism as a public policy, the views of the majority group dominate. Their secular-modernist view expects immigrants, particularly from more traditional societies, to assimilate through the processes of secularisation and individualisation. This view is founded on the premise of secularism—the diminishing significance of religion—and forces religion from the public sphere into the private domain. The modern public sphere is purported to be premised on the notion of equality—not so much socio-economic equality as liberal equality within the context of political theory. The modern public sphere is a bourgeois public sphere where the conception of formal equality is somewhat constricted and narrow. The Australian public sphere is inescapably bound up and connected to a formal equality that serves as a precondition for the creation of a modern democratic public sphere. However, the purported existence of this formal equality, even as a precondition to delineating the public sphere, is inadequate in averting the public sphere from being narrow and constricted. Resultantly, it ends up serving to exclude rather than include.

Hence, what we witness on the ground is the expectation that immigrants, perhaps those from second and third generations, will eventually assimilate and embrace the modern public sphere as individuals and become divorced from their ethnic roots. It remains true, of course, that modern Australians have traditionally seen themselves as part of the 'Christian world', but Australia is a remarkably secular nation, and after Catholic–Protestant tensions eased (from the 1950s onwards), religion has occupied less of the public space, and only Christian sectarian movements have shown any 'militant reactivity' against modernity.[41]

With regard to Islam, Humphrey argues that this secular-modernist attitude sees Islam as a homogeneous culture that is resistant to modernity.[42] In the discourse of multiculturalism, a discussion on Islam is to some extent usually framed around concerns of cultural resistance and self-alienation. In Australia, Islamic organisations and culture have their origins and development in settlement and immigration processes connected in a complex way to working-class immigrants' experience of cultural alienation, social marginalisation and economic deprivation.[43] For Muslims, this immigration experience has forced them to negotiate their Islamic identity within the Australian state and society. Muslim immigrants and their children as a socio-religious community need to be taken into consideration in the design and development of public policy, and that public policy cannot persist in being indifferent to their existence. A denial of Muslim community or group identity in public places cannot be sustained, because doing so fails to recognise and acknowledge Muslims and their role, and the role of their religion, in society.

Recognition and acknowledgement by the state have to be qualitatively different from what current multicultural policies offer. The state needs to recognise and acknowledge the role Islam and Muslims play in society and, therefore, proceed to ensure inter-group equality, which in the current climate is missing. In relation to this, Humphrey argues that Islam in Australia is a reflection of the politics of multiculturalism, which limits both pluralising and homogenising tendencies:

> It is pluralising through the migration process that has generated local, ethnic community-based Islamic religious institutions which, in turn, helped decentre and localise the religious authority of tradition. It is homogenising through a multicultural politics of 're-traditionalisation'—the essentialisation of culture as a defensive, as well as representational, strategy that tends to place ethnic culture in compartmentalised social space.[44]

The conceptualisation of multiculturalism we have in Australia is inherently limiting. Obvious limits of multiculturalism can be recognised in the social and economic markers that show that more recently arrived migrants, including Muslims, are relegated to the bottom of the Australian social structure. The limits are also evident in the ways in which citizens from non-Anglo backgrounds are framed in governmental and popular ideas of Australianness. The multicultural narrative has never completely replaced white Anglo-Saxon and Anglo-Celtic Australia. The country remains Anglo-Australian, where 'belongingness' is hierarchicalised and the entitlement of migrants such as Muslims is placed below that of Anglo-Australians. It is the Anglo-Australian 'host' group who possess the power to determine who enters Australia and who doesn't, and who is accepted and who is not. Many Muslims find themselves at the mercy of Anglo-Australians who reject Muslims rather than accept them as part of the national mosaic. Muslims find themselves the subjects of unpunished vilification, public assault, open discrimination and negative stereotyping, and are told to 'Go back to where you came from'. They are seen as unsuitable members of Australian society and their religion is regarded as incompatible with Australian values. They are stereotypically caricatured as 'backward' and violent,[45] bent on to 'taking over' Australia,[46] irrational,[47] incompatible with Judeo-Christian culture,[48] and part of an extremely religious community that is counter to the Australian modern secular tradition.[49] Although Muslims belong to different ethnic, parochial, linguistic, cultural and ideological groups, making them vastly diverse, they are frequently essentialised, as noted by Humphrey,[50] and their heterogeneity is often ignored in the media[51] and public and political discourses.

For many Anglo-Australians, Australia embodies *an accomplished and privileged good* that they represent themselves; therefore, they are model hosts to all cultures. Yet in this Australian imagination, Muslims as Australian citizens are not permitted a voice in the so-called equitable Australian multicultural space: in fact, they are voiceless. The result is that the universality of the egalitarian imagination of the 'good' Australia only helps to highlight prevailing inequalities.

Thus, the negotiation by Muslims of their Islamic identity in the context of Australian multiculturalism has left Muslims to be reduced to the 'Other' in the national imagination, which is both defined and predominantly represented by the culture of the hegemonic group. It incorporates Muslims in Australian society only insofar as they contribute to the 'cosmopolitanism' of the dominant group and, therefore, merely as the 'Other'.

The widespread perception of threat and mistrust and such stereotyping of Muslims in Australia is not without consequences. One of these is a decline in interaction between Muslims and non-Muslims.[52] This in turn shapes popular notions of Australian identity and 'Australianness', resulting in discussions of Australian multiculturalism in which the compatibility of Islam with Australian values is questioned and concerns are raised about Muslims posing a potential cultural threat. While it is true that state-enforced assimilation is no longer an official policy, religious groups such as Muslim communities are still expected to comply with Australian Anglo-Saxon tradition and become absorbed in the secular system.[53] This aspect of multiculturalism is thus essentially a policy for the management of ethnic minorities. According to Ghassan Hage, it involves strategies of exclusion alongside the rhetoric of inclusion.[54] In a sense, then, this form of multiculturalism maintains the marginality and liminality of immigrants and their descendants.

Muslim marginality

In the Australian multicultural panorama, being Muslim means being located in the 'immigrant working class' and labelled as religiously 'conservative'.[55] This class description of Muslims has developed from the origins of Muslim immigrants and their real experience in the Australian labour force. A vast majority of Muslim immigrants have arrived from poor rural and urban backgrounds from mostly underdeveloped or developing countries.[56] After arriving, they are largely engaged in unskilled or semiskilled jobs in the manufacturing and service industries.[57] Muslim immigrants with academic qualifications and professional experience are usually forced by the processes of immigration to take up non-professional menial jobs. Australia considers some qualifications from underdeveloped and developing countries comparatively substandard and thus refuses to recognise them;[58] in some instances employers perceive qualifications from underdeveloped and developing countries to be inferior and thus unacceptable.

Furthermore, Wendy Lowenstein and Morag Loh assert that 'Often Australia does not recognise the overseas trade and professional qualifications of migrants, so skilled people are forced to work either at unskilled jobs or to carry out skilled work at unskilled rates of pay.'[59] As in the context of immigrants in general, the demand by Australian society for cultural accommodation of Muslim immigrants entails a slow transition. Muslims are required to initiate social and cultural adjustments to their daily social and vocational rituals by accepting the routines of the manufacturing industry where they work, and take more than one job to maintain their family or depend on limited welfare benefits with some income derived from working in the 'black economy'. The whole process of cultural accommodation imposes upon Muslim immigrants a modification of the rituals of their daily life in accordance with the practices of broader Australian society; in so doing, it impacts on the entire basis of Muslims' social existence. The impact is felt on all aspects of social life, including marriage, social networks, residency, gender relations, housing and consumption patterns. This makes reconciliation between ethnic culture and customs and new social and work rituals challenging and even problematic.

These are the demands of the class culture[60] and when Muslim immigrants fail to fulfil them, they also fail to meet, as a group, their expected economic participation and are consequently censured for not making a fair contribution to the national economic growth and development of the whole society. Their over-representation in the statistics of welfare benefits, workers compensation claims and unemployment give them a negative image and push them to the lowest strata of the social hierarchy.[61] Mario Peucker and colleagues note that:

> The persistent pattern of Muslim under-performance on key socioeconomic indicators holds significant implications for the sense of belonging and citizenship. The most immediate consequence of socioeconomic marginalisation is limited access to the resources that facilitate civic and political engagement ... Australian Muslims demonstrate significant gaps in the infrastructure, and this could undermine identification with Australia and active citizenship. High unemployment rates, low income and a persistent sense of being on the margins of society make Muslims less inclined to aspire for full citizenship. Continued disparity in

wealth and prospects of prosperity, evident in the 2001, 2006 and 2011 Censuses, work against the sense of belonging.[62]

This highlights Muslims' peripheralness in urban structures and social status in Australia.

Given their marginality to the labour force, many Muslim immigrants have been pushed into a situation of mutual dependency. The requirements of social and community reciprocity due to Muslims' social marginalisation and fear of loss of family and cultural identity often force families and communities to guard the environments in which traditions are nurtured.[63] While on the one hand family and community are strengthened as principal cultural capital through the immigration policy and social and economic marginalisation, on the other hand they are rendered tenuous by a fear of loss of cultural heritage and identity through the process of immigration. Thus, Muslim community organisations and Islamic culture, which are the focus of the next chapter, emerge to organise the affairs of Muslims and establish Islamic values and institutions.

In postwar political and public discourses, the expected outcomes of the settlement process have always been shrouded in dispute. In other words, who should and who should not enter Australia has been under constant disagreement. However, one focus has remained constant: assimilation of immigrants.

Immediate postwar immigrants were expected to settle into the pre-existing sociocultural milieu without making noticeable changes to it. The assimilationist orientation of the settlement process expected immigrants to learn and speak English, attend Australian schools, develop an appetite for Australian food, and practically blend in. Preference was given to immigrants with white skin who would keep Australian society 'white' and would not disturb Australia's essentially British/European culture. Preservation of Australia's whiteness was a social phenomenon that anticipated and expected that immigrants would slowly give up their cultural traditions and opt for the new Australian ways. At a societal level there was no expectation of a permanent development of any new religious traditions or cultural patterns.

The influx of immigrants in the 1950s and 60s, and then in the 1970s with the abolition of the White Australia policy and finally in the 1980s, fundamentally changed the overall sociocultural structure of Australia. From descriptively a monocultural country, Australia became practically a multicultural society. Among the immigrants were Muslims who brought with them their own ethnic values and religious traditions, adding to Australia's diverse population and multiculturalism and forever changing its socio-religious mosaic.

However, the Muslim influx to some extent evoked fear and prejudice among a small section of the Australian population, which has led to enduring Muslim economic and social marginalisation. Although multiculturalism is about celebration of diversity, protection of egalitarianism and promotion of sociocultural pluralism, Muslims have been subjected to harassment, legal limitations and suspicion of their activities by some Australians. One way of understanding this is that for some, multiculturalism is about relationships between 'equals'. This kind of thinking detracts people who hold this view from focusing on pressing issues faced by minority and oppressed groups such as Muslims. They make assumptions that issues or problems facing Muslims are of Muslims' own making as they are products of their own culture. In other words, the problems Muslims face originate from their distinct culture: Islam. In this framing of multiculturalism, the same analysis is made for all group-related problems as problems seen to emanate from culture. Consequently, the analysis offered that is supposed to help develop multicultural strategies is constantly familiar and revolves around symbolic cultural equality, which ends up in systematic neglect of alternative causes of Muslim marginalisation and disadvantage. One very significant impact of this, as I discuss in some depth in the next chapter, is the establishment of substantial Muslim community enclavements complete with their own social structures, welfare services, organisational support services, and culture.

Chapter 3

Muslim community and organisational development and the institutionalisation of Islam

An exploration of Muslim community and organisational development and the institutionalisation of Islam in Australia is relevant for an improved understanding of Islam and Muslims in Australia as well as for a global comprehension of human settlement and multiculturalism. Muslim community and organisational development and the institutionalisation of Islam in Australia, which has not been studied sociologically, reflect a range of issues that go beyond the local context and include Muslim integration and adaptation to a new pluralistic and cosmopolitan society, as discussed in some depth in the next few chapters.

Muslims have a rich, inspiring and productive history in Australia. This chapter briefly covers the Afghan Muslim settlement period and then moves on to cover more extensively the period since World War II, when large numbers of Muslims arrived in Australia. In particular, I look at early Afghan Muslim settlement patterns and then Muslim settlement patterns more generally; Muslim encounters with the broader Anglo-Celtic Australian population and involvement in multiethnic Muslim communities; and the gradual development of Muslim communities, establishment of sociocultural or Muslim civic society organisations (CSOs), and institutionalisation of Islam.

The Muslim community is one of numerous different ethnic communities in Australia. Despite their minority status, Muslims have been able, together with various other communities across the nation, to maintain their ethnic and religious identities and develop their social and religious institutions, and engage with the broader community as part of multicultural Australia. The Muslim community's Islamic religious characteristic is one element in the overall fabric that forms the diversity of the Australian population and its multiculturalism.

Australia's distinctiveness is reflected in its embracing of multiethnic, multi-racial and multi-religious groups and their meaningful support as belonging to humanity and social harmony. Australian multiculturalism rejects prejudice, racism, social exclusion, suppression of minorities and extremism in all forms, including Muslim terrorism, which these days seems to have caused serious damage to social harmony between Muslims and non-Muslims who otherwise have been living peacefully in plural secular modern Australian society.

This chapter provides a narrative account of the emergence of the Muslim community and Muslim organisations, and the institutionalisation of Islam within this highly profiled population. It delineates the key social and religious trends that have shaped institution-building and relations with wider Australian multicultural society. It begins by offering a background to Australia's first pronounced and visible Muslim community, the Afghan cameleers, and contextualises the types of Muslim institution-building that have emerged with the increasing population of Muslims since World War II. This is followed by a discussion of the importance of internal Muslim diversity and different theological and cultural trends and Muslim religious needs that have shaped civic society infrastructure development and identity formation. I argue that in the absence of proper state support and resourcing, it became necessary for separate organisations, associations, councils and civic institutions to emerge to accommodate the complex and multiple aspects of Muslim community life and lay the foundation for the institutionalisation of Islam in multicultural Australia.

Muslim religious needs in Australia

Since Federation in 1901, the Australian Constitution has prohibited the Commonwealth Government from intervening in the free exercise of any religion, making Australia a secular nation-state with a sharp demarcation between religion and politics. In this framing, the state must take a religiously neutral stance: religion, therefore, is a private affair outside state control, and the state is not responsible for providing religious support or fulfilling the religious needs of its citizens. This is reflected in government policy, including immigration policy. All aspects of religion and its requirements, then, are managed by individuals or religious groups themselves. Religious organisations and institutions operate through the voluntary efforts and financial contributions of their members.

Demographically Australia is Christian, but with Muslim immigration, especially since World War II, an enormous change has occurred in the configuration of Australia's religious edifice, particularly through the establishment of a sizeable Muslim community with its own social arrangements, organisations and cultural norms and practices. Some Muslim-majority countries have noted this Australian reality and recognised the religious needs of their people and provided *sheikh*s (Muslim theologians) for assistance, especially in dealing with religious matters. For example, Turkey, Saudi Arabia, Libya, Iraq, Iran and various other Muslim states have been involved in providing financial support to *imam*s (Muslim religious leaders) to lead prayers and teach the Qur'an and Islamic studies, and for mosque-building. They have been motivated to provide this kind of support due to concerns about the wellbeing of their people, to avert competition from other Muslim states, to protect Muslims as a minority group in a Christian-majority country, and to keep open the links between home country and host nation for their former residents and citizens. It is worthwhile to note that when home states of Muslim immigrants have not been able to provide support, in some instances the Muslim residents of the new country have themselves sponsored the immigration of imams and sheikhs from the homeland.

All this, of course, is part of a gradual process. Once Muslim immigrants settle into the patterns of life in Australia, they realise their religious needs. Some people may argue that such religious needs do not exist: secularists, for example, are quick to dismiss the significance of religion in people's lives. This cannot be any further from the truth. The vitality of religion and religious organisations and institutions continues in modernity and postmodernity: people are still interested in religion and religious issues, including practising religion.[1] It took some time for Muslim immigrants to come to the realisation that existing institutions in Australia were inadequate when it came to fulfilling their religious needs. When Muslim immigrants arrive, many realise that life in Australia is not easy, and that when it comes to pursuing religious life, it is even harder.

Muslims who immigrated in the 1960s and 70s and even long before this, during the Afghan period, came with the intention of spending a brief time (say, three to five years), making some money and returning to their homeland, as can be seen from an immigrant quoted by Gary Bouma:

> In the early days we had strange feelings—no language, no mosque, no community, no organisations, no relatives, no friends. We were getting very tired of working. I was doing such hard jobs that couldn't be compared to an *Imam*'s work. But I could still be considered happy because I believed I was making good money

and I was saving a reasonable portion of it. After all I was planning to go back home in five or six years. As long as we were making reasonably good money we could put up with certain hardships. We knew that nothing comes easily. We anticipated some hardship. In later years we made friends, real good friends. We used to go to picnics together and have good times. We established community organisations, we built mosques and we began to have some social and spiritual satisfaction and our lives started to change and become more fulfilling.[2]

Not all Muslims who arrived in Australia returned 'home'. The number of those who stayed gradually increased, and over a period of time a significant Muslim community emerged. Muslims are not only an immigrant community but also a religious community. For Muslims, a religious identity is critical as it defines them. Muslims started to build their own communities along ethnic, parochial and linguistic lines and establish their own organisations, associations, councils and mosques.

Afghan cameleers and the colonial era

The first Afghans came to Australia in 1860, and Afghans continued to arrive until the 1930s. They were recruited during initial British exploration and development of Australia's scrubland and the desert centre, and played a pivotal role in opening up the vast Australian outback to Europeans and non-Indigenous settlement. Afghan men were forbidden to bring their wives to Australia, and therefore the Afghan demographic during this period was almost entirely male. During the enforcement of the White Australia policy from 1901 until the 1970s, further Afghan migration was extremely minimal.

The cameleers were widely called 'Ghans' despite the fact that many were from British India or what was referred to as northern India (which is now Pakistan) and others were from Afghanistan, Egypt or Turkey.[3] Afghans were mainly Muslims but some were from other faiths, such as Hinduism and Sikhism.[4] With their arrival, a significant semipermanent Muslim population was formed. They were employed as camel drivers in the great national project of the construction of the Overland Telegraph Line from Adelaide to Port Darwin between 1870 and 1872, which finally connected Australia with London via India. They worked on other projects, too, such as the Queensland Border Fence and Western Australia's Rabbit Proof Fence and Canning Stock Route. Another major project in which Afghan camel drivers were pivotal was the development of the transcontinental rail link between Port Augusta in South Australia and Alice Springs in the Northern Territory. Some of these exploratory and construction missions were in the most inhospitable parts of Australia, and their successful completion was only possible due to Afghans' expertise and endurance. From then on, Afghan camel drivers were in great demand.

When gold was discovered in Western Australia and other minerals in remote Queensland in the early 1890s, Afghans were employed regularly in these industries and their employment proved considerably profitable for the white camel owners, colonialists, capitalists and employers. Camels proved more resilient than horses and were better suited as the mode of transportation, particularly in rough terrain and semirural areas. The cameleers were viewed by whites as an inferior race and were therefore easy targets for exploitation.[5] They were often employed at low wages.[6]

By 1901 there were between 2000 and 4000 Afghan drivers in Australia.[7] They provided services across Australia's inland pastoral industry by carting goods, transporting wool bales by camel train, and servicing the mining industries. They set up camel-breeding habitations and rest-house stations, called caravanserai, throughout the outback, creating a lasting connection between coastal urban centres and remote sheep and cattle stations until the 1930s. From this process a succession of 'Ghan' towns were established along the railway and became commonly known as 'Ghantowns'. Afghans were not permitted to live with the white community and resided in rough makeshift camel camps in segregation.[8] Ghantowns occupied a single section at the edge of a town and consisted of a constellation of camps, sheds, cabins and houses. They were not commercial centres as such because Ghantowns harboured camels, which were kept away from the town centres ostensibly to separate rural or farm areas from the town and maintain the town's urban character. Many of the towns had at least one mosque that, in contrast to brick-and-mortar structures, was typically built from sheets of corrugated iron interposed with a small minaret. Having no government support, Afghan Muslims raised funds from within their community to purchase land and build a mosque on it. The first mosque was built in Marree in northern South Australia in 1861. Twenty-six years later, in 1887, the Broken Hill Mosque on Buck Street was built in New South Wales. The first large mosque, known as the Central Adelaide Mosque, was built in Little Gilbert Street in Adelaide in 1890, followed by one in William Street in Perth in 1904–05, and the Holland Park Mosque in Brisbane in 1907. All these large mosques are still in operation.

With the introduction of the railway in the remote interior, the advent of the automobile, particularly the T-Model Ford in the 1920s, and the introduction of motor lorry transportation, cameleers were made redundant, bringing the end of an era.[9] In 1901, when the colonies were federated, the nation's early commitment to the White Australia policy barred most non-Europeans from gaining citizenship and this further marginalised the cameleers. Without citizenship and with no prospects for employment, many old cameleers returned to their homelands.[10] Those who stayed took up other trades and ways of making a living and settled in areas near Alice Springs and various other parts of the Northern Territory.

With their numbers dwindling through repatriation and natural causes, it became 'more difficult for those who remained to retain their Islamic identity'.[11] Separated both religiously and culturally from the main white Anglo-Celtic society, a vast majority of this generation of Muslims abandoned their Islamic conviction,[12] resulting in the public disappearance of Islam.[13] Today some descendants of the Afghan cameleers can still be found in various parts of remote Australia.

Muslim communities and the establishment of mosques

Although the White Australia policy was abolished in 1972, supposedly making migration of non-whites easier, the reality was that assimilationism was still very much active. Migrants, including Muslim migrants, were still required to adopt Australian norms, values and ways of living and at the same time were expected to abandon their cultural values and practices and religious rituals and observances and blend in with Australian society, leaving it free from 'foreign' accretions.[14] Some Muslims fulfilled these assimilationist expectations, but the vast majority held firmly to their ethnic traditions and religious values. Religious identity and practices were important for many and they made every effort to maintain them, particularly through community and religious activities.

Family and village communities formed the original basis for Muslims in Australia and the re-establishment of Islamic life in their new country. In many cases, Muslim CSOs emerged from the activities of village community organisations. Michael Humphrey asserts that these Muslim community organisations were the product of family and community ties.[15] He argues that for the Muslim immigrant community, religious life emerged as one aspect of the continuation of prior village community activities in their homelands, and that as the community grew in the new context, so did the people's needs. This made necessary the establishment of separate organisations, associations, councils and civic institutions that could cater for multiple aspects of Muslim community life.[16] For example, ('post'-) village social centres or community meeting places frequently developed into provisional prayer halls and, subsequently, as the population grew and demands increased, into mosques. Islamic immigrant cultures and practices emerged from these localised sets of contacts in multicultural Australia. These contacts selectively fostered the re-creation of religious culture in a context where Muslim immigrants found their status transformed from a majority to a minority group.

The key religious interest for first-generation Muslims, as discussed in Chapter 2, was with the arranging of what might be collectively described as Muslim life-cycle rituals—birth, marriage and death—within the local community framework. Muslim village associations were important institutions for community life and played a key role in the process of settlement.[17] Consequently, mosques assumed a significant role in the Muslim settlement process. They have emerged in direct response to the growth in the Muslim population and the needs of the Muslim community. Ryan Edwards says that 'Throughout the history of a permanent Muslim presence in Australia, Muslim communities have retained a focus on establishing and maintaining local Islamic infrastructure. Historically, this has meant an emphasis on the construction of mosques'.[18] Humphrey notes that in the context of Muslim immigration, mosques were significant, but not the first, Islamic institutions in Australia.[19] He asserts that mosque associations came into being alongside various other voluntary Muslim immigrant organisations during the early period of Muslim settlement. For newly arrived Muslim migrants, settlement often proved a difficult experience. Difficulties included homesickness, culture shock, language barriers and job insecurity. The mosques performed a variety of different functions.

As in many parts of the world where Muslims are in a minority, in Australia mosques cater for multiple needs of the Muslim community and have become more than just places of worship. They have become spiritual centres for symbolising the existence of Islam, collectivising Muslims, teaching, and training Muslims in religious values and practices. Mosques also act as centres of religious, educational, cultural and social activities and welfare services. Bouma asserts that:

> After many Muslims had come, they began to discover each other. Then, with the formation of Muslim immigrant communities in, primarily, Sydney and Melbourne, there emerged mosque facilities and communities as well. The building of a mosque was often mentioned as a significant feature in the settlement of immigrants who had arrived before a mosque was established. The existence of a mosque provided an emotional resolution, or focal point, for some Muslim immigrants. They finally felt that Australia had become home for them.[20]

Apart from facilitating the coming-together of the community through regular ritual prayers and other aspects of ritual worship, mosques serve as centres for religious and social activities. They further serve as venues for the Friday congregational prayer or *jum'ah*, and the celebrations of Eid al-Fitr (festival celebrated at the end of Ramadan) and Eid al-Adha (festival of the sacrifice); and act as centres for activities and accommodation of Muslims engaged in *dawah* (preaching) work. Thus, Humphrey states:

> in the evolution of immigrant cultural institutions the mosque has often functioned as a pan-village organization, in which the culture of Muslim family and [prior] village relations become incorporated into a wider Muslim immigrant community through religion.[21]

According to Humphrey, mosques as symbols of collective Muslim presence in Australia emerged in one of the following three ways:
1. from existing community- or 'village'-originated social venues, or what may be called community meeting places
2. from an already-existing place of worship, such as a church
3. from purchasing a site and constructing a mosque on it.[22]

In regard to financing mosques, Bouma says that 'mosques in Australia have been financed by the local Muslim communities, sometimes with assistance from Muslims overseas'.[23] In either case, even though the way each mosque is established is distinct (for instance, one comes into existence through communal life, and another is based on broader community support both in terms of finance and lobbying of the local council), the purpose for establishing it remains the same: to fulfil the social and religious needs of the Muslim immigrant community. Bouma summarises this as:

> For Australian Muslim immigrants then, building mosques has been an essential part of settlement. Australia is not home for them until there are mosques in which to pray, until there are Islamic symbols atop buildings, until there are communities in which *halal* food can be obtained and Islamic education is available for their children. Moreover, although each mosque may be limited to one or a few ethnic backgrounds, the Islamic symbols cut across ethnicity and provide the basis for a kind of trans-ethnic unity grounded in religious identity.[24]

Muslims do not have to have a mosque to pursue a religious life: Islam permits the offering of prayer anywhere, such as in an office, at home, or even on the lawn in a park, as long as the place is clean. Nora Amath says:

> It is important to note that Islamic rituals do not necessarily need to be carried out or performed in a 'sacred' place of worship. Therefore, for many Muslims, the building of a mosque extends beyond a need for a sacred place; it conveys a deeper sense of community and establishes their permanency in a land.[25]

Similarly, Mario Peucker observes:

> Most mosques and other Islamic community centres in Western non-Muslim majority societies are more than just places of worship where Muslims go to perform their ritual prayers. They typically pursue a much broader agenda encompassing cultural, social, civic or even political advocacy activities. This is not only in response to the contemporary needs arising from Muslims' diasporic situation, but it is also rooted in the Islamic tradition of mosques being multi-purpose sites and centres of the community.[26]

Thus, mosques play a role beyond being merely places of ritual prayer. Classic mosques such as Masjid al-Aqsa (the grand mosque in Jerusalem) and Masjid al-Nabawi (the Prophet Mohammed's mosque in Medina) have always played spiritual, educational, social, cultural and political roles in Muslim community life. In relation to Masjid al-Nabawi particularly, Qari Asim reminds us that it was not just a place to pray but also served as a centre for Islamic teaching and learning, socialisation and interreligious engagement, lodging for travellers, and a venue for civic and political discussion.[27] Prayer is only one aspect of Islamic life, and given that Islam is a complete way of life, Muslims require mosques for other religious and social needs—particularly in the context of immigration. In this sense, the mosque as a local community institution that fulfils religious, welfare, educational and social functions assumes a role beyond a place for worship. As Humphrey remarks of the Australian context:

> As the pre-eminent community institution, the mosque becomes the domain for the assertion of separate identity and status within a pluralist political environment in which ethnicity has legitimacy. It is a centre from which demands are made on Australian political, legal and bureaucratic structures about the needs and rights of the 'community' vis-à-vis other groups.[28]

Through the mosque, Muslims make demands regarding those aspects of life considered essential to uphold religious and moral values. Such demands can include the right of Muslim girls to be allowed to wear the hijab to public schools, legal recognition of the right of imams to conduct marriages and perform burial services according to Islamic precepts, and acknowledgement of the right to pray at work. These demands symbolise the restoration of Muslim cultural tradition and Islamic practice to the public domain in the context of immigration.

In the post–World War II period, the first mosque to be built in Australia was the King Faisal Mosque in the inner Sydney suburb of Surry Hills. The site on which it sits was originally two terrace houses, which were transformed into a mosque in the 1960s by some Pakistani professionals. In the same decade, in 1969, the Albanian Australian Islamic Society built Melbourne's first mosque in Drummond Street, Carlton North. A little over a decade later, in 1977, Imam Ali bin Abi Taleb Mosque was built in the western Sydney suburb of Lakemba by the Lebanese Muslim Association; it has been claimed as Australia's largest mosque. The Auburn Gallipoli Mosque in the western Sydney suburb of Auburn is another important mosque in Australia; it was originally a house but was turned into a mosque in 1979. In 1986 a committee constituted by Turkish Australians started replacing this mosque with an Ottoman-style structure; it was completed in 1999. Unlike in other Muslim communities in Australia, mosques in the Turkish community are funded by the Turkish Government and their imams are Turkish Government employees.[29]

In Australia the largest Muslim population lives in New South Wales in the western suburbs of Sydney. In 2014, according to the research report *Mosques of Sydney and New South Wales*, there were 167 mosques in the state.[30] Out of this total, 82 mosques or 50 per cent held jum'ah and the five ritual prayers. The remaining 50 per cent were either used only for daily ritual prayers or only for jum'ah. The vast majority of the mosques in New South Wales—approximately 64 per cent—were built between the 1990s and 2010s. The report found that the number of mosques in New South Wales has increased steadily at a 4 per cent growth rate since 2010. Table 5 shows the percentage of mosques built in each decade.

Table 5: Years of establishment of mosques in New South Wales

Year	Prior to 1970	1970 to 1979	1980 to 1989	1990 to 1999	2000 to 2010	Post-2010
Percentage	8%	12%	12%	31%	33%	4%

Source: Husnia Underabi, *Mosques of Sydney and New South Wales: Research Report 2014*

Table 6 shows the number of mosques in different locations in New South Wales.

Table 6: Mosque locations in New South Wales

	Mosque locations			Total
	Inner and northern Sydney	Western Sydney	Outer Sydney	
Number	11	31	7	49

Source: Husnia Underabi, *Mosques of Sydney and New South Wales: Research Report 2014*

The vast majority of mosques built in the 1980s and after are divided along ethnic lines, as Edwards notes:[31] 'Thus, mosques in Australia are widely considered to be that of a specific cultural group.'[32] This means that mosque committees are essentially constituted of individuals from a particular ethnic group who form an association to manage the activities of the mosque and the affairs of the local Muslim community.[33] Edwards claims that:

> However, even though the mosque board or committee is representative of one cultural group, the congregation of the mosque is usually diverse. Mosques don't turn worshippers away based on their cultural heritage, so many Muslims will simply worship at a mosque based on its location and convenience.[34]

Mosques in Australia are very much set up like organisations, with either a board or a committee responsible for their management and operation. The board or committee collects funds to run the mosque and also collects and distributes donations. It is also responsible for recruiting an imam or imams to service the mosque in terms of leading the daily and congregational prayers and, in some instances, running Islamic studies and Arabic classes.

The course taken in the establishment of a mosque reflects the distinctive ethnic, linguistic and regional backgrounds of Muslim communities in Australia. For the vast majority of Muslims, religion continues to be deeply rooted in class structure and ethnic sources. As a corollary, local community politics based on old family and sectarian rivalries in 'home' communities continue to play out in mosque politics.[35] The claim of 'Muslim' as an identity and the stipulations for acknowledgement of Muslim religious and legal practices in this political milieu are effectively competitive and get drawn into the politics of a community's reputation and protection of cultural autonomy. The organisational focus of a community association, however, is not fixed and can be transferred to that of a mosque. The quintessential character of cultural capital and political resources undergoes transformation as demands originally made based on parochial attachment to kinship, friendship and community networks are located in totally distinct political and institutional frameworks. The mosque, which is established in light of a legal framework that demands a formal organisational structure and the establishment of proper management processes, becomes a central focus and serves as a base for the mobilisation of Muslim immigrants within a political arena.

Figure 3: Mosque activities in Australia

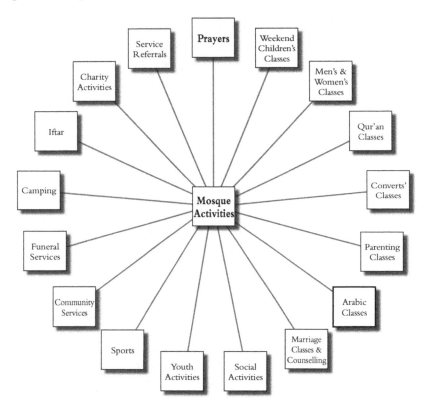

Many mosques are linked to Muslim schools. For example, in western Sydney the Rooty Hill Masjid in the suburb of Mount Druitt is linked to the Australian Islamic College of Sydney, and the Green Valley Jami Masjid in the suburb of Green Valley is associated with the Green Valley Islamic College. Mosques are also linked to scripture and language classes and the provision of social and cultural services critical to the Muslim ethnic community. The organisations and associations connected with mosques are often developed by Muslims to provide members with a platform to connect and work with one another, offer social support, and create opportunities to influence public policies. They even manage various projects depending on community and local needs, such as welfare services, health support, settlement assistance, housing, grief and marriage counselling, family dispute resolution, and help with relationship problems. Mosques in Australia have often turned into wider associations and institutions that play an important role in offering congregations and community members not only religious services but a variety of other provisions and a social network. Many of these and other mosque activities are captured in Figure 3.

Thus, mosques have become integral to the geographic landscape of urban centres in Australia following postwar immigration of Muslims from various parts of the globe, including many from the Middle East and Turkey. Mosques were originally established in existing buildings, but a growing number are purpose-built. Internal mosque activities, mosque management, and how mosques are connected to local Muslim communities and what kind of relationship they have with society in general are frequently debated by politicians, the media, academics and ordinary citizens, including even some Muslims. Mosque-building has often been a contested issue in Australia that causes community tension and political conflict, particularly in the post-9/11 era, with debates about mosques as hubs for homegrown terrorism, religious extremism and lack of Muslim integration.

Nevertheless, mosques have always 'served as vehicles to preserve the community's religious identity, to help build and empower the community as well as develop outreach programs to serve the wider community'.[36] Their establishment enables inter-communication between Australian Muslims and government departments and agencies. Both mosques and Muslim CSOs have helped Australian Muslims to understand Australian 'values', political and social systems, laws and public policies. At the same time, they have enabled both local and overseas government departments and agencies to come to better appreciate Islamic values and precepts and understand issues facing Muslims in their respective communities.

Institutionalisation of Islam

Various ethnic civic institutions or Muslim CSOs have come into existence, in order to look after the affairs of Muslims in Australia, empower them and build their social capital, and to institutionalise Islam. Given their diverse ethnic, parochial, national, sectarian and ideological backgrounds, the civic bodies established have essentially been within the confinements of specific ethnic groups and very much removed from one another, with limited to no inter- or intra-communal interaction. Even within a particular ethnic group, numerous lines of division and fragmentation have existed, preventing intra-communal interaction from occurring. For example, Sunni and Shi'ite Lebanese had separate community organisations and were spread across different Australian cities but grouped around various homeland villages, regions and urban centres; and Turkish Muslims in Sydney, although from Sunni backgrounds, had two separate mosques—one in the inner-city suburb of Erskineville and another in Auburn—with very little intra-communal interaction.

As a consequence, there are many small Muslim CSOs from different countries, including India, Pakistan, Afghanistan, Bangladesh, Malaysia, Indonesia, Fiji, South Africa, Yugoslavia, Bosnia, Albania and numerous Middle East states, and of course the two largest Muslim CSOs, founded by Turkish and Lebanese Muslims respectively. Ordinarily, individual Muslim CSOs have opted for the maintenance of separate identities rather than coming under a single national body. Muslim CSOs and mosques have emerged from specific communities and ethnic pride has always played a divisive role, rendering Muslims in Australia a heterogeneous community.[37]

Muslim immigrants started establishing CSOs as early as the 1950s. The Islamic Society of New South Wales, for instance, was established in 1957. Then, in 1960, the Lebanese Muslim Association of Sydney emerged. The Islamic Society of Victoria in Melbourne and similar societies in Adelaide, Perth and Brisbane were all established in 1962. In 1973, the Islamic Council of New South Wales was formed in spite of the existence of a national Islamic body, the Australian Federation of Islamic Societies (AFIS), which was established in 1964 and in 1976 changed its name to the Australian Federation of Islamic Councils (AFIC). Before we enter into a detailed discussion about Muslim CSOs, let us first focus our attention on AFIC, which has claimed to be the peak body representing all Australian Muslims for almost half a century.

Australian Federation of Islamic Councils

AFIC was restructured in 1976 into a three-tiered organisation comprising local societies and mosques, state and territory councils, and a national federation.[38] During the restructuring, the organisation changed its name from AFIS to AFIC and its headquarters was moved from Melbourne to Zetland, an inner-city suburb of Sydney where it has since remained.

The idea behind the formation of AFIC as the peak body was to bring together all the disparate Muslim CSOs under one national umbrella to create a sense of unity among Australian Muslims. By bringing together different Muslim CSOs, the aim was to make Muslims feel a real sense of belonging to a single ummah and have a united sense of direction, and to give Muslims a strong single voice. Although it seems that AFIC had the best of intentions, it never succeeded as a national force in uniting Muslim CSOs and Australian Muslim communities. The division between the CSOs and a lack of Muslim unity persisted, as we will see in the next section.

When AFIC was initially established, its interests and activities were not firmly linked to broader Islamic practices, arrangements, and provision of religious guidance and directions within the Muslim CSOs. In fact, it was more firmly focused on the certification of halal meat, particularly for export to Muslim countries in the Middle East. This was the basis for much of its initial success as it was relatively well-resourced.[39] Saudi Arabia and a coalition of Gulf States recognised AFIC as the only Australian authoritative body permitted to issue halal certificates. Revenue from issuing halal certificates and further financial support from the Saudi Arabian Government—initially $1.2 million to develop Islamic infrastructure such as mosques and Islamic schools—placed AFIC on a sound financial footing and helped its steady growth in structural development and activities.[40] In the late 1980s, King Fahd gave AFIC a gift of $1 million to purchase a parcel of land in the south-western Sydney suburb of Greenacre to build a Muslim school; the Malek Fahd Islamic School, named in the king's honour, was established in 1989.[41] In the 1980s AFIC also established King Khalid Islamic College in Melbourne, but due to internal wrangling and poor management it lost the school to the shrewd school board, who changed its name to Australian International Academy and turned it into a private commercial venture.

As its success grew, AFIC started to forge closer links with Muslim CSOs. A connection was also established with Australian government officials, who were regularly invited as honoured guests to Muslim social and religious functions. Contacts were established with overseas Muslim countries and Islamic organisations who were later lobbied for material and financial support to reinvigorate and increase religious activities in Australia. In addition, the publication of a multilingual quarterly journal, *Minaret*, was started; it remained in circulation for some time.

The Saudi and Middle Eastern preferential treatment of AFIC came to a halt in the early 1990s when halal certification was rationalised.[42] However, by now AFIC had cemented its financial foundation and embarked on a mission of Muslim school-building. It built several schools around the country, including the Islamic College of Brisbane in 1995, the Islamic College of South Australia in 1998, Langford Islamic College in Western Australia in 2004, the Islamic College of Melbourne in 2011, and the Islamic School of Canberra in 2015. As Muslim community-based schools or schools for the Muslim community, they proved to be very profitable for AFIC.

Despite AFIC's various successes, it has frequently been criticised by Muslim activists and former-member and non-member Muslim CSOs for internal wrangling, mismanagement, aloofness from Muslims at the grassroots level, and failing to develop close bonds with Muslim CSOs and members of the clergy. Its serious troubles became more public in 2015 when the Australian Broadcasting Corporation (ABC) aired an investigation into what might be termed the 'paper societies gate scandal' when allegations were made against AFIC for creating 'fake societies' or 'fake councils' for the purpose of filing relevant paperwork with Australian authorities so that certain individuals could maintain control or secure their powers within AFIC.[43] In March 2017 an independent audit on behalf of the Australian Charities and Not-for-profits Commission found that AFIC lacked proper governance mechanisms consistent with the protocols of its not-for-profit status, and gaps in the financial controls environment were found that were likely to expose AFIC to serious financial risk.[44]

In the last few years AFIC has been in a constant media spotlight for controversy surrounding its schools, school boards and particularly its president, Hafez Kassem, a former backyard mechanic who migrated to Australia from Lebanon, for misconduct. Several of its affiliated schools have faced accusations of malpractice, non-compliance and financial mismanagement, leading to an investigation by the federal Department of Education of all AFIC-affiliated schools. In the process, AFIC had to close the Islamic College of South Australia in June 2017 due to a federal government funding cut, and it lost the management of Australia's largest Muslim school, Malek Fahd Islamic School, to a newly created school board constituted of a mixture of Muslim and non-Muslim unsuitable, incompetent and unqualified individuals.[45]

At the time of writing, AFIC's three-tiered organisational structure continued to exist but its operational function remained fairly obscure and limited. Even though it is continuously working towards improving its national and international profile and exercising greater influence over the Muslim community, group pressures for improvement are always afoot. Potentially, it can attempt to exercise even greater and stronger influence over Muslims in Australia, particularly in terms of overcoming the many barriers that divide Muslim ethnic communities. Given this, the roles of Islamic cultural and organisational structures—particularly the roles of the family and community—in the process of enculturation need to be understood in the context of immigrant culture.

In this context, the relationship between the maintenance of male authority and the establishment of Muslim CSOs and religious institutions is significant. It reflects the intimate connections between secular and Muslim CSOs in ethnic politics and shows how the discourse of ethnic struggle and deprivation is reflected in the political and religious orientation of individual and independent mosque communities and Muslim CSOs. In the arena of ethnic politics, the maintenance of autonomy of Muslim communities is an important issue because autonomy is directly related to ethnic identity. Therefore, issues relating to leadership and the maintenance of ethnic and sectarian character in mosque associations and Muslim CSOs gain greater importance in ethnic politics and reinforce the need for autonomy and separate identity of Muslim communities, which AFIC has constantly struggled to address and diffuse.

Muslim civic society organisations

As discussed earlier, in an immigrant context mosques are a form of community centre despite being considered as faith spaces that serve as places of worship. They also serve as formal or social meeting places and resource and information centres.

Mosques aside, all community centres, societies, associations and councils are referred to as Muslim CSOs in this book. In the context of Muslim immigration it is possible to suggest that while every Muslim organisation is a Muslim ethnic organisation, not every Muslim ethnic organisation is a Muslim immigrant organisation. Muslim ethnic organisations constitute a broad grouping that includes not only Muslim immigrant organisations but also organisations of the descendants of Muslim immigrants. Thus, these organisations are called Muslim CSOs to encompass them all under a single description for the purpose of convenience.

Muslim CSOs are generally non-profit, formal, self-governing, voluntary, and founded by new and long-term immigrants at all stages of immigration principally to service Muslims and Muslim immigrant communities. According to Amath, in 2014 there were 486 Muslim organisations in Australia that fell under the description of CSO,[46] and with more Muslims migrating every year and the Australian Muslim population growing, this number will no doubt grow incrementally. With the constant flow of Muslim immigrants from various parts of the world and the consolidation and growth of their communities in Australia, manifold Muslim CSOs, some connected to mosques, have come into existence, working to assist with the various social, cultural and religious needs of their community members. Muslim CSOs in a variety of ways complement mosques as they provide services that extend beyond those typically linked to mosques. Although there are certain shared characteristics, what is distinct about Muslim CSOs is that they usually have a grassroots reach to their members and communities that extends much wider and deeper into social lives, social health, informal social networking, and interaction processes such as problem-solving, decision-making and conflict resolution.

Various organisations can be described as community centres or societies. Some of them are related to ethnicity, such as the Sydney-based Bangladesh

Association of New South Wales or the Perth-based Afghan Islamic Association. Then there are some that are multiethnic or non-ethnic, such as Crescents of Brisbane, which promotes healthy lifestyles through sport, entertainment, education and culture for Muslims across Queensland, or the Sydney-based Islamic Friendship Association of Australia, which offers a range of services, including education, recreation and youth activities and classes, to all Muslims regardless of their ethnicity.

To give an insight into how Muslim CSOs describe themselves, the descriptions range from 'Muslim umbrella organisation' and 'Islamic education organisation' to 'Muslim social and/or cultural organisation', 'Muslim youth organisation' and 'Muslim student organisation'. Other self-describing Muslim CSOs call themselves 'Muslim *dawah*/spiritual organisation', 'Muslim relief organisation', 'Muslim sports organisation' or 'Muslim charity organisation'.

Some Muslim CSOs have a long history, but the vast majority are relatively young. Many cooperate with mosque associations or mosque committees, and therefore there is some crossover in their activities.[47] Muslim CSOs are mainly located in the metropolitan centres where most Muslims live. Those who service these organisations are largely volunteers who do not receive a wage or salary, but in rare cases they are employed as paid staff.

Muslim CSOs often have multiple functions in the community they serve and have a crucial role to play, particularly in the lives of newly arrived Muslim migrants and refugees, offering them support and information and organising much-needed resources, especially during the settlement phase of their lives. While these services have retained their importance due to the ongoing arrival of Muslim migrants and also due to the continuous growth, based on local births, of Muslim communities, the configuration of Muslim CSOs in Australia has become much more complex, diverse and dynamic over the years. Muslim CSO services often cross from religion and economic status to address practical and cultural issues related to the settlement process in Australia. Not all of these organisations have the same purpose and aims, and therefore several different purposes and functions are combined within them, making them multipurpose and hybrid entities that are difficult to classify into definite categories.

Muslim CSOs fulfil a wide range of social, cultural, economic and political needs of both Muslim immigrants and locally born Muslim individuals. They act as a type of shelter providing support, a way of representing the community, and a sense of belonging through responding to the feeling of alienation widely prevalent in modern cities such as Sydney, Melbourne and Brisbane; and serve as a place for the creation of a distinct collective identity through celebration of festivals and the practice of customs from the country of origin.

The Muslim community in Australia is a product of mass migration that commenced in earnest in the 1970s. Immigration is the principal circumstance leading to the development of the Muslim community, the emergence of Muslim CSOs and the institutionalisation of Islam. Multiple dimensions have been operating to shape this.

Generally, migration from home country to host country makes it difficult for immigrants to participate in already-established voluntary organisations in the host country. Language and cultural barriers, non-recognition of overseas skills and qualifications, lack of work experience, and discrimination are the key hindrances. Furthermore, the objectives of existing organisations in the host country may not fulfil immigrants' specific needs. This leads to the establishment of ethnic and immigrant organisations.

Muslim CSOs are established to provide a response to the special needs that Muslim migrants and individuals share with other Muslims but not necessarily with the broader local community. Muslim migrants require not only practical guidance but contact with fellow Muslims with whom they share the same language and the desire to preserve and continue their home culture. In other words, Muslim CSOs constitute a space for familiar communication and sharing of language and culture of the home country; they eliminate the complexity associated with and the effort required to communicate, especially in a new language, in the host country. Moreover, the role of Muslim CSOs extends beyond merely serving the Muslim immigrant community to engaging in the process of strengthening and shaping Muslim ethnic collective identity and representing the community in the host country.

One of the pivotal explanations for the founding of Muslim communities and CSOs in Australia is the fact that Muslim immigrants bring their own culture, traditions, language and religious norms that may be different from each other and from those of wider Australian society. Given these gaps, Muslim communities and CSOs serve as a framework for the formation and maintenance of ethnocultural minorities.

As discussed in this chapter, the presence of Muslims in Australia has gradually become visible since World War II as the Muslim community has grown in size and developed religious and civic society infrastructure to cater for the public observance of Islam and the transmission of faith to future generations of Muslims. Religious and civic society infrastructures have resulted from the maturation of individual Muslim ethnic communities who organised to represent their members' concerns to the government and broader society. The institutionalisation of Islam in multicultural Australia has occurred through the establishment of Muslim communities, mosques and CSOs. These institutions have acted as sources of community mobilisation and as mediators with local, state and federal governments to cater for the religious needs of Muslims in the public sphere.

Part 2

Muslim exclusion and inclusion in Australia

Chapter 4

Muslim experience of social exclusion in Australia

Social exclusion is a process that produces complex and varied social disadvantages, preventing certain types of individuals or human collectivities from accessing resources, exercising various civil rights and having common opportunities, and thereby precluding their full and meaningful everyday participation in the society in which they reside. The process may target and discriminate against race, skin colour, appearance, social class, religious affiliation, ethnic origin, educational status, living standards or political stance, producing individual or group marginalisation, alienation, disenfranchisement and capability deprivation. The overall impact of this is that person's or group's relegation to the fringe of the society they call home, and the erosion of their universally shared forms of social citizenship.

Individuals or groups who seem to deviate in any way from perceived or real usual patterns of living may become victims of subtle or abrasive forms of social exclusion. This can occur due to social or structural factors. For example, at a social level, non-Muslim female workers at a department store may not share a table in the staffroom during the lunchbreak with their hijab-donning colleague because of the perception that all hijab-donning women are backward, uneducated, subservient or even uncivilised. At a structural level, long-serving bearded Muslim bureaucrats in a government department may not be promoted to senior positions because of the perception among senior management that bearded Muslim men are conservative and narrow-minded and will have an intellectually damaging influence on junior staff.

When it comes to Muslims in Australia, across the society individual Muslims and Muslim communities have experienced social exclusion on the basis of their religious belief. Australia is a multicultural society that prides itself on being accommodating, tolerant, compassionate, liberal, egalitarian and socioculturally inclusive. So why is there social hostility towards Muslims as a religious minority group? Why do Muslims suffer communal violence? And why do many Muslims feel a sense of isolation and disenfranchisement? Why do Muslim Australians, who constitute the second-largest religious group in the country and many of whom are citizens, largely remain disengaged from and apathetic towards many mainstream social and cultural processes and activities? Why have Muslims not participated actively in politics? Why are Muslims not involved in a substantive way in policy design, development and implementation? Why don't Muslims hold senior positions in public office or have chief roles in large corporations and government departments?

Generally, Muslims have remained on the periphery, away from the social core of Australian society. They are often perceived and identified as the 'Other' and described implicitly or explicitly in the media and in public and private discourse, and even in some scholarly literature, as people who are disembodied from the broader society. The events of 11 September 2001; the Bali, London and Madrid bombings; Australian Lebanese gang rapes of women in Sydney in 2000; the 2009 terror plot connected to al-Shabaab at Holsworthy Barracks in Sydney; the 2014 Sydney hostage crisis; the shooting of New South Wales Police employee Curtis Cheng in Parramatta in 2015; and the 2018 Melbourne stabbing attack—to mention but a few—have intensified and accelerated the tendency of 'othering' Muslims, resulting in their exclusion from many socioeconomic and cultural processes.

Despite the Australian Government's vision of a socially inclusive society in which all Australians, based on their permanent residency or citizenship status, feel valued and have the opportunity to freely take part in the norms of everyday living, research indicates that Muslims in Australia, in many instances, continue to experience a series of social disadvantages and struggle to participate in the broader Australian socioeconomic and political landscape, with the real possibility of this experience being also felt by future generations of Muslims. Muslims continue to struggle to access social rights, suffer material deprivation, face limited social participation and experience a lack of normative integration.

This chapter examines Muslim experience of social exclusion in Australia in an attempt to better understand the much bigger phenomenon of Islam and Muslims in Australia. Muslims experience social exclusion in a variety of ways, and there are many prevailing causes of their exclusion from wider Australian society. Looking at some of these causes and how they impact on Muslims will give us some sense of why Muslim social exclusion is a concerning social issue in Australian society and that political and policy actions are necessary to ameliorate its impact. It also offers insights into Muslims' relationship with non-Muslims and with key institutions, and Muslims' overall status in Australian society. I argue that Muslim social exclusion is detrimental to Australia's general wellbeing, and that when the society emphasises differences in social integration that designers of inclusion create to control and manage how socially deprived individuals occupy social space, then the final outcome is not social freedom but, ironically, maintenance of many of the attributes of the existing state of affairs. For Australia to build for itself a strong and inclusive society, it must facilitate Muslim social cooperation and coexistence and bring into play governing forces with liberating effects.

Social exclusion

Despite social exclusion increasingly having become central to policy and academic discourse in the West and in other parts of the world, it is a highly contested concept with multiple meanings. It suffers from a definitional problem as well as the fact that the meaning of social exclusion varies from country to country[1] and is embedded in different intellectual traditions and political epochs.[2] However, according to Jane Mathieson and her colleagues, there is some consensus that 'social exclusion' is a multidimensional concept because it is dynamic and involves social, cultural, economic and political dimensions and operates at different social levels.[3]

Traditionally, certain targeted individuals or communities have experienced exclusion from the prevailing social system in either absolute or relative terms, leading to the attenuation of their rights and privileges and intensification of their poverty and non-belongingness. This has been made possible either through commonly held beliefs and customary practices, or by enacting specific laws. Eric Robinson, for instance, notes that Greek democracies established ostracism and analogous laws as early as the fourth century BCE that made it possible for people 'to vote into exile for several years leaders who seemed to have grown too powerful, troublesome, or threatening to popular order'.[4] Some were excluded, but generally the laws encouraged a strong sense of belonging and inclusion among the majority who were part of the democracies and, therefore, the laws won popular support. Much later, in Nazi Germany, we see the policy of exclusion being applied, by 'status groups' or by people in a privileged position, against Jews. Thus, social exclusion is all about marginality, social polarisation, lack of participation, and ruptures or disconnectedness in solidarity and the social bond. The society rewards those who carry out their personal responsibility with inclusion, and those who commit personal irresponsibility with exclusion.[5]

However, more recently the focus on social exclusion has come from France, as 'a result of France's postwar transition from a largely agricultural society to an urban one'[6] and 'the effect of the failure of integrative institution'[7] in the 1970s, which accelerated through the 80s and 90s and at the turn of the second millennium. Dan Allman asserts that:

> In its initial contemporary use, the exclusion terminology adopted in France and subsequently diffused elsewhere, was meant to refer to those individuals who were considered to be on the margins of French society of the 1970s. That is, individuals considered society's social problems, who tended to share a particular social reality, a less than successful material existence compounded with real barriers in accessing benefits provided by the French welfare state.[8]

Nabin Rawal says, 'This concept, which first emerged in the policy discourse in France, and its adoption later by other European countries have had an increasing impact on the analyses of social disadvantages in Europe over the last couple of decades.'[9] Around the same time, 'social exclusion' was conceptualised as an alternative to poverty, deprivation and social disenfranchisement by European Union policymakers in their discourses of urban social policy development.[10] When the phenomena of poverty, unemployment and crime became critical issues for the EU, policymakers' attention turned to social exclusion as a response to the crisis of the welfare state. Social exclusion also became a mainstream policy framework by the end of the twentieth century, particularly in the United Kingdom under the prime ministership of Tony Blair when it was incorporated into the country's Social Exclusion Unit.[11]

Generally speaking, exclusion conveys the notion of a failure to achieve the sound working and developing capacities that are viewed as constructive and indispensable in an inclusive society. Although the concept of exclusion is multidimensional, the focus on poverty and inequality features prominently in almost every debate.[12] Due to this, it is often found that research focuses on the concept of exclusion emphasising economic exclusion, especially extreme poverty.[13] Tamiru Berafe says, 'There is no unanimous consensus among scholars on whether poverty is a cause for social exclusion or social exclusion results in poverty.'[14] It is possible that poverty may be the consequence of exclusion, but exclusion is not poverty. For instance, exclusion can be the basis for rejecting the common norms[15] and materialisation of splinter groups or subcultures.[16] Likewise, exclusion that leads to withdrawal from the labour force[17] may also manifest itself in retreating from the mainstream social and political structures of society.[18] Rawal suggests that 'The strength of the concept ... lies in the fact that in distinction to poverty, which has been primarily thought about in economic terms, social exclusion also takes into consideration deprivation in a number of spheres, of which low income is but one.'[19] Hence, there can be a great variety of outcomes and expressions of exclusion. However, we still need a reference point for social exclusion. According to Dragana Avramov, social exclusion is:

> a condition of deprivation that is manifested through the generalised disadvantages facing individuals of social groups due to accumulated social handicaps. It is experienced by people as the overlapping of objective deprivation with their subjective dissatisfaction with life chances due to inadequate means and limited access or poor participation in several of the most important domains of human activity ... Exclusion is as a rule associated with social stigmatisation, blame and isolation, which translate to low self-esteem, a feeling of not belonging and not having been given a chance to be included in society.[20]

Social exclusion invokes imagery of social entrapment, of being caught in an unending series of hardships with no real prospect of escaping them. It conveys a persistent sad state of affairs and a probable source of turmoil, discord and crime. Social exclusion is the inability of individuals or groups to participate and access opportunities and resources in society because of the imposition of various forms of restrictions.

The exclusion of some individuals or groups from mainstream society is often about resource monopolisation and unequal power relationships.[21] Those with power always get to determine the distribution of resources in society, which affects the 'underclass' or the exclusionary groups not only in accessing economic resources but in their ability to participate in collective action and society-building. People in positions of power and members of privileged groups use social closure that results in restricting underprivileged groups from accessing social capital. Individuals and groups who experience social exclusion inevitably, as a consequence, feel its impact on both their current and future access to a variety of resources—none less so than in economic and social spheres.[22]

Exclusionary practices and experiences impact not only the underclass and dependency culture but the entire society. It is a common social-scientific fact that those individuals and groups who experience exclusion tend to suffer from under-education, unemployment, poverty, inequality, limitations in accessing the labour market, and social, economic and geographical isolation from active engagement in politics; they also have lower incomes and inadequate services compared to others in society.[23] Moreover, they appear to have poor living standards, increased health issues and reduced prospects for the future. Younger people from the underprivileged sector experience further negative consequences of social exclusion by being unable to freely access social and economic resources and enjoy their full benefits as members of society. At a societal level, the consequences of this impact heavily, leading to rising poverty, crime rates and antisocial behaviour; and a reduced level of social inclusion severely costs the society economically.

But who are the underprivileged and underclass group who suffer from social exclusion? Can it be a large community, or simply a section of it? In order to explore this very broad question, it is worth looking at migrant Muslims in Australia, especially those from working-class backgrounds, as a case study.

Social exclusion for migrants in Australia, particularly Muslim working-class migrants, is a concerning matter. Marginalisation or social exclusion affects these Muslims directly, leading to a multiplier effect in their communities. This is evident in rising poverty, homelessness, unemployment and income gaps, and restraint on upward social mobility, which in turn result in an increase in youth crime, higher representation in welfare receipts, and participation in the 'black economy'. Like any migrant group, for working-class Muslims social exclusion means a disconnection from social life in general and the labour market in particular: a form of severance from the social core of the society.

Causes of Muslim social exclusion

Capability deprivation or social exclusion impacts on Muslims directly, leading to their disconnectedness from others in broader Australian society. They get stuck in a chain of exclusions resulting from the systematic stratification of access to resources. Like any migrant group, for Muslims social exclusion means restriction from being able to move from the periphery or outside to the social core, and being consumed by social and economic malaise and decreasing quality of life.

Muslim social exclusion is a serious issue. It raises questions about Muslim wellbeing and their status in the society but also has a lot to do with the appropriateness of social, welfare and health service provisions, which often differ from those constituting the mainstream. What causes Muslim social exclusion, or how Muslim social exclusion occurs, provides important insights into the challenges Muslims experience in accessing resources, socialising and developing capability as a minority group, and highlights other broader issues surrounding social exclusion in Australia. What follows, then, is an analysis of the barriers to social inclusion experienced by Muslims in Australia. It draws on an empirical study entitled *Muslim-Australians and Local*

Government: Grassroots Strategies to Improve Relations between Muslim and non-Muslim Australians conducted by Amanda Wise and me in 2007–08.[24] In the study, some of the causes of Muslim disengagement with wider Australian society are discussed. The purpose of using this work is to explore the causes or reasons for Muslim disconnectedness in some systematic fashion to better understand the phenomenon of Muslim social exclusion in Australia.

Bear in mind that the focus of this chapter is to develop an understanding of the barriers to social inclusion experienced by Muslims in Australia, and therefore it is critical to study the motivations behind Muslim disengagement and withdrawal from community-building as well as the general barriers to mixing with non-Muslims and the impact of this on social cohesion and an inclusive society.

Our study found that the causes of disengagement were the result of the negative aspects, or lack thereof, of the process of socialisation. Interview participants who had this experience represented a cross-section of the Muslim-Australian community. They highlighted the difficulties in negotiating their cultural identity and the factors restricting them from becoming an integral part of the larger community and mobilising them from the periphery to the centre. As I will demonstrate, these causes of disengagement and withdrawal appeared to create real barriers for these Muslims to get to know non-Muslims and socialise with them, and as a consequence restricted their capacity to participate in and contribute to society-building and open social exchange.

Many of the significant barriers identified regarding mixing with non-Muslims were related to 'everyday' cultural and religious differences. In ranked order, the most common barriers identified were:
1. gender
2. language barriers
3. experiences of discrimination and racism.

Gender

The last several decades have seen a global rise in Muslim religious consciousness, known as Islamic revivalism—including in Australia. Muslims, particularly those who are nominal in nature, have been returning to the basics of Islam and its scriptural teachings in increased numbers and trying to fashion their everyday living according to *sharia* (Islamic law). One aspect of this increased Islamic consciousness is a strict observation of Islamic gender norms and rules that generally leads such Muslims to avoid interaction between genders and limit their socialisation to same-gendered individuals and to their *maharim*.[25] According to one prophetic tradition narrated by Abu Huraira, regarding women in Islam, he notes that the Prophet Mohammed said, 'It is not permissible for a woman who believes in Allah and the Last Day to travel for one day and night except with a Maḥārim.'[26] Such an interpretation of the prophetic tradition can be challenging to the process of socialisation between men and women from both Muslim and non-Muslim backgrounds, as demonstrated in the Australian context but applicable globally in these extracts:

> Mustafa: Well, in our culture, we mix mostly with our own gender. For social order, you know? Men mix with men, and women mix with women ... So if someone comes and visits, for example, if me and my wife are living in a certain house and our friends are coming to visit, normally the procedure that we'll go by is that men will sit in this lounge room and the women will be in another living room. Socialising is done that way.
>
> Dalia: It's not a problem. But the fact, like, with a man, they don't know. I don't shake hands with men, so that's a minor problem. And another problem ... Because like ... sometimes the other person feels embarrassed or ... it's still embarrassing? For both of us ... like, I get embarrassed, too ... because I feel ... I don't feel sorry for the other person, but ... you know ... like ... he's trying to make an effort to be friendly and ... to say: 'Oh, no ... sorry, I don't shake hands.'
>
> Mustafa: ... if there's a picnic or a barbeque, we'll go and have a barbeque, but in a way that doesn't affect the sensitivities on each side. For example, there won't be alcohol. If I want to have a picnic, I want to bring my wife, I'll ask my non-Muslim friend if he can respect our way of ... segregation. The women sit on these chairs on this side, the men on this side ... it will work, you know? So that's mostly how I interact with my non-Muslim friends.[27]

While there are many Muslims, both male and female, who quite comfortably and freely mix with the opposite gender and pay less or no heed to Islamic gender norms and rules, there are a considerable number who do. For the latter, gender segregation is important because such a practice is seen as part of *taqwa* (piety) and is often linked to *'ibadat* (worship). Of course, this practice alone does not epitomise the model Muslim individual, but from these Muslims' perspective, the practice reinforces the image of a 'proper' Muslim in a very potent and important way. To give the subjects—in this case the interviewees—their own voice, one must understand their agency and subjectivity and how they pattern their everyday lives. The subjective meanings they assign to their natural daily environment and the 'real' social processes they undergo cannot be ignored. Appreciating interviewees' bodily behaviour and their engagement with reality construction is critical sociologically, and those involved in bringing Muslims and non-Muslims together and creating a socially inclusive society—such as community leaders, bureaucrats and policymakers—must pay attention to this important sociological process and fact.

Muslims' own interpretation of their bodily behaviour is absolutely critical in understanding issues surrounding gender relationships and how gender norms, rules and identity are negotiated in a social context. Their rituals of piety are not just about how they are enacted but explain the way they are embodied and expressed experientially in an attempt to construct or maintain a religious-oriented identity. Hence, Muslims' commitment to gender rules is part of the bodily behaviour that is at the very centre of their proper realisation of 'true Islam'. Saba Mahmood reinforces this point by arguing that:

> in this program of self-cultivation ... bodily acts—like wearing the veil or conducting oneself modestly in interactions with people (especially men)—do not serve as manipulable masks in a game of public presentation, detachable from an essential interiorized self. Rather they are the critical markers of piety as well as the ineluctable means by which one trains oneself to be pious.[28]

Open social interaction is difficult for particularly 'religious' Muslim men and women. Handshaking, for instance, makes it even more difficult. When a non-Muslim is refused a handshake, offence can easily be taken. However, this can be remedied with education and raising awareness in the broader community about gender norms and rules, which vary from culture to culture. Gender segregation should not be seen as unique to Islam. Muslim gender norms and rules and the practice of gender segregation, which often restricts relationship-building, particularly between Muslims and non-Muslims, can be overcome with better education and strategic socialisation.

Gender segregation in a secular environment such as Australia doesn't have to be taken as anti-modern or anti-secular and therefore resisted at social and policy levels. Instead, its facilitation will help reduce Muslim experience of social exclusion. In Australia, more appropriate opportunities can be created where Muslims and non-Muslims can gather without breaking Muslim gender rules. As shown in the extracts above, these rules are not impossible or impractical to uphold, and a well-planned occasion or event can both keep the rules intact and allow socialisation to continue.

Language barriers

Language barriers can pose a major obstacle to socialisation, constructive dialogue and building relationships. Unable to effectively communicate a point of view or a message and have meaningful discussion can be not only frustrating and embarrassing but challenging, with consequences for all involved. Language barriers can become a real ordeal for people, because understanding and being understood are critical to exchanging information and building relationships or rapport. When people fail to communicate with each other due to language differences, it can impact directly on equal access to resources and important opportunities. For instance, an Australian Department of Immigration and Multicultural and Indigenous Affairs (DIMIA) longitudinal study of immigrants found that those with a sound command of the English language had a better chance of being employed.[29] Instead of coming together to establish a shared bond, language barriers can hamper this process or even, in some instances, destroy it:

> Iqbal: I try to talk English, but that's hard. Sometimes, maybe he understands but he doesn't accept it, you know what I mean? ... Sometimes you can explain an easy thing for him ... But he doesn't accept it, especially because of the accent.[30]

Iqbal's experience relating to language barrier is neither unique nor culture-specific. In other sociocultural contexts people have demonstrated similar experiences. For example, Nina from Eastern Europe states, in Brotherhood of St Laurence research:

> I've had no English classes ... It is very uncomfortable because I can't say what I want and when you go to a different country and you can't speak it makes you feel bad, very bad, very uncomfortable, like you are more down than the other people.[31]

Language barriers are not just a problem for the speaker but also for the listener. While the speaker may find it embarrassing not being able to speak the language fluently with the appropriate accent, it can be equally problematic for the listener who can't understand the other person. Mario Peucker, Joshua Roose and Shahram Akbarzadeh, in relation to Muslim active citizenship in Australia, say that, 'Being able to speak the language of the country of residence is crucial for many forms of civic engagement, in particular for those that require inter-community interaction with mainstream stakeholders in the political arena or civil society.'[32]

When English proficiency is lacking or language barriers exist, then many forms of civic engagement suffer; exchange and meaningful discussion are abandoned; and hope for social exchange and interaction is all but dashed. Also, without proficiency in English many migrant Muslims are easily excluded from a variety of aspects of life, including education, employment, services and social exchange. Government services that have the potential to overcome the problem of language barriers are often few and far between, allowing for the maintenance of Muslim social exclusion to continue.

Discrimination and racism against Muslims
Discrimination and racism are subjective feelings in individuals. They are not easily quantifiable and are difficult to prove. They occur for a variety of reasons but are largely due to ignorance about and 'fear' of the 'Other'. Many Muslims, as we will see below in interview extracts, due to the experience of racism express reluctance to engage with the broader community from non-Muslim backgrounds and opt out of visiting certain predominantly Anglo-Celtic suburbs for shopping and other purposes. The types of racial taunt or slur that discourage many Muslims from leaving their own suburbs include racist remarks from passengers or drivers in cars, staring, and being ignored for service in stores. For example, Jasmina, an interviewee in Brotherhood of St Laurence research, states:

> Well, it happened to me once, OK? But in the city, when I go to the city, I truly, truly feel different. Like, I know around Bankstown, I feel like I'm in Syria, OK? My country. But when I go to the city I just feel different. I get the sense that they look at you differently. They don't even care, but it's just that feeling. And even out of the city, we go in the car and then this group of people started pointing. They were all Aussies. It was like, 'Get off' or something. And it was just so embarrassing, and I poked my head down in the car![33]

Jasmina's experience in the city centre highlights the fact that people are often territorial, and when someone enters a 'foreign' territory—the size of the locale doesn't matter—their presence may be unwelcome and in some instances even rejected. This can be seen in a much larger Australian context when migrants do not always receive a warm welcome, leading to their alienation and disenfranchisement. Racism is a severe form of non-welcomeness and can be expressed both verbally and non-verbally, as the experience of Jasmina reveals. Due to fear of racism, which in some cases can be severe physical abuse, many Muslims navigate non-familiar boundaries with great caution or avoid them totally. Instead, they restrict their movements to familiar areas where they feel safe and secure. That is why we find predominantly Muslim suburban enclaves in almost all major capital cities in Australia, such as Bankstown in Sydney and Hume in Melbourne. These enclaves are in part the result of exclusionary processes operating in society.

Jasmina's is only one example: there are many other instances of reported and non-reported experiences of racism. Mubarak's experience reinforces that racism against Muslims is not rare but quite widespread in Australia:

> When I'm travelling on public transport, for example. On a train or a bus, and the seat next to me is empty, if any Australian is coming—and you can see it's a purely Australian person, a white person, for example—they will tend not to sit next to me. They will give you a look which is probably ... OK, maybe I'm wrong in my perception, but I think so far I'm right in a sense, that they don't want to sit next to me ... when I have sat next to someone who is purely Australian, a white person ... I have seen it, they change seats, on many occasions! As soon as I sit, they change seats! It's like, OK! Sorry! That's fine! I have to sit, anyway! ... But that's the kind of negative feeling I get. I feel like there is something going on.[34]

These are real human experiences that shape Muslims' perception of Anglo-Celtic Australians and Muslims' place in society. The treatment they receive from some Anglo-Celtic Australians has serious social consequences. In a 2004 survey, Scott Poynting found that 43 per cent of his respondents had been subjected to racial abuse while driving. Of these, 50 per cent of Muslim respondents said they had been subjected to abuse while driving compared to only 16 per cent of non-Muslim respondents. Many respondents stated that they had been victims of racial abuse on public transport or while travelling as passengers in private vehicles.[35]

Approximately fifteen years later, not much has changed. In their report *Islamophobia in Australia II (2016–2017)*, Derya Iner and her colleagues examined 349 vilification incidents against Muslims over a 24-month period from January 2016 to December 2017, noting that:

> Women, especially those with Islamic head covering (79.6% of the female victims), have been the main targets of Islamophobia and more than 30% of the female victims had their children with them at the time of the reported incident ... 98% of perpetrators

were identified as ethnically Anglo-Celtic, as indicated by the reporter, and the typical perpetrator tended to be male ... Most reported physical assaults (offline incidents) occurred in NSW (60%) and VIC (26.7%) ... 48% of offline attacks occurred in crowded spaces that were frequented daily—shopping centres, train stations and mosque surroundings were the most common.[36]

These experiences show the targeting of Islam and Muslims in Australia. Constructions of the 'Other'—inferiority and incompatibility—are principal implements of racism in Australia today. Many scholars describe this as a type of 'new racism'.[37] Kevin Dunn and his colleagues observe that 'This is a form of racism where individual (and group) rights are confined on the basis that a cultural group's ways of life are judged as nefarious, or on the basis that a cultural group does not fit or belong within the society as defined by a protagonist.'[38] These racisms emanate from the discourses of 'Otherness' and inferiority. Anti-Islamic and anti-Muslim attitudes are forms of racism that racialise religion and culture, and privilege hegemonic culture. New racisms still operate essentially to buttress structures of inferiority (hierarchies) and differentiation (exclusion).[39]

As a result, Muslims effectively take a somewhat defensive position about how they see and relate with Anglo-Celtic Australians, and attempts to form relationships with them are often made with much care and caution. Racism is an unwholesome experience, and when Muslims suffer from it at the hands of a handful of perpetrators, not only the perpetrators but those associated with them are held in low esteem. Hence, Muslims with experiences of discrimination, Islamophobia and racism naturally show reluctance towards mixing with Anglo-Celtic Australians, which hampers attempts at building bridges between Muslim and non-Muslim Australians.

Muslim experience of social exclusion and its consequences

At the very heart of this chapter has been concern over the situation of centre-periphery cleavage in Australia in which many Muslims find themselves trapped. Muslims feel a strong sense of isolation and disenfranchisement in a country that calls itself liberal and multicultural. In such a free society, many permanent members, including Muslims, remain disengaged from the processes of social inclusion or open social exchange. There are numerous reasons and causes of this, some of which I have discussed above.

Structural and organisational changes and unceasing social, cultural, economic and political development and reforms that have effectively facilitated people movement (migration) from developing to developed countries have raised concerns about an inclusive society or social inclusion of all members of a society. Therefore, experimentation with social inclusion or integration in migrant-receiving Western countries, including Australia, is not a new phenomenon and was undertaken as early as the 1930s.[40] As discussed in Chapter 2, in Australia assimilationist policies designed for social integration of migrants, with the expectation that they would blend in and become members of the dominant society, operated until 1972. Assimilationism or assimilation policy with an underlying assumption of the inferiority of immigrants created racism and ethnocentrism[41] and, as a result, the policy was abandoned and replaced with multiculturalism, in which diversity was apparently celebrated.[42] Australian multiculturalism meant that pressure was released from forcing migrants to abandon their cultural inheritance, and their social inclusion was sought through permitting them the right to keep their language, traditional values and ways of life. Social inclusion translated to civic citizenship. It was hoped that by bestowing equal rights on migrants and permitting them to practise their culture, social inclusion would occur naturally.

Although multiculturalism was an attempt to produce social inclusion of migrants and ethnic groups, its success has always been open to question,[43] as demonstrated by the interview extracts above. Riaz Hassan and Bill Martin say that 'Muslims are a particularly striking example of how a growing cultural subpopulation experience disadvantage ... Australian Muslims are educationally high achievers, but underemployed and underpaid.'[44] Peucker, Roose and Akbarzadeh note that 'The overall socioeconomic situation of Muslims continues to be characterised by substantial disadvantage and poor access to resources and human capital, compared to the total population.'[45] This may be because multiculturalism privileges rights over responsibilities and intensifies political disintegration:[46] essentially, as a policy it places emphasis on political participation and not necessarily on socioeconomic inclusion.[47] Multiculturalism does not necessarily lead to social inclusion, as the interview extracts clearly demonstrate, and therefore no meaningful social inclusion occurs in the society even though it assists members—particularly those from ethnic backgrounds—to take part in a variety of political activities and processes, such as running in elections at local council level.

For Australia to be a proudly inclusive society, one in which tolerance, understanding, egalitarianism, civility and justice are purported in the rhetoric of multiculturalism or, more recently, in the political discourse and public policy of social inclusion, then exclusionary processes and marginalisation of Muslims—or any group of individuals, for that matter—ought to be eradicated. In Australia's Old Right conservatism, the cherished cohesive society in which component groups and ways of life come together in some form of organic unity can no longer be sustained. Australia is an integral part of democratic capitalism and a global free market in which individuals belong not to one but many ethnic communities and whose demands are different and often conflicting. No one way of life can assert to be self-justifying when the group or groups over whom a society attempts to exercise authority are beholden to other values, cultural norms and life patterns. In a modern liberal capitalist society like Australia, subordinate and hybrid members—individuals who belong in part to various cultural traditions but wholly to none—are widespread. In these circumstances, patterns of living or lifestyles must make sense or hold meaning themselves to those who practise them. They must demonstrate themselves receptive to people's needs, show tolerance and respect, and be open to the growing sense of justice in the broader society.

It is for this reason that social cohesion cannot mean a flat acceptance of one's place and duties in society; nor can it be sustainable. It needs to be replaced with social cooperation and coexistence or social inclusion that values individuals equally and equitably, because modernity has greatly altered social institutions and, as John Gray writes, 'No one nowadays can hold to his station and duties, for no one has a fixed station or the duties that might go with such a position.'[48] The social inclusion or inclusive society I am proposing is one that encompasses a broad-based consensus on fundamental human rights and values and seeks to substantially reduce—or even eradicate—widespread disenfranchisement, alienation, marginalisation, disaffection, elitism and anomie, and where there is true large-scale unification of all Australians in a cooperative enterprise.

It is worthwhile to note that material and labour-market deprivation has been the central focus of social inclusion policies in many countries, including Australia, rather than the social, cultural and political aspects of social exclusion.[49] Peucker, Roose and Akbarzadeh assert that 'Muslims in Australia often lack access to relevant resources that facilitate civic and political participation and are therefore less likely to get involved in formal types of civic engagement.'[50] This explains why many Muslims feel disenfranchised and alienated. Their retreat from society-building is fundamentally because social integration or inclusion policies, it seems, aim merely to '[make] social and economic deviants fit into dominant norms and institutions, as well as to give them opportunities for political participation, educational development, and welfare benefits',[51] while ignoring processes of exclusion such as cultural intolerance, racism and economic exploitation.

Muslim experience of social exclusion in Australia is a serious issue that highlights the need for important policy reform, not only in the economic sector but also in social and political arenas, and the need for appropriate social, welfare and health service provisions. Muslim social exclusion is about not only economic exclusion—especially extreme poverty—but marginality, lack of social engagement, and fluid social bonds in society.

Many Muslims in Australia find themselves marginalised and neglected by Anglo-Celtic Australians and by socioeconomic and political institutions and processes because of their faith and cultural norms and practices. The obligations that society has to its members, particularly Muslims, to provide reasonable livelihoods and a sense of belongingness are grossly lacking. In a sense, the mutuality and reciprocity evident in elements of Australian multiculturalism reflect a social contract that favours the already-included in its conceptualisation of society. The role of reciprocity in the Australian context has implications for producing biases against the failings of the Muslim excluded, who are seen to veer away from society's includable norms. Whether these considerations will lead to action is yet to be seen. For Anglo-Celtic Australians, the Muslim excluded may very well represent the punished sector of a society against whom they, the included, have failed to hold up their end of the bargain in the social contract.

Chapter 5

The need for Muslim social inclusion

During the 1940s and until the 1960s, under the slogan 'Populate or perish', and then during the 1970s and 80s under the multiculturalism policy, migration was a source of positivity in Australia. More recently, however, migration has been described, particularly by conservative politicians, as a source of discontent, fear and instability in a modern liberal nation-state.

The shift in the framing of migration can be explained in terms of the changing global socioeconomic and political context. The last several decades have seen the world experience deindustrialisation, the decline of the nation-state, falling productivity, growing unemployment, poverty, marginalisation, inequality, violence, and the expansion of neoliberal political economies. Some global events have been specifically linked to the changing perception of migrants with Islamic faith, such as the Israeli-Palestinian conflict (1948 to the present), the Iranian Revolution (1978–79), the Rushdie affair (1989), Gulf War I (1990–91), the Bosnian War (1992), the September 11 terrorist attacks (2001), the Afghanistan War (2001), Gulf War II (2003) and the Danish cartoon crisis (2005–06). All these events have, in some direct or indirect way, moulded the ways in which Muslims have been comprehended by the West, including Australia, and in which Muslims have conceptualised the West.

Muslims and Islam prior to the tragic terrorist attacks in the United States on 11 September 2001 were almost 'invisible' in Australia. Events like the Rushdie affair, Gulf War I and the Bosnian War brought spasmodic and short-lived attention, but the 9/11 attacks produced an unprecedented and ongoing focus on Muslims and Islam. Since the period of the Crusades, Islam has been a 'problem' and an 'enemy' in the Western gaze, but this has intensified since 9/11. In other Western countries as well as in Australia, Muslims have been increasingly represented by anti-Muslim and anti-Islam activists as people who 'beat their wives', 'cut off hands', 'commit honour killings' and 'bomb people'; whose religious laws permit 'suicide bombing' and 'stoning adulterous women to death'; and where men can take 'child brides' and 'four wives'. These prejudiced perceptions about Muslims and Islam have been further reinforced by the impact of more recent events such as the Arab Spring, the Syrian civil war, and the emergence of the Islamic State of Iraq and the Levant (ISIL or ISIS). Consequently, it has become inevitable for some Australian—and by extension Western—individuals to have the urge to defend Western civilisation against Muslim migrants and their offspring, whom they perceive as the 'enemy within' and as culturally and religiously different from 'civilised' Western people.

This kind of perception and feeling has opened up debate about Muslim migration to Australia, the nature of Australian multiculturalism, and the compatibility of Islam with the civic and moral values of modern Australian liberal secularism. Given this, questions have been raised as to whether or not Muslims as a religious minority group can be politically and socially incorporated into the Australian liberal democratic nation-state.

In this chapter I address this by exploring Muslim social inclusion. In Chapter 4 I examined Muslim experience and some of the causes of social exclusion in Australia, and shed light on how the emphasis placed on social and cultural differences in the model of social integration leads to further Muslim marginalisation and not its elimination. In this chapter I expand on this and redirect the discussion to how reduction in socioeconomic disparities between Muslims and the mainstream community could potentially be the way forward to Muslims' further social integration in Australian multiculturalism. I posit that Muslims in Australia are already integrated in society and that the call for their social inclusion is not about integration but about better state and civic facilitation so they can experience a greater sense of belonging and anchorage in Australian multiculturalism.

Australian multiculturalism is limiting as a form of minority protection because group inequalities are attributed to cultural incompatibility and not correctly to socioeconomic disparities that prevent many Muslims from attaining social inclusion or a greater level of it. There is a critical need for Muslim social inclusion in the wider Australian social system, and this can be achieved, among other means, in three interrelated areas: comprehensive social security, effective participation, and egalitarian economy. Muslim social inclusion has a national benefit that has not been recognised in the conceptualisation of Australian multiculturalism or in the formulation of multicultural policy and integration and the social cohesion model.

Social inclusion

Every society aspires to maintain the principle that all its members should equally enjoy the benefits of prosperity and procure minimum standards of wellbeing. Based on this, it is expected that all segments of society are free from poverty and hunger and, among other things, are assured of healthy lives and access to education, medical services and justice. These may not be easy to achieve unless processes are in place and institutions are properly designed and managed so they can work for everyone, particularly those who are most vulnerable and needy in society. Also beneficial in this endeavour is the embracing of broad targets aimed at fostering the rule of law, ensuring equal access to all public services and justice, and generally cultivating inclusive and participatory decision-making processes.

These goals and targets, when properly conceptualised and effectively put into action, become vital functional elements of social inclusion processes. However, social inclusion encompasses a wide range of complex concerns, and no single goal-setting program or strategy can adequately address the multidimensionality of exclusion from which inclusionary reaction emanates or comprehensively promote inclusion, particularly given the diversity and complexity of conditions in a given society. The concept of inclusion, therefore, is opposite to exclusion and focuses on countering and remedying the negative consequences of exclusion.

Social inclusion generally is about the elimination of exclusion, the removal of any 'structure damaging'[1] barriers, through bringing members of a society in from the margins, having a positive human development approach to wellbeing, and creating strong and animated communities within a society.[2] For many concerned with issues of inclusion, priority is given to reducing poverty across generational and geographical divides: their focus, therefore, is on the economic sphere. For them, social inclusion is a process through which 'the underprivileged are ... [brought] into the mainstream market economy'.[3]

However, another essential element of the process entails creating access to social capital, which involves capacity-building of individuals and communities to empower them so they can work with each other and change the existing divisions between 'status groups'. There is no competition between the economic and social dimensions of inclusion; rather, the idea is collaboration between economic and public policies[4] with a proclivity for involving all segments of society in planning, designing and developing the inclusionary process.[5]

Irene Bloemraad, Anna Korteweg and Gökçe Yurdakul downplay the importance of this and place greater emphasis on the political aspect of inclusion, arguing that engagement in politics is critical and constitutes a major marker of full membership and belonging in the nation-state.[6] According to them, there are a range of individual and group behaviours that can be used to determine especially migrant groups' commitment and access to the political process. Taking out citizenship is the clearest marker of commitment to the political process, along with voting in elections and engagement in civic life through membership in civic organisations.

For social inclusion to be successful and effective, removing barriers is not enough. It requires making investments in laws and legislative changes and reforms, policies, processes, institutional developments, strategies and programs, and facilitating structural developments. As an ideal, social inclusion needs to be a long-term endeavour with both a local and a national focus that seeks to provide equity across diversity, remove social isolation and disenfranchisement, create access to material resources, and facilitate participation in community decision-making. In Esuna Dugarova's conceptualisation, social inclusion refers to 'a goal, process and outcome':

> As a universal goal, it aims to achieve an inclusive society that entails respect for human rights, cultural diversity and democratic governance, and upholds principles of equality and equity. As a process, it enables citizens' participation in decision-making activities that affect their lives, allowing all groups to take part in this process, especially marginalized groups. As an outcome, it ensures the reduction of inequalities, elimination of any forms of exclusion and discrimination, and achievement of social justice and cohesion.[7]

In scholarly discussions, social inclusion is always about creating an inclusive society as seen in Dugarova's definition, so it is often considered in conjunction with parallel concepts of social integration and social cohesion. As such, these concepts and social inclusion are used interchangeably in this chapter. It is worth noting that some scholars and community service delivery workers use the term 'social capital' in social inclusion discussions to describe networks with shared values, customs and understandings that enable collaboration within and between groups, and this is comprehended as a means to an end rather than a core goal.[8]

Social inclusion is often 'treated both as a goal which aims for a more stable, safe and just society for all, and as a process which entails the participation of stakeholders in decision making that affects their lives'.[9] In terms of a goal, social inclusion attempts to enable all members of a society to engage in social development, creating a society for all in which discrimination is outlawed; all human rights are promoted and protected; tolerance, respect for diversity, equality of opportunity, solidarity and security are actively sought and provided; and participation of all members of the society, irrespective of race, class, age, ethnicity, cultural background, political and religious persuasions and other differences, is facilitated at local and national levels. As a process, social inclusion is understood as a dynamic and principled course of action involving the promotion of the shared norms and values, relations and institutions that facilitate member cooperation and participation in all aspects of everyday living—social, cultural, economic and political—on the basis of equality of rights, equity and human dignity.

Thus, social inclusion is a multidimensional process aimed at creating conditions that enable full and active participation of people in society-building, including combating poverty and social exclusion—which is an involuntary exclusion of certain members of society from political, economic and societal processes leading to the prevention of their full participation in the society. It also includes empowering poor and marginalised people so that they have a voice in decisions that affect their lives and have access to the opportunities and resources needed for full participation in societal activities.[10]

In discussing social inclusion, inclusion of whom, inclusion into what, and how are important issues. 'Inclusion of whom' is about which groups or communities are being targeted for social inclusion; 'inclusion into what' asks whether inclusion is sought in the labour market, the welfare system, social spaces, or social, cultural and political processes; and 'how' refers to the processes and strategies that must be used or designed to achieve social inclusion. Care needs to be exercised when implementing social inclusion. Sometimes impoverished and oppressed people are included in a process but to their detriment, and therefore the inclusionary process may not be automatically beneficial for or necessarily wanted by such a group.[11] Social inclusion services for some people may be made available but the manner in which they are delivered may be inappropriate: for example, staffing a female-based nursing home with only male staff may undermine the elderly residents' way of living.

Social and political inclusion also has a positive impact on state security, which partly explains why various Western governments, including in Australia, show interest in promoting social inclusion as a policy and approach. A commitment to social justice and equity is another reason for countries to emphasise the merits of social inclusion. In Australia's case, both the Commonwealth and state governments have made contributions to the literature that stress the importance and usefulness of supporting social inclusion policies and strategies while at the same time refining popular understanding of the inclusion and exclusion processes.

The South Australian Government was the first to initiate a social inclusion program, establishing the Social Inclusion Unit within the Department of the Premier and Cabinet in March 2002. The aim of the initiative is to improve outcomes for highly vulnerable and disadvantaged members of the broader community. The Social Inclusion Unit's focus has been on promoting ongoing cooperation across government and with other stakeholders to jointly develop solutions to problems relating to social inclusion.

Several years later, in 2008, at federal government level under Deputy Prime Minister Julia Gillard, the Australian Social Inclusion Board was established as part of the government's commitment to reducing disadvantage and building up capabilities to help the broader community to take advantage of the choices and opportunities being created in modern Australia. Following the board's establishment, a number of government departments started concentrating on social inclusion issues in Australia.

These initiatives demonstrate state concern around and focus on social inclusion as an important approach to the political and civic incorporation of members of society. However, how much of it is symbolism? And are these approaches and mechanisms yielding real benefits for Australian Muslims? I attempt to address this, to some extent, in the ensuing sections.

Models of integration

Muslims in the countries of the West, including Australia, are minority communities and therefore, as some scholars[12] argue, are expected by their host societies or dominant cultures to conform to essential values and institutions. In the Australian context, this has been described by Ryan Edwards thusly: 'the dominant perspective of Australian multiculturalism, which is based on the assumption that public religion is on the decline, remains that immigrants will be assimilated into Australian society through individualism and secularisation'.[13] The recent calls for 'schools for imams' in Europe as well as in Australia to educate imams in the values and traditions of their host society is an expression of this expectation.[14]

However, conformity is neither a simple process nor necessarily desired by immigrants. Jørgen Nielsen[15] suggests that Muslims in the West have opted for one of three choices when it comes to the questions of integration and assimilation: they opt for integration/assimilation or reject it outright, or take a middle position.[16] He claims that those who opt for integration/assimilation are mainly the second-generation children of immigrant families, who tend to adopt Western social norms in family and social behaviour, business practices, language and dress, and in a sense are Westernised in their way of life and attitude.

At the other end of the scale are those who reject integration/assimilation outright and prefer to maintain their traditional lifestyles.[17] Settled in communities that keep consistent links with their home countries, they maintain a clear ethnic identity and the customs and social practices of their home countries. Nielsen argues that for them, practising Islam as understood in their homelands and drawing clear similarities between Islam and ethnic traditions are closely tied to their identity and thus many perceive themselves in terms of their ethnic or national origin. They continue to have religious and political loyalties to families, friends, communities and political parties in their homelands.

In the middle are those who have integrated/assimilated into the public and private spaces of their host society and use *ijtihad* (independent reasoning) to interpret Islam.[18] This group blends Islam with Western values, leading to the creation of a new hybrid Western–Islamic identity that Olivier Roy calls EuroIslam.[19] This new identity has its roots in a liberal and innovative form of Islam that accommodates Western material and individualistic, secular and social values. Nielsen claims that these Muslims, with their secular and individualistic outlook on life, make religious compromises so that they can fit in with the expectations and rationalities of their host societies and thus pave the way for a more syncretic and diasporic version of Islam. For these Muslim immigrants, Islam is a changeable system that can be modified and reshaped to suit their lifestyle and mode of existence and the demands of the epoch, rendering it a secular, individualistic and private religion with no necessary link to a religious movement or caliphate or to the ummah. Nielsen claims that those who fall in the middle category are in the majority. To adopt a middle ground is not necessarily a conscious choice but, rather, taking part in 'a process of continual negotiation between individual personality and circumstances'.[20]

Apart from Nielsen, scholars such as Yvonne Haddad and Jane Smith[21] and Gary David and Kenneth Ayouby[22] have also argued that those Muslims in the West who adopt a middle position towards integration/assimilation are in the majority. David and Ayouby show this to be true through their work with Muslims in Detroit in the United States. They claim that certain Muslims, especially locally born second- or third-generation migrants (or both) from Arab backgrounds, find themselves in the 'middle ground' as they seek both to identify with their cultural heritage and try to conceal it.

For Muslim immigrants, integration into the culture of Western societies is clearly problematic. Pierre Van Den Berghe suggests that immigrants in general are 'Subordinate minorities ... under constant pressure to acculturate, because becoming like the dominant group almost invariably confers social advantages.'[23] Ake Sander,[24] whose work focuses on Muslims in Sweden but has relevance to the Muslim situation in general in the West, sees the integration of Muslim immigrants as a serious problem. He claims that it is not that Muslims resist integration but that, as in many Western countries, Swedish structures are largely unfavourable to them, and notes that as part of the Western monolith, Sweden sees itself as built on the idea of 'One nation, one people, one religion'.[25] He connects the separation of Muslims in Sweden to this notion of 'a common culture and religion, including common manners, norms and value system, as well as a common way of thinking in general'.[26] Sander further argues that the state's officially declared 'multiculturalism', where equality, freedom of choice and partnership are important features, is understood in different ways by the Swedish non-Muslim and Muslim population. Swedes in general understand multiculturalism basically through the principle of equality, denoting 'equality between universal individuals regardless of culture, ethnicity, race, religion and gender'.[27] Muslims, however, are likely to see multiculturalism in terms of equal rights to freedom of choice. Sander argues that for Swedish authorities the idyllic 'multiculturalism' is one in which public life is characterised by equality, denoting similarity, while religious and cultural expressions should be restricted to the private sphere. Hence, while officially an integrationist model is promoted, in reality the expectation is for an elevated degree of assimilation.

Muhammad Anwar, a sociologist from the United Kingdom, presents a similar argument for the case of Muslims in Britain when he suggests that integration in Britain means one thing to the majority of Britons and another to immigrant Muslims.[28] He claims that immigrant Muslims conceive of 'integration' as 'acceptance by the majority of their separate ethnic and cultural identity'.[29] However, from the majority perspective, 'integration' echoes the 'ideology of the dominant group', which implies that 'any group unabsorbed, or not assimilated, is considered to upset the equalisation of social relations in the society'.[30]

In Australia, Rosalie Atie, Kevin Dunn and Mehmet Ozalp found in their research that:

> there is a strong willingness of Muslims wanting to integrate to Australia and feel part and parcel of the country and its society. The more religious Muslims are and the more they are educated in the Islamic scholarly tradition, the more likely they are to see the consistency between Australian norms and Islamic practice. Muslims are expected to integrate to multicultural Australia. Multicultural policy has a reciprocal expectation that non-Muslims show a willingness to allow and support that integration to take place.[31]

Australian Muslims and the need for their social inclusion

Scholars have argued that Australian Muslims are a marginalised minority group in Australia who 'continue to occupy a socioeconomically disadvantaged position' and that following the terrorist attacks of 11 September 2001 and the subsequent bombings in Bali, London and other places, 'Muslim citizens have come under extreme scrutiny'.[32] Many Australian Muslims find themselves on the margins of society, alienated and disenfranchised, but as difficult as this is, they are still somehow either directly or indirectly involved in a broader network of social relations. With regard to social inclusion, their problem is not so much that they are unintegrated into the wider Australian social system but that the prevailing patterns of inclusion foster unjust or damaging outcomes in certain situations. The challenge, therefore, is for social policy, inclusionary processes and strategies, and state initiatives to ensure that patterns of human relations in Australian multiculturalism promote justice, offer fair opportunities, and ensure equitable outcomes for all, including Muslims.

Thus, policies have been developed aimed at inclusion through economic efficiency that focus on cultivating individual wellbeing and alleviating poverty. In doing so, they ignore the social relations that underpin exclusion and the realisation of rights connected to security and social protection, adequate living standards and participation in all spheres of life. In this context, measuring social inclusion has been restricted to indicators that reflect an individual's access to resources, programs and services but hardly provides explanations of the nature of human relations, social processes and institutional functions. Like social ills such as poverty and inequality, exclusion is multifaceted: in other words, its causes are many and it takes varied forms, and therefore it cannot be addressed predominantly through economic means.

Critical to note is the fact that individual outcomes—for instance, in education or health—do not necessarily lead to social inclusion, and that policies and strategies that work in one socioeconomic and political context may not work in another. They may not even help to tackle unfair and unequal power relations in society. It is, then, crucial to adopt a more wide-ranging approach to inclusion, with policies and programs based on the principles of solidarity and reciprocity promoting equal opportunities and fair outcomes, and guaranteeing entitlements to services-based rights. Also included should be the capacity of social groups such as Muslims to participate in society, taking into account social, cultural, religious, economic and political factors.[33] Under this consideration, social policy needs to focus on the welfare and rights of individuals as well as facilitating the growth of social relations, institutions and structures, while at the same time stressing the importance of broad-based societal levels of analysis and not merely focusing on economic or individual indicators.[34]

Thus, I argue that there is a need for Muslim social inclusion in the wider Australian social system and that this can be achieved through three interrelated areas: comprehensive social security, effective participation, and egalitarian economy.

Comprehensive social security

Social security will involve averting, managing and overcoming scenarios that negatively impact on Muslims, particularly the most vulnerable. As a paradigm for Muslim social inclusion, it needs to comprise policies and initiatives that provide access to basic human services such as housing, health and education, and ensure adequate provision for numerous contingencies of life such as unemployment, sickness and old age. Social security is a vital means of alleviating poverty among vulnerable Muslims and can be employed as a powerful tool to promote Muslim social inclusion. It can not only act as a preventive mechanism for individual Muslims and Muslim families from entering poverty or remaining in it, but also empower them with rights and pave the way for their active participation in societal processes.

Effective participation

Without participation in socioeconomic, cultural and political processes either as individuals or a community, success and life satisfaction are limited and in some instances non-existent. Andrew Pearse and Matthias Stiefel define participation as 'organized efforts to increase control over resources and regulative institutions in given social situations, on the part of groups and movements of those hitherto excluded from such control'.[35] It denotes engagement in diverse facets of life, ranging from sociocultural to economic to political, by all members of the wider community, based on equality of opportunities, fairness and rights.

In relation to Muslims, particularly those who are disadvantaged, effective participation denotes not only giving them a voice as a group but strengthening their capacity to take part in decision-making processes and influence outcomes, particularly those relevant to them as a minority and disadvantaged community. It also involves them being able to exercise claims on external entities and institutions that impact on the realities of their everyday living. In this sense, Muslim participation is a prerequisite for inclusive processes and development.

Egalitarian economy

Egalitarian economy is an ethical and values-based approach to economic development where the production of commodities by manufacturers and businesses is undertaken for human and social good and not for profiteering. It privileges the welfare of people and environment over profits and blind growth, and involves cooperative and associative relations and democratic forms of management. Egalitarian economy is built around a core of ethical principles and espouses values of egalitarianism, cooperativism and sharing, with a systemic and transformative agenda.

In egalitarian economy, the crises related to Muslim poverty and social exclusion can be solved through the development of various bottom-up programs that are based on the egalitarian principles shared by different social groups in an attempt to resolve their own problems. Apart from Australian governments at all three levels, other actors in developing inclusive strategies have to start recognising the need to shift from an approach that focuses on providing direct material assistance to needy Muslims to an approach that empowers these Muslims through productive activities, training, skills development, and social organisation and management. As Atie, Dunn and Ozalp write, 'Promoting education and facilitating employment of Muslims would further increase social inclusion and cohesion, especially for those that are struggling to enter the labour market.'[36]

Muslim integration into Australian multicultural society is a complex endeavour requiring what is often described in the literature as a Muslim-centred integrated approach. Due to limitations of space here I will not explore this in depth, but I have tried to offer a glimpse into it. In an attempt to facilitate Muslim integration in Australia, the overarching objective needs to be the identification and addressing of the root causes of Muslim social exclusion and, therefore, promoting policy and practical solutions, investing in the human potential of vulnerable and marginalised Muslims by upgrading their skills and thereby creating for them stable employment and income opportunities. Investments need to be made in continued learning and vocational resources, education, skills development and employment facilitation in order to equip young Muslims especially with the skills needed for a rapidly changing labour market. In addition, discrimination, marginalisation and exclusion are major causes of Muslims' reluctance to fully participate in society and the economy, and must be removed through better and fairer anti-discrimination laws and social policies. Muslims need to be empowered through integrated economic and social policies and Muslim-centred social inclusion programs and initiatives.

Australia needs to develop a national 'model' of integration for minorities such as Muslims in order to facilitate their political and civic incorporation. Such a model will help Muslims take up Australian citizenship with ease, unlike the current cumbersome system with its unreasonable citizenship test, and participate in voluntary associations, including co-ethnic ones. The current laws relating to citizenship and voting shape Muslims' political membership and participation by regulating access to formal methods of engagement. Citizenship laws, it seems, have symbolic consequences in that they promote a hierarchical citizenship by restricting and even denying the advantages of 'Australianness' to those who are seen as permanent 'Others'.[37] Mario Peucker, Joshua Roose and Shahram Akbarzadeh state that in Australia:

> Legal citizenship status grants individuals full civic, social and political rights and responsibilities, including the right and duty to vote and the entitlement to run for public office. Muslims remain, however, severely under-represented in political decision-making processes.[38]

The current seemingly symbolic approaches or mechanisms, in contrast to well-thought-out and well-worked-out ones connected to opportunities for civic and political engagements, do not significantly shape or facilitate Muslims' political and civic incorporation across wide-ranging Australian settings.[39] To give Muslim social inclusion any chance of success, they must be revisited and reformed. A way forward with this is to institute a political dialogue involving all three levels of governments, key non-government organisations, and peak and non-peak Muslim community civic organisations, with a view to achieving better integration of social inclusion and social protection processes in national and subnational policymaking.

At the moment, much Muslim political and civic incorporation occurs through association membership because the design and implementation of prevailing social inclusion models are inadequate. Through association membership, Muslims—especially the young cohort—establish a meaningful sense of belonging in the face of precariousness. Although Muslim political and civic participation is occurring through association membership, it is only one component of the more general process of Muslim integration that is required and that must involve social, economic and cultural dimensions, all of which are affected by Muslims' minority status based on religion.

Part 3

Sharia and Muslim clergy in Australia

Chapter 6

The formal accommodation of sharia in Australia

Sharia is a hotly debated subject in Australia among people from all walks of life, including conservative and bigoted politicians, ignorant journalists, militant far right white supremacists, and biased academics. For many, it is seen as a draconian and outdated religious law—particularly in the field of criminal law—that is inimical to the common law system, anathema to human rights, the main obstacle to progress of Muslims, and the cause of Muslim experience of social exclusion. Those with such views denounce sharia as incompatible with democracy and modernity and, therefore, having no place in a country like Australia that is characteristically modern and secular.

Based on such views, in Australia the recent movement to right-wing politics has brought demands to impose controls on the implementation of sharia, advocating restrictions on public veiling by Muslim women, curbing of mosque-building and private Muslim schools, halting halal certification, and the imposition of firmer limits on Muslim immigration. However, attempting to control the spread of the practice of sharia is not viable because in a Muslim's daily life, sharia is the legal foundation and a comprehensive code. It has laws governing all aspects of life, from the physical to the intellectual and from the spiritual to the mundane.

As a legal system of Islam, sharia is a corpus of rules, considered to be of divine origin, implemented by practising Muslims to govern their 'ibadat (private worship) and mu'amalat (social relations and human transactions). Abdul Ansari confirms this: 'In its restrictive sense, the Sharia comprises rules governing relations between man and Allah (s.w.t.),[1] commonly known as rules of ibadat, and rules governing human relations and human behaviours, commonly known as rules governing muamalat.'² This set of rules specifies the directions and regulations that govern the lives of faithful believers, and also encompasses moral and spiritual values. Sharia does not separate matters relating to this world from those relating to the hereafter, and the sacred and the profane constitute one whole universal complex. Any attempt to restrict these rules would not only be extremely problematic and difficult but could potentially provoke the ire of Muslims as Australian citizens.

For Muslims, imposing restrictions on the implementation of sharia is counterproductive. Instead, many Muslims, under the influence of Islamic revivalism,³ want a more open implementation of sharia; some even want legislative changes to be made so sharia can be formally accommodated in Australia. In the latter case, in 2011 the Australian Federation of Islamic Councils (AFIC) made a submission to the federal Parliamentary Joint Standing Committee on Migration requesting a change in legislation so Islamic law could be adopted as mainstream legislation.⁴ A year earlier, 'During an open day at Sydney's Lakemba Mosque ... the Australian Islamic Mission's president, Dr Zachariah Matthews, called for aspects of sharia law to function as a parallel legal system.'⁵ Whichever way one looks at it, a discussion of sharia is inevitable in Australia.

One very key problem in such a discussion is what Muslim leaders and activists and Muslims in general from different ethnic, parochial, sectarian and ideological backgrounds mean by sharia.

For some, it is 'God's law' or 'revealed law' and by nature essentially a non-negotiable text-based law originating from the sacred sources—the Qur'an and Sunna (words, deeds and actions of the Prophet Mohammed, and his implicit approval or disapproval of others' actions around him)—and whose authority lies outside human purview and certainly outside the authority of a modern nation-state. Those with this view, then, present sharia as a set of immutable rules designed by God that cannot be compatible with democracy and modernity, which operate under human-made legal systems: 'The shari'a, according to this line of thought, is the revealed law of God and is, therefore, the perfect set of rules for human conduct, which needs no supplementation by man-made laws.'⁶

This belief is detectable from media depictions of Islam as well as from Muslim individuals and groups claiming to speak for Islam. One such group is Hizb ut-Tahrir (Liberation Party), a small but very vocal movement that originated in Jordan in the 1950s as an offshoot of Al-Ikhwan al-Muslimin (Muslim Brotherhood)⁷ and that since the 1990s has found small but powerful support in Sydney and Melbourne, especially among Muslim students.⁸ Boko Haram (sometimes translated as 'Westernisation Is Sacrilege') is another very vocal and hardline Islamic sectarian movement, founded in 2002 by Mohammed Yusuf in Maiduguri, the capital of the north-eastern Nigerian state of Borno.

In its initial proclamation, Boko Haram revealed its intentions of uprooting corruption and injustice in Nigeria, which it blamed on Westernisation and modernisation, and advocated the imposition of sharia on Nigerian society. It reportedly has links with al-Qaeda and ISIL and has secured small but strong support in Sydney and Melbourne, especially among Muslims from African countries such as Nigeria, Ethiopia, Kenya and Somalia.[9]

Hizb ut-Tahrir and Boko Haram reflect only one of several understandings of the nature of sharia. Some Western scholars take the view that after sharia's formative and classical periods of development, it ceased to evolve.[10] Some say, for instance, that in the late Mamluk and Ottoman periods and through much of Islamic history,[11] it was not the specific solutions or legal rulings that were considered critical but how solutions were developed and decisions were taken within the generally accepted framework of thought, utilising commonly accepted intellectual know-how and methods.

Discussion of sharia is now much more complex and contested, not only at intellectual, legal and theological levels, but also at social, cultural and political levels. Muslims who are seeking to keep the practice of sharia alive today fall into two categories.[12] The first is conservative traditionalists: Muslim ideologists, sometimes referred to as Muslim puritans, who seek to keep sharia 'fixed'. The second is secular modernists, or Muslim moderates, who want to see sharia undergo reform. The latter are divided into two groups. One is often described as modern secularists: they substantially advance more inclusive, pluralistic and vibrant civil societies with an understanding of sharia as a flexible and time/space-friendly legal system. The other is portrayed as critical-progressive Muslims with a broad-based outlook on contemporary Islam: they focus on reinterpreting normative Qur'anic teachings in light of a global viewpoint and in a way that promotes the wellbeing of people in accordance with their specific context.[13]

In this chapter I explore Muslim calls for the formal accommodation of sharia in Australia. Muslims all over the world have been practising sharia for over 1400 years, as it is one of their central resources. In Australia, the call for formal accommodation of sharia is a way for Muslims to deal with modernity and globalisation as they pursue life in a constantly changing liberal multiculturalism. I posit that Australian Muslims' call for the formal accommodation of sharia raises important questions about Muslims wanting to practise sharia as an integral part of their religion in a free society. They are not demanding, as antagonists of sharia would have it, to constitutionalise sharia but, rather, to allow its wider recognition as an ethico-moral structure in Muslim communities and broader Australian society. I suggest that the formal accommodation of sharia in Australia is a worthy legal and political consideration but one imbued with great complexity.

A basic framework of sharia

To understand Islam, or Muslim religious practices, one needs to understand the basic framework of sharia (pronounced SHAH-ree-ah). Sharia is an antediluvian Arabic word that has been used to designate the code of conduct or the law of religion of Islam. It literally means 'a path to a waterhole, way or well-trodden road', and in terms of Muslim usage is a metaphor for achieving salvation for God's ordained total way of life.

In the English language, the word is normally translated as 'Islamic law'; however, in Arabic-speaking contexts it denotes a much broader meaning of comprehensive guidance and a divine rule of law. Religiously speaking, this equates to a pathway to be followed seeking felicity and salvation.[14] Muslims believe that it puts righteous believers on the right path—siraat al mustaqeem—and this right path, which the believer has to tread, is the way to the source of life. Like water is a source of life, sharia is the source of the Islamic way of life, which Muslims believe is ordained by God. In other words, sharia is a source of the ordained way, and guidance for humankind in how to conduct their material and spiritual affairs.

The etymology of sharia as a 'path' or 'way' derives from the Qur'anic verse 'Thus we put you on the right way of religion. So follow it and follow not the whimsical desire [hawa] of those who have no knowledge.'[15] At the time of the revelation of this verse, sharia did not exist as a legal code; the Qur'anic reference here is to its literal sense of an explicit faith in Allah's designated way—Islam.[16] The religious character of Islamic law emanates from divine sources—the Qur'an and the divinely inspired Sunna—representing God's design for the correct ordering of all human activities. Although Muslims generally agree that they are bound by sharia, there is no single understanding of it.[17] Instead of sharia, in Arabic the terms al-Qanun al-Islami or al-shari'at al-Islamiyya (both meaning Islamic law) are often used.

Interpretations of sharia and its requirements have differed over time, historically influenced by sectarian divisions and the existence of a wide spectrum of jurisprudential schools. In the modern era, interpretations have been impacted by the question of how to design and apply sharia to constantly and rapidly changing contemporary human conditions and circumstances under the processes of modernisation and globalisation. These have left sharia as a legal system with a dynamic nature and without a unified code, which means that there is no single set of legal rulings or book of statutes.

Despite this, sharia is the fundamental religious concept of Islam, the essence of Muslim faith, and a path to guide Muslims on how to live in this world and prepare for the next. Although it takes diverse forms of observance, it is understood to describe Muslims' personal responsibilities as believers, wherever they live: 'In the Qur'an, sharia corresponds to the idea of God's

Way—divine exhortation about the ideal way to behave in this world—thus, "God's Law".[18] In the Qur'an, sharia is used, as mentioned earlier, in relation to a way towards or a purpose of faith[19] as well as in relation to the whole system of law and jurisprudence within the religion of Islam. The principal Islamic ethos demands Muslims to surrender to the will of Allah in totality, and Allah's command for the Muslim ummah is expressed through sharia and constitutes a system of duties that all faithful believers must fulfil.

Sharia as a term only appears once in the Qur'an,[20] yet for Muslims it is believed to be the revealed word of God and the basic text that provides the guidelines for his law. Muslims believe that sharia is 'God's law'[21] or 'revealed law'[22] and by nature a text-based law originating from the sacred sources of Islam: the Qur'an as the literal word of Allah and Sunna of the Prophet Mohammed. The Qur'anic revelation is seen by Muslims to have laid down the basic standards of conduct upon which the Prophet established his first ummah. The Qur'an, Muslims believe, provides a variety of ethico-legal teachings, of which some have a universal application and others are specific to particular circumstances and material conditions. Ism'ail Raji al Faruqi advises that:

> Muslims have recognized the imperatives and desiderata of the Qur'an as falling into different orders of rank or priority. Although they all belong to the divine will and are constitutive of it, Qur'anic values do not all enjoy the same degree of normativeness. Some are more fundamental and important than others. Some are direct and specific in what they demand of man; some are indirect, pointing to general directions. Some are explicit and comprehensible on first reading; others are implicit and have to be deduced from one or more Qur'anic premises.[23]

Wael Hallaq sheds further light on this:

> The traditional count of all legal verses comes to about five hundred—a number that at first glance seems exiguous, considering the overall size of the Quran ... these verses represent a larger weight than the number may indicate. It is common knowledge that the Quran repeats itself both literally and thematically, but this tendency of repetition is absent in the legal subject matter. The proportion of the legal verses, therefore, is larger than that suggested by an absolute number. And if we consider the fact that the average length of the legal verses is twice or even thrice that of the non-legal verses, it is not difficult to argue ... that the Quran contains no less legal material than does the Torah.[24]

The Qur'an is taken by Muslims to hold the key elements of legislation and legislative powers: 'There are close to 350 legal *ayat* in the Qur'an, most of which were revealed in response to problems that were encountered.'[25] Various Qur'anic verses are testimonies to this, but mentioning two here will suffice: 'The command rests with none but Allah'[26] and 'And whoever judges not by that which Allah has revealed, they are disbelievers'.[27] These and other verses form the basis of a distinct concept of law in Islam that fundamentally differs from the notion of law in a modern national constitution. A duality is envisaged in a modern constitution where the state is the lawgiver and is also subject to the law—but not so in sharia: 'In *Sharia*, both the state and the individual are subjects of the *hukm* (law) issued from the Hakim (Lawgiver) who is Allah (swt), and whatever legislative powers exercised by the state are considered conferred upon the state by the Hakim, and do not emanate from it.'[28] It is for this reason that Dominic McGoldrick explains that sharia is the fundamental religious concept of Islam and the essence of Muslim faith:

> Shari'a can be understood as an abstract philosophical concept or overarching meta-norm approximating to the rule of law. Alternatively, Shari'a can be understood as more of a moral conception ... It can be more narrowly conceived as embodying Islamically derived rules and norms. Finally, it can also be understood as a flexible general system of law ...[29]

Sharia, then, is understood to be a corpus of rules of divine origin implemented by human agency to govern private worship and social relations. It specifies the rules and regulations governing the lives of faithful believers. It is thought to be a way of life, a complete exchange, in which all important religious, legal, moral, ethical, social, cultural, economic and political institutions find simultaneous expression. Sharia, 'historically and at the present, is associated with its function as a language of justice. It is not just "law" in the modern sense, but a total discourse of religion, morality and justice.'[30] From a Weberian perspective, it exhibits a 'substantive rationality' within which morality, ethics, law, religion, economy and politics are enmeshed, in contrast to a 'formal rationality' (which Weber associates exclusively with Western capitalism) within which law is separate from other parts of societal structure and operates under its own distinct code of conduct and conventions.[31]

Along with the two canonical sources (the Qur'an and Hadith) that constitute the basis of sharia, there are three others, *ijma*, *qiyas* and *ijtihad*, that complete the sources of sharia—particularly in Sunni Islam, which the majority of Australian Muslims follow. A number of verses in the Qur'an identify the sources of sharia and their order of priority. However, there is one passage in which, with the exception of the last source, all other sources are indicated: Chapter al-Nisa' (Women), which says, 'O you who have believed, obey Allah and obey the Messenger and those in authority among you. And if you disagree over anything, refer it to Allah and the Messenger, if you should believe in Allah and the Last Day. That is the best [way] and best in result.'[32] 'Obey Allah' refers to the Qur'an, and 'obey the Messenger' refers to the Sunna. Obedience to 'those in authority among you' refers to *ijma* (scholarly or juristic consensus in which scholars and jurists rely on *'aql* [intellect] to generate general principles based on the Qur'an and Sunna); and the final part of the verse, which requires that all disputes be referred to God and to the Messenger, gives *qiyas* (reasoning by analogy) legitimacy as a source. In this way, qiyas is basically an extension of the injunctions of the Qur'an and Sunna. The appropriateness and utility of qiyas may be indicated in these sources or may be identified by way of *istinbat* (inference). Whatever the case, qiyas basically involves the discovery of a rule that already exists in the divine sources.[33]

The final source—often described as the human source—is *ijtihad* (individual reasoning, which is an intellectual property for increasing *ilm* [knowledge] of traditional practice and the trained capacity to deduce from it, using *ray* or juristic opinion), and its legitimacy emanates from various Hadith such as the following, narrated on the authority of Thawban that the Messenger of Allah (s.a.w.) said: 'A group among my Ummah will continue to follow the truth and prevail, and those who oppose them will not be able to harm them, until the command of Allah comes to pass.'[34] 'A group among my Ummah' refers to people of *fiqh* (jurisprudence), knowledge and Hadith.

In a discussion of sharia one will often find a number of different concepts being explored; one is fiqh. Many people, including countless Muslim theologians, erroneously use the terms sharia and fiqh interchangeably. Amanullah Fahad states: 'The Arabic words *Fiqh* and *Shariah* are frequently used in Islamic literature as the interchangeable terms.'[35] However, sharia is different from fiqh. Fiqh, which is an Arabic term, literally means 'understanding' or 'knowledge' and what is commonly known as 'Islamic jurisprudence' in English. It is the human attempt at understanding sharia and a tool used by *fuqaha* (Muslim jurists) to extract *ahkam* (legal rulings) from the sacred sources of Islam. Khaled Abou El Fadl distinguishes between sharia and fiqh:

> Shari'a is the eternal, immutable, and unchanging law as it exists in the mind of God. Shari'a is the Way of truth and justice as it exists in God's mind. In essence, Shari'a is the ideal law as it ought to be in the Divine realm … . Thus human beings must strive and struggle to realize Shari'a law to the best of their abilities. In contrast, fiqh is the human law—it is the human attempt to reach and

fulfill the eternal law as it exists in God's mind. As such, fiqh is not itself Divine, because it is the product of human efforts. Fiqh, unlike Shari'a, is not eternal, immutable, or unchanging. By definition, fiqh is human and therefore subject to error, alterable, and contingent.[36]

When sharia and fiqh are distinguished from each other, many Muslims find the basis for the claim that sharia is the expression of God's will for human behaviour and, therefore, immutable. What is not fixed is fiqh, and this is critical in understanding the relationship between the two. Fiqh is the process of human interpretation of that revealed will, the divine law, the extrapolation of the immutable sharia into guiding principles and rules for everyday living. This is totally different from what is generally understood as legislation in modern secular Western societies, where the actual law and laws can be changed by humans.

In Islam, in both the majority Sunni case and the minority Shi'a case, fiqh is a large collection of juridical opinions that were given by various early jurists from multiple jurisprudential schools, often called madhabs—such as Hanafi, Shafi'i, Maliki and Hanbali in Sunni Islam and Twelver, Zaidi and Ismaili in Shi'a Islam. This jurisprudential corpus was mainly produced in the second and third centuries of Islam by ulama (Muslim scholars) or private scholars, with unique methods of reasoning and argument. It effectively became the corpus of sharia as developed from canonical sources and implemented to address issues facing Muslims relating to their practices of worship and social relationships. The juridical opinions were formulated to assist in the application of sharia to Muslims' real-life situations after the death of the Prophet Mohammed. Fiqh is the human understanding of the sharia or an Islamic jurisprudential tool used to assist in a better understanding of sharia and implemented by jurists' rulings called fatwas. Fiqh, which literally means 'understanding' or 'knowledge', is Islamic jurisprudence used to define rules and methodologies of law. It is the methodology employed to work out and apply the law.

In essence, then, fiqh is a science of ascertaining a sound understanding of sharia, and a discipline that permits academic discussion and exegetical analysis of Islamic practice. Thus, while sharia is believed to be immutable and infallible, fiqh is understood to be fallible and changeable yet helpful in making sharia clearer and more understandable, and ultimately implementable in everyday living. It is for this reason that many different opinions exist on what is permissible and what is not in Islam, and why sharia is practised by Muslims in a large variety of ways.

The differences between sharia and fiqh are summarised in Table 7.

Table 7: Differences between sharia and fiqh

Sharia	Fiqh
Broad and general	Narrow and specific
Fixed	Open to change
Sources are the Qur'an and Sunna	Source is sharia—the Qur'an, Sunna, qiyas, ijma and ijtihad

The Muslim case for formal accommodation of sharia in Australia

The question of whether sharia can be formally accommodated in the Australian legal system and, more broadly, in the Australian multicultural way of life is a complex yet pertinent one. What follows is an exploration of this important question in some depth.

It is important to start by asking what is meant by formal accommodation of sharia in the Australian legal system and in the Australian multicultural way of life. The response to this is not all that clear, but it seems that from Muslims' perspective it doesn't mean the constitutionalisation or legislation of sharia: it means the ability to freely practise sharia and non-punitively implement the principles of Islam in their everyday living. Ghena Krayem, a sharia expert in the University of Sydney Law School, claims that sharia is already accommodated in Australian society without legislative changes, and that Muslims are not seeking to establish a separate legal system but want rules of sharia integrated in the current Australian common law system.[37] This means that there is an assumption that the principles of sharia are compatible with the principles of common law; and that sharia doesn't have to become the primary source by inserting its elements into the common law system or the Constitution but only to be presented in spirit or as an inspiration.

As far as the Australian Constitution is concerned, citizens have the right to freedom of religion and therefore Muslims have the right to practise their faith freely. Section 116 states:

> The Commonwealth shall not make any law for establishing any religion, or for imposing any religious observance, or for prohibiting the free exercise of any religion, and no religious test shall be required as a qualification for any office or public trust under the Commonwealth.[38]

Likewise, as members of Australian society Muslims have the constitutional right to seek justice in the nation's common law system. If they have constitutional rights to practise religion freely and to seek justice in the common law system, why would Muslims then want a formal accommodation of sharia? Muslims claim that it is precisely under the right to freedom of religion that they seek formal accommodation of sharia. Another claim is that the current common law system doesn't cover or deal adequately with certain Islamic matters in a manner that complies with sharia or Islamic legal rules.

In the latter case, looking at divorce, for example, helps to shed some light on the problem. Divorce in Islam involves a high degree of complexity as there are different legal processes applicable to men and women. In a husband-initiated divorce, the process is rather straightforward as men generally can divorce extrajudicially through a unilateral pronouncement of divorce, called *talaq* in Arabic. Under sharia, the man has to wait three months before the divorce comes into force and subsequently can remarry in accordance with sharia. However, as Ann Black and Kerrie Sadiq write, 'Under Australian [common] law he would need to be separated and wait a further nine months.'[39] If a wife seeks divorce from her husband and secures it, in sharia court she is required to return the *mahr*[40] (dower) but not so in the Australian common law system under section 79 of the Family Law Act 1975 (Cth). These scenarios highlight the complexities and problems associated with setting a procedural form of power and accountability into the Australian common law system.

Many Australian Muslims already implement various aspects of sharia, such as *nikah* (marriage), *janaza* (Islamic burial), *zakat* (alms) and *sawm* (fasting), in their everyday living and on this basis support the idea of formal accommodation of sharia in the Australian legal system as it would make their everyday lives easier to pursue. They argue that since this is already occurring, it is only logical to make the practice official. What they wish to happen is to be able to continue living their lives this way without any prejudice, fear or public admonishment and with state support when it is needed. However, this is not always easy and many external social and institutional hurdles (hurdles created outside the Muslim community) exist.

To expand on this, let us take Muslim women's dress as an example. In the post-9/11 period in Australia, Muslim women's clothing, particularly the hijab, *niqab* (face covering) and *burqa* (full loose body covering), has become the most controversial and commented-upon issue. The likes of One Nation leader Pauline Hanson, New South Wales Legislative Council member Fred Nile, leader and founder of the Jacqui Lambie Network and Tasmanian senator Jacqui Lambie, former member of the Liberal Party of Australia and leader of the Australian Conservatives Cory Bernardi, former 2GB radio presenter Alan Jones and right-wing shock jock Ray Hadley have all called for a ban on wearing burqa by Muslim women. It is not an exaggeration to postulate that few, if any, other cultural elements have received as much attention in Australia as Muslim women's dress.

The pressing question here is: why has the way Muslim women dress become such a bone of contention? Perhaps it is not so much the dress itself but the meaning assigned to it or the representation it holds. It may even be more about accommodating or not accommodating Muslims as a minority group in multicultural Australia than about Muslim women's dress code. Women wear a large variety of attire, but for Muslim women the veil is a powerful signifier. It is construed by some to signify not only a backward, anti-modern Islam and a threat to national security, but also women's seclusion and relegation to a private sphere, women's passivity and submissiveness, and their invisibility in the public space. Ultimately, it comes to represent a patriarchal religious system in which women have an inferior role and status and are oppressed subjects.

This kind of image is particularly common in the mainstream media, especially print and television. Julie Posetti attests:

> Ubiquitously portrayed as veiled, [Muslim women] are concurrently represented as oppressed and radical non-conformists, as threatened and threatening, as passive sex-slaves and exotic, erotic beings. Symbolised generically by the distinctive religious clothing some choose to wear, Muslim women of all cultures have become the most recognisable visible targets of racism on the streets, yet at the same time they are almost invisible and voiceless in news coverage.[41]

The issue of dress is very concerning for Muslim women and of great significance to them in multicultural Australia, where Muslims generally constitute a minority community. This concern originates from recent attempts in Australia to regulate and even ban Muslim women's veil.[42] The reasons for calling for such a ban vary, but they seem to revolve around the idea that the veil undermines Australian values and erodes the values of liberal democracy. Take the following statement by the former South Australian Liberal senator Cory Bernardi calling for the banning of the burqa:

> the burka has no place in Australian society. I would go as far as to say it is un-Australian ... the burka separates and distances the wearer from the normal interactions with broader society ... Equality of women is one of the key values in our secular society and any culture that believes only women should be covered in such a repressive manner is not consistent with the Australian culture and values.[43]

Another politician who is an incumbent member of the New South Wales parliament said, as he introduced a bill attempting to ban Muslim women from dressing according to Islamic precepts, that the veil was oppressive of women and had no place in Australia.[44] Others have sought to proscribe Muslim women's dress because they see themselves as saviours of Muslim women who need rescuing from themselves and from others.

Whatever justification and reasons anti-veiling campaigners may provide, it is not difficult to see that such representation of Muslim women is extreme and associated with generating fear in the community. Their portrayal as either a threat to society on the basis that the practice is detrimental to the values of liberal democratic states such as Australia or a threat to themselves is baseless and an attempt to rob Muslim women of their agency. Many Muslim women veil because it gives them agency, and in some instances because it enhances their agency. They observe veiling not because they are made to veil (there are some exceptions, where Muslim women have been forced to veil by their husband, father, grandfathers, brothers or uncles) or lack the capacity to think for themselves, but because it is their right to veil according to the principles of sharia.[45]

In this regard, the key source of sharia, the Qur'an, instructs women as follows: 'And O Prophet, tell the believing women to lower their gaze, and protect their private parts, and not show off their adornment except only that which is apparent and to draw their veils all over their bodies.'[46] The banning of Muslim women's veil would deny women their agency and the spiritual significance of their dress. Veiling for them is a spiritual exercise and an act of worship as they show obedience to God. Katherine Bullock argues:

> [Condemned] forever as the victim, as the submissive, oppressed Muslim woman, negative stereotyping has denied that Muslim women have agency, that they have autonomy and even that they have any critical perspective on their own situation. Any support for Islam and its prescriptions is frequently taken as an example of false consciousness.[47]

The right of Australian Muslim women to veil has been contested in terms of seeking to have veiling banned or heavily regulated, or having support withdrawn for multicultural policies that endorse its accommodation. This contestation arouses fear in Muslim women of losing their civil liberties and religious identity, closely connected with their fear of being undeservedly targeted. In response, many Muslim women in Australia have spoken out in support of their right to veil or dress according to their religious teaching.[48] There is no denying that some Muslim women do experience oppression and veiling is forced upon them; however, this does not mean that all have the same experience or that Muslim women's dress is incompatible with the values of liberal Australian multiculturalism. It is due to such kinds of treatment of Muslims in Australia that formal accommodation of sharia in the Australian legal system is sought: to give them not only social and cultural power but also the legal right to practise their faith and observe its rules freely and without judgement or punishment.

The call for formal accommodation of sharia in Australia raises critical issues of cultural and religious pluralism and is a test of freedom of religion. Australia prides itself on being civilised, rational, tolerant, compassionate, understanding and accepting of cultural diversity. It purports to hold open values and to confer freedom of religion on all citizens. Under these provisions, Muslims who seek to pursue an 'Islamic way of life' in full light of sharia should be able to do so. However, in reality this is not the case. For example, when Muslims have sought to establish mosques and schools or express their Muslimness through attire and religious rituals (prayer at work), they have found their citizenship rights challenged. When Muslim citizens have attempted to exercise their constitutional right to freedom of religion, they have often found that there is a limit to such freedom. This leads to their exercising only those Islamic practices and rituals that don't impact particularly upon public space, and those Islamic values that are seen as of direct benefit to the Australian economy, such as Islamic finance and banking;[49] other practices and rituals are forced into the domestic sphere.

This is not the end of the extent of complexity regarding the formal accommodation of sharia in the Australian legal system and more broadly in the Australian multicultural way of life. 'Islamisation of Muslim life' in Australia and globally manifested in movements such as Hizb ut-Tahrir and Boko Haram has become a strong basis for calls for formal accommodation of sharia in the Australian legal system. Islamisation of Muslim life involves proselytisation, a process whereby increasing number of Muslims have set themselves to learning new Islamic knowledge, becoming more aware of their religious obligations and adopting Islamic teachings in a variety of facets of everyday living. A growing number of mosques, prayer halls, Muslim businesses, Muslim schools and educational centres, after-hours Islamic classes under certain sheikhs, and Arabic classes for young and adult Muslims have emerged in recent years in Australia and impacted upon Islamic identity and practice.[50] Many Muslims who were previously inconsistent in implementing sharia, or who pursued a life in which observance of sharia was absent or minimal, are now observing it in their everyday life with increased vigilance, austerity, rigour and consistency.[51] Their identity is rooted in what they claim to be the 'proper' religion, and they project an Islam whose essence is largely the scripture and not ethnic and parochial values, which have been removed through the process of Islamic revivalism. They claim to practise a sharia-based scriptural Islam. While their religious rituals and practices are by no means homogeneous, a vast majority of them follow similar and very strict religious rules and regulations.[52]

It is many of these strict Muslims in cooperation with like-minded Muslims from the general Muslim community (who may not have necessarily undergone 'Islamisation') who demand, with the authority and power of their citizenship, the formal accommodation of sharia in the Australian legal system. They are fluent in the official language of Australia and have a sound education and an excellent understanding and even experience of the operational functions of key institutions such as the bureaucracy, judiciary and the education system. The premise of their claim is that to live a proper life as a Muslim one has to adhere to God's orders, and this is only possible with God's rules governing personal affairs as well as social relationships and exchanges. They argue that Islam is a religious system revealed by God for the entirety of humanity and for all time. In this way it covers all facets of the life of individuals and society. Sharia, according to them, is a divine law given by God and therefore the most ideal set of directives for human conduct. They believe that since Australia is a liberal democracy and they are citizens of Australia, they have the right to practise their religion freely—a religion whose essence is the divine law of sharia. Formal accommodation of sharia is a mere exercise of their citizenship rights in a liberal democracy. If they are successful in their demand, they will be able to lead what they perceive to be a true Islamic way of life.

However, formal accommodation of sharia in the Australian common law system or Constitution would have serious conceptual and practical problems. One solution could be to permit a dual legal system to exist, but this comes with its own complexities and practical hurdles—internal hurdles created within Muslim communities. A dual legal system exists and works in Malaysia and Indonesia. Would it work in Australia? Most likely not, because Australia is home to Muslims from 183 different countries[53] and interaction between them is limited and in some instances non-existent. To get such a heterogeneous group or different community representatives together is a huge logistical task involving costs, human resources, coordination, and so on. Coupled with this are strong differences of opinion on matters of religious practice and religious law among Australian Muslims, not to mention ethnic, parochial, sectarian, ideological and theological conflicts that exist within and between Muslim communities. Furthermore, there exist different interpretations of Islamic historicity, the sacred texts and classical literature on Islam. There are also significant gender and generational differences within the larger, differentiated Australian Muslim population: to assume that they share a common view on Islam and its law and how sharia should be designed, formulated and implemented in everyday living is not only simplistic but problematic.[54]

Within the total Muslim population, those calling for formal accommodation of sharia form a very small, mainly young group whose knowledge of sharia is based in large part on learning about it informally as part of growing up in a Muslim family, which in itself is inherently problematic; and the support for their campaign is evidently weak. To campaign for such a course there needs to be a demonstrably sound understanding of sharia and fiqh, which are not simple concepts, and for the campaign to be successful there needs to be a solid community support. Also, many so-called sheikhs and imams who support the idea and are actively engaged in the process not only lack Islamic knowledge and practices themselves because their learning has been informal, rote and imitational, but are madrasa dropouts who demonstrably don't cooperate and consult with each other and with the wider Muslim community. In addition, many qualified sheikhs and imams who are graduates of great centres of Islamic learning such as the University of Al-Azhar are not trained in classical Islamic jurisprudential methodologies[55] to properly and adequately guide their congregations. The University of Al-Azhar, the great Sunni mosque-madrasa, for example, although over 1000 years old and the most important centre for higher learning, has been gradually modernised and reformed since the late nineteenth century.[56] Sami Zubaida explains that:

> In 1961, under Nasir [Gamal Abdel Nasser, president of Egypt 1956–70], the educational component was converted into a modern university, offering curricula in the religious sciences alongside modern faculties of science, arts and technology, and under its own rectorship. The Shaykh of al-Azhar, now appointed by the president, and not, as previously, chosen by his peers, presided over the religious institution. In effect, religious personnel were largely converted into state functionaries, and official religious authority firmly subordinated to the political directorate.[57]

According to Bernard Botiveau, during educational reform in 1961 the Faculty of Law at the University of Al-Azhar became the Faculty of Sharia and Law.[58] The implication here is that the reform significantly altered the historical role of Al-Azhar, whose central function and focus was to provide training in the expertise of the law, and substantially weakened an important part of the university's religious authority. The reform process also produced a sharp separation of the profession of the law and religious discipline and piety. Serious attempts by the modernisers to keep 'ibadat separate from mu'amlat by suggesting two separate modes of application removed crucial facets of jurists' training and education: that of religious conviction, ethical standards, moral virtue, and rectitude gained from regular and routine participation in a series of key religious rituals and practices within a sacred institution. Consequently, individuals receiving training in this modern system inevitably seek to maintain its operation and existence because it is in their interests to do so. Even those lawyers and judges who are passionate revivalists and support a systematic Islamisation of the law and complete implementation of Islamic law often become disinclined to pursue the revival of the legal institutions of courts, *qadis* (the magistrate or judge of a sharia court) and juridical law (instead of state law typical of the early Islamic period) because of their fear of being taken over by 'progressive' and 'modernist' lawyers and judges.

As mentioned earlier, the call for formal accommodation of sharia requires community and organisational support. Australian Muslim community organisations provide a mixture of important religious and non-religious activities. However, there is no coordination of activities among the organisations and in many instances they are managed and run by Muslims with limited knowledge and practice of Islam. For example, Muslim schools in Australia teach the generic curriculum supplemented by Arabic and Islamic studies but are called Muslim or Islamic schools, giving the impression that they are religious schools providing a complete Islamic education as a pedagogical process. In fact, Muslim schools in Australia are secular institutions that operate with a corporate ethos.[59]

Muslim community organisations represent Islam and are at the forefront of Muslim activities. However, given that there is an absence not only of coordination among them and their activities but of any interaction among them, one can deduce that the current state of affairs is not capable of lending support to the call for formal accommodation of sharia. Which organisations would lead the charge? How would they gather and mobilise community support? And what would be the nature of sharia in Australia? Without consensus and cooperation among Muslims and Muslim community organisations, any work towards the formal accommodation of sharia is unlikely to yield a positive outcome.

One area that is very important when it comes to the implementation and application of sharia for Australian Muslims is dispute resolution and mediation. In the absence of formal accommodation of sharia, this area has been covered by what are known as local suburban sharia tribunals and sharia courts.[60] Of course not all Muslims use these services, but many do. In Australia a vast majority of disputes are resolved by state-instituted courts of law or arbitration regulated by state law, but for many Muslims these processes are inappropriate and inadequate. This is because for Muslims, wherever arbitration and law are involved in dispute resolution, morality and social ethics are interlinked; but 'in the legal culture of Western and, increasingly, non-Western modern nation-states, morality and social ethics are strangers'.[61] Therefore, many Australian Muslims use the services of local suburban sharia tribunals and sharia courts.

The danger is that these tribunals and courts are self-funded and self-managed and therefore raise critical issues of qualification, professionalism, accountability and transparency. Are the service providers in these local facilities qualified experts with proper training and adequate skills? How do they fund the services? If they charge fees, how are they regulated? Ann Black asserts that:

> The ad hoc system in Australia where informal tribunals and certain Imams hold themselves out as possessing authority and knowledge to make legal decisions for Muslims based on their understanding of Islamic law is neither transparent nor professional. These legal determinations are done 'behind closed doors'.[62]

Despite these and other issues, the sharia tribunals and courts provide important avenues for Muslims to settle their conflicts, and sheikhs and imams play critical roles in them. However, they could be better organised and managed with government support.

Critical to note is that sharia is an important and integral part of the Islamic way of life and shapes the lives of Australian Muslims, their individual community undercurrents and, ultimately, their relationship with broader Australian multicultural society. Although it seems that the arguments for formal accommodation of sharia in Australia are weak, sharia is nevertheless being practised here by observant Muslims. Practised in a variety of ways and dictated by a diversity of scholarly opinions, sharia remains indispensable in the lives of observant Muslims and, therefore, is central in arbitration and mediation of disputes in their daily lives.

In a legal system like that of Australia, centralisation could potentially work in favour of a sharia-based legal pluralism if state authorities and policy-makers can be convinced that Muslims as a minority group should be formally permitted to run their own legal dispute resolution and mediation system to settle personal and domestic matters, and to deal with other religious issues such as marriage, divorce and animal slaughtering. Here, the roles of prominent Muslim voices who are versed in sharia and respectful of Australia's common law system are particularly useful. Mobilisation of these voices could make formal accommodation of sharia in the Australian legal system successful. If the legal system is antagonistic in nature, this might be achieved with some degree of ease if Muslims unite to engage a prominent 'just' third party to fight their legal battle, or if prominent individuals or groups within mainstream society are found and asked to assist in influencing the decision-making process and, consequently, in establishing a conflict resolution and mediation system for the Muslim community. Also, if the judiciary was relatively autonomous and judges shared egalitarian views and pluralistic ideals, had sufficient knowledge about Islam and were conversant with the principles of sharia, then they might consider accepting sharia-based arguments in their courts and also might permit the operation of a sharia-based conflict resolution and mediation system serving Muslim communities whose decisions would be legally binding.

The formal accommodation of sharia in Australia is a weak case for a variety of reasons. However, equally weak are the arguments advanced against it: namely, that sharia poses a threat to Australian values, liberal democracy, and a secular and impartial legal system. The national political debates and media discourse that continue to be consumed by an exclusionary 'us' and 'them' binary about Islam and its adherents, where Islamic law in particular is perceived as a threat and therefore must be rejected in all its forms, are doing more damage than good to Australian multiculturalism and social cohesion and to Australia's liberal democratic way of life.

Sharia is here to stay in Australia as Muslims continue to make the country their permanent home and the Muslim population grows. It is true that the Muslim community that has emerged in Australia is different in terms of certain religious values and norms, but the overall differences are highly exaggerated and the similarities and shared values are often understated and sometimes completely ignored. Sharia regulates the legal relationships many Australian Muslims enter and exit as they see fit, but this does not mean that they reject Australian laws. In fact, the evidence shows a desire on the part of Australian Muslims to conform to sharia in addition to the common law system wherever possible.[63] Ignoring the fact that sharia is being practised by Australian Muslims and overlooking how sharia operates within some Muslim communities can prove problematic, particularly for less empowered groups such as women and children within those communities. Also, the dominant cultural avoidance of sharia and, therefore, an unwillingness to engage with its importance and normative relevance to Australian Muslims not only perpetuates fiction and stereotypes surrounding sharia but heightens the possibility of miscarriages of justice for minorities within Muslim communities by driving sharia practices out of public sight.

Bound by one law in Australia, Muslims regularly and successfully interact with the mainstream legal system to resolve issues in everyday living as well as participate in established but legally unenforceable community negotiations conducted by religious leaders that have similar principles of conciliation and mediation to, for example, the family dispute resolution provided for by the Family Law Act. Contrary to the claim, sharia is not a threat to Australia's multiculturalism and social cohesion. A better understanding of the way in which Australian Muslims generally successfully navigate their way through different legal systems is very important. Equally important is acknowledging the challenges Muslims face in doing so. Such acknowledgement and understanding could enhance Australia's multiculturalism and social cohesion.

Chapter 7

The role of Muslim clergy in Australia

In Australian public debate and Muslim community discourse, Muslim clergy (religious experts including muftis, sheikhs and imams)[1] is presented as a powerful institution constituted of influential theologians who dominate not only their own mosque communities but also the Muslim immigrant population. Australian Muslim clergy is thought to have many more responsibilities than its counterparts in Muslim-majority countries, and consequently has become the agent of religious authority and leadership in Australian Muslim communities. Its role in Australia generally has been to provide Muslim communities with religious guidance and leadership; in the process, it has 'assumed' the authority that speaks for Islam and Muslims in Australia.

Apart from Muslim clergy, many organisations, including the Australian Federation of Islamic Councils (AFIC) and the Islamic Council of Victoria, Islamic movements such as Hizb ut-Tahrir, and individual Muslim activists such as Yassmin Abdel-Magied claim to represent Islam and Australian Muslims. Hadi Sohrabi notes that there are others, too: 'From within, subgroups such as Muslim youth and Muslim women contest the incumbent leadership, striving to impose a new image and definition of the Muslim identity in the Australian public sphere.'[2] Emerging as new authoritative voices within the community, they compete with the clergy and therefore raise questions around Islamic authority and leadership in Australia: who really speaks for Islam and Muslims, and with whom does the state deal and interact in Australia?

One key advantage Muslim clergy has over others regarding authority and leadership is that its individuals undergo credentialed learning and training. As religious scholars they have the right to interpret holy texts and sources and deliver fatwas, and by virtue of this the clergy is the proper and appropriate authority to speak for Islam and Muslims. Given its legitimacy, the clergy is appropriately placed to influence the direction, shape the vision, and produce the voices and discourses on Islam and Muslims in Australia. However, in this chapter I demonstrate that this is not as straightforward as it sounds and the role of Muslim clergy is complicated, and often overshadowed by factors such as the emergence of new authoritative voices, Muslim community heterogeneity, and an absence of deep and regular consultation among Muslim theologians and coordination of their activities.

In the context of secular liberal democracy since World War II and subsequent migration and refugee flows, Australian Muslim clergy has faced numerous difficult changes and challenges, particularly in connection to secular-liberal institutions and adaptation, or lack thereof, to the multiculturalism that characterises Australian society. The realities of globalisation and transnational migration, and different interpretations of secularism, have led to people questioning and often rejecting the existence of religion in public spaces in multicultural Australia, placing Muslim clergy in a very precarious position—especially in terms of how it exercises its authority and articulates Islam. This has forced the clergy as the religious authority to revisit its organisation, governance and internal hierarchy. It has struggled to negotiate its place among the institutions of the modern state in the age of secularism, and is currently experiencing a shift of roles and functions not only in Muslim communities but in Australian society more broadly.

The above notwithstanding, in the last fifteen years or so some non-government organisations from Muslim communities and from broader Australian society and some policymakers have entertained the idea that perhaps Muslim clergy as a part of the problem can be turned into the solution to the problem. They have suggested that Muslim clergy take a more direct and active role in civic religion, projecting more conspicuously its civic virtues and interfaith tolerance and showing greater levels of professional managerial and preaching skills, and possibly becoming involved in inner-city renewal as an agent of social integration and cohesion, particularly on behalf of vulnerable Muslim youths and in the fight against violent extremism.

It should be highlighted that although government support is welcome in this endeavour, the Muslim clergy must grow organically out of community incentives and concern for the religion of Islam and the community, and not from pressures exerted by the government. Since this is apparently the case, current clergy practices are problematic although they have nothing to do with government security concerns. Rather, they are to do with community concerns, prevailing issues facing especially young Muslims and women, and the possession or lack of credentialed qualifications and proper leadership skills.

This chapter explores the role of Muslim clergy as complex, incoherent and underdeveloped. Although Islam doesn't have an initiatic clergy or an institutionalised priesthood, Muslim clerics in Australia, apart from operating as theologians, have assumed important diverse functionary roles. As an institution the clergy is self-regulated and hugely heterogeneous, and has no legal obligation to accountability or transparency. It appears to have assumed the role, in large part, of deliberating on the functionality of law in terms of what is permissible and what is not under sharia. The central argument of this chapter is that Muslim clergy as the custodian of sharia, representative of Islam and Muslims and an agent of religious authority and leadership in Australia, has failed to unite its members and by extension Australian Muslims. This lack of unity within the clergy class as well as in the broader Muslim community must be the focus in building Islam and the Muslim community in Australia.

The concept of clergy in Islam

It is often said that Islam has no 'clergy' or religious authority.[3] Unlike Catholicism, Islam doesn't have an organised and institutionalised religious authority, essentially because religious specialists in Islam do not perform sacramental or priestly functions.[4] Muslim clerics do not serve as intermediaries between human beings and God or go through a process of ordination or carry out sacramental functions; instead, they serve as teachers, guides, judges and community leaders. This is particularly true for Sunni Islam, where no formal or structural hierarchy of religious scholars exists.

The Prophet Mohammed himself steered away from establishing a priesthood in his ummah. Centuries after the Prophet died, roles and personalities emerged to teach recitation of the Qur'an and explain Hadith to various students and audiences. Jurists and qadis appeared who engaged in developing legal methodological principles and systematising Islamic legal rules, and an increasing number of theologians were tasked with explaining and defending Islam, particularly against heresy. As their number, status and power grew, they came to be recognised by dynastical authorities, notably during the Abbasid dynasty (749–1258), and were given positions in educational institutions known as madrasas, in courts as qadis, and in state bureaucracies. Collectively, they became known as the ulama: scholars with Islamic knowledge and expertise in chosen fields, including Islamic doctrine and law.

The individuals constituting Muslim clergy or the ulama can be variously identified as alims, sheikhs, muftis, imams, khatibs and mullahs. An alim—which literally means 'the one who knows'—in a broader sense refers to an individual who has studied a wide range of Islamic disciplines for several years. A sheikh—literally meaning 'old' or 'elderly', especially in a tribal context in the Arabic-speaking world—is a learned person who plays an institutional role, such as Sheikh al-Azhar at the Al-Azhar Mosque in Cairo. A mufti is an Islamic scholar with the authority to issue fatwas (legal opinions on specific points of law). During various Muslim empires, such as the Ottoman Empire (1299–1923), the function of the mufti was institutionalised and entrusted to the highest office of the religious structure; this is still the case in many contexts, where he is the highest religious dignitary of the state. An imam—an Arabic word meaning 'leader'—leads the prayers at mosques, particularly in Sunni Islam. Pre-Islam, a khatib (an Arabic word) was a man who spoke for a tribe with authority; with the advent of Islam he became a figure who proclaims the *khutba* (sermon) during the Friday congregational prayer and on other special occasions, such as during the month of Ramadan. A mullah is a term derived from the Arabic mawla (lord or guardian) that generally means a person who possesses religious knowledge or charisma.

Islamic religious leaders have traditionally been educated and qualified individuals who, as part of the clerisy, mosque, madrasa or government, perform a prominent function within their community or country. However, this has changed in the modern period, particularly in the contexts of Muslim minorities in non-Muslim countries and in secularised modern Muslim nation-states—for instance, Indonesia and Turkey—where Muslim clergy may assume a range of informal roles. In many contemporary Muslim societies, while clerical institutions exist, their roles and structures differ vastly. The clerics may perform several roles and hold various titles, but the majority of those operating in Western Muslim communities such as Australia and the United Kingdom are called sheikhs or imams. They can perform numerous duties, such as:

- leading prayers
- conducting marriages
- conducting funeral rituals
- divorce and bereavement counselling
- offering spiritual advice
- teaching classes for adults and children
- offering couple and family mediation and arbitration
- dealing with drug abuse and youth problems
- discussing mental health issues
- business dispute resolution
- offering fatwas.

For various reasons it is difficult to count the number of Muslim clergy in Australia today. First, a range of formal and informal centres exist for Islamic religious education and training that offer a series of curriculums at different levels, with emphasis placed on the acquisition of specific sets of skills or knowledge—for example, memorisation of the Qur'an, learning prophetic traditions or studying sharia. Second, the heterogeneous character of Muslim clerisy in Australia means that there is no official national directory of religious scholars and no systematic process for recording the details of individual scholars. However, among Australian Muslim communities, an informal process of collective recognition of the scholarship and piety of particular religious personalities is well established; it is manifested in those individuals' public speaking, media interviews and mosque networks. Third, there are some Muslim religious scholars in Australia who are not directly attached to a Muslim centre, organisation, *musalla* (place for prayer) or mosque and operate from 'home' independently or work informally in the community through networks.

Compared to Muslim-majority societies such as Indonesia and Pakistan, in Western societies such as Australia sheikhs and imams experience a very different, complex set of realities. For one, they do not have state support and are not part of the state bureaucracy. In Australia they are very much on their own and rely heavily on their communication and leadership skills and personal efforts to connect with the Muslim population and exercise influence over them. Another issue is that Muslims in Australia are not a homogeneous population and differ from one another culturally, linguistically and nationally yet coexist; hence, sheikhs and imams require distinct communication, leadership and negotiation skills in order to connect with the very diverse local communities. In addition, the rise of Muslim radicalism and religious violent extremism and state securitisation has brought new focus on sheikhs and imams in Australia, complicating their religious role and authority in Muslim communities. Due to state intervention, many sheikhs and imams in Australia have become unwitting sentinels in Muslim communities, extending their traditional roles as religious guides, leaders and authorities to state 'managers'.

The Australian Government and Muslim community leadership

In the landscape formation of Islam and Muslims in Australia, particularly since the late 1960s, the state has been an enthusiastic actor through exercising influence over Muslim community leadership. As Australia emerged out of a monocultural framework to multiculturalism in the 1970s, the government found resourcefulness in Muslim ethnic leaders and turned to them for information, welfare allocation, and political representation and support.[5] Paul Tabar, Greg Noble and Scott Poynting state that this is generally because:

> Since the emergence of multiculturalism in Australia in the 1970s, ethnicity has not only become an issue of cultural and social importance in a diverse society, but one which has political consequences as groups mobilise around 'ethnic communities' and as governments increasingly seek to structure social policy around cultural differences. The lines of political patronage and funding central to Australian multiculturalism led to the development of organisations and leaders whose task was seen to be to not only service the needs of specific 'ethnic communities' but to represent them in the wider political field ... The relationship of ethnic leaders to the State, as well as to their respective 'communities', became a crucial element in the overall strategy of the government to manage and make use of 'ethnic politics'.[6]

In his important sociological work on immigration, Michael Humphrey[7] explains the part played by the government post-1975 in Sydney in consolidating Lebanese community leadership. He describes how Christian Lebanese had a centralised leadership structure while, in contrast, Muslim Lebanese from the Sunni denomination had formed groupings around regional, village and religious (Sunni and Shi'a) associations. The state involved itself in the debate about Muslim leadership at the mosque in an attempt to exercise influence over what kind of Islamic values, organisations, leadership and politics should occur in Australia. Its attempts to intervene in Islamic religious authority were an indirect way to shape Muslim organisations in the image of Australian state bureaucracies and centralised institutions. By encouraging the formation of bureaucratised and centralised Islamic institutions with centrally organised authority structures and hierarchies, the state sought to ease their regulation and make them better understood and managed. However, state intervention in the Muslim leadership debate and formation did not always go the government's way as it was seen by the Muslim community as a way of impinging upon their religious values and community autonomy. In fact, it triggered a defensive reaction from the Muslim community that saw the mobilisation of:

> a community previously unable to unite because of family, village, regional, sectarian and ethnic divisions ... [An] important outcome of mobilisation [was the exposure of the] Muslim community to political, legal and bureaucratic processes of the Australian state. In other words, one important outcome of resistance—defence of

religion—[was] the political socialisation of a community, and individuals, to enter into mainstream Australian society and politics.[8]

The Muslim religious leaders who took steps to serve their communities assumed roles in addition to their religious duties that involved them catering for the settlement needs of new arrivals: for example, they concentrated on securing accommodation and employment for newly arrived Muslims from Lebanon. Alongside them in these communal activities were some well-known personalities who emerged from earlier waves of immigrants. Muslim Lebanese immigrants relied on the assistance of these community leaders because the leaders had already gone through the experience of settlement in the host society. In the process, important relationships were formed on the basis of family, village, ethnicity, locality and religion that then helped to provide networks for these services. Delivering the services effectively and diligently helped those involved to develop good reputations and status and strengthened the grounds from which leadership developed among Muslim immigrants. From this kind of situation, then, Muslim leaders emerged who were not religious scholars—for example, Shafiq Khan, chair of the Australian Islamic Cultural Centre; Qazi Ahmad, founder of the Islamic Foundation for Education & Welfare; Adib Marabani, founding member of the Lebanese Muslim Association; and Sheikh Taj El-Din Hilaly, former Grand Mufti of Australia and Imam of Masjid Ali Bin Abi Taleb.

More recently, with the 'securitisation' of the Muslim community in the Australian legal system[9] and public policy[10] since the events of 9/11 and subsequent terrorist bombings, much interest has been shown in the public role of Muslim clergy and the training and qualifications of its members. In recognising the important role Muslim clergy plays in the community, the Australian Government has acknowledged in the past ten years that Muslim clergy is the agent of religious authority and leadership but has said that it requires structural remoulding.[11] Despite this acknowledgement, Muslim clergy was viewed as part of the problem rather than the solution, driven by security concerns and a counterterrorism agenda.[12] The concern with Muslim clergy and its members' training is not confined to Australia: it has also been the subject of much discussion in the United Kingdom[13] and Europe.[14]

Finding prudence in developing ways of training Muslim clergy, the Australian Government took more active steps to restructure Muslim leadership and clergy. In 2005, Prime Minister John Howard convened a meeting in Canberra with selected so-called moderate Muslim leaders and theologians to discuss concerns about the radicalisation of Muslim youth.[15] It led to the formation of the Muslim Community Reference Group and laid the foundation of what became the National Action Plan to Build on Social Cohesion, Harmony and Security.[16] A year later, in 2006, the Reference Group released its final report, which showed that the government had allocated $35 million to fund a wide variety of programs and initiatives in Muslim communities to address marginalisation and radicalisation, employment, education and training, community engagement, and leadership.[17] The government was also involved in setting up the Australian National Imams Council in an attempt to harmonise the activities and voices of imams in Australia.[18]

The role of Muslim clergy in the Australian sociocultural landscape

It is important to note that migration brought Islam and Muslims to Australia. Today, Islam is the second-largest religion after Christianity and the biggest minority religion in Australia. As discussed in Chapter 1, there are in Australia 604,200 Muslims[19] who come from 183 different countries.[20] As such, they are the most ethnically and nationally diverse community in Australia. Muslim migration has produced ethnic enclaves in Australian urban centres in which networks have emerged to cater for the needs of new immigrants relating to social capital.

Muslim migrant networks are essentially systems of interpersonal relations through which Muslims can exchange valuable resources and knowledge. They can then take advantage of these social interactions by transforming information into tangible resources and consequently reducing the costs of their migration. What can be exchanged is useful information as well as knowledge about employment opportunities, cheap housing, government assistance schemes, free medical and education services, and helpful non-government organisations such as the Salvation Army and Mission Australia. Thus, by stimulating and maintaining social connections, Muslim ethnic enclaves produce a set of intangible resources that prove useful for the promotion of social and economic development among their members.

By providing a space for fellow ethnics to produce potentially valuable relationships, Muslim ethnic enclaves help members to attain economic mobility and social solidarity in Australia. They produce a substitute labour market that is ethnic-specific and doesn't have the strict criteria for employment typical of mainstream Australia. By removing language and cultural impediments, enclave economies offer employment exclusively to co-ethnics and hasten the incorporation of new Muslim immigrants into a thriving economy.

However, despite their immediate benefits, there are some long-term issues associated with Muslim ethnic enclavement. Their economies have the potential to limit Muslim growth and socioeconomic upward mobility. While participation may help to secure upward mobility through easy access to the substitute labour market, it may at the same time rob Muslim immigrants of opportunities to acquire the social and cultural skills offered by the mainstream labour force, which can benefit them in the long run. Such lost opportunities or delays restrict Muslim immigrants to working only within the enclaves and isolate them from the larger economy. Opportunities available to those operating in mainstream society are not available to Muslim immigrants who have no experience of or familiarity with that society's complex workings. Consequently, the quick path toward economic mobility that attracts new Muslim immigrants into enclave economies may restrict them from achieving bigger and better success in mainstream society. Integration into an ethnic enclave may delay and even cease cultural assimilation, inhibiting Muslim immigrants from profiting from mainstream institutions.

The role of Muslim clergy needs to be understood in this context as well as in the context discussed in the previous section. There is no doubt that the role of Muslim clergy in Australia is complex and multifaceted, and has been constantly changing. Australia is a multicultural and secular modern nation-state that plays no role in religion or religious management; therefore, each religion and its clergy or leadership is responsible for managing the affairs of its faith and faithfuls independent of the state. Unlike in many Muslim-majority countries, where Muslim clergy receives state assistance in a number of ways, in Australia it relies heavily on Muslim communities for its own preservation and that of the Muslim population. Muslim clergy and communities in Australia have a strong symbiotic relationship.

Because of the Muslim ethnic enclaves, members of the clergy do not represent the Muslim population in Australia but instead represent specific ethnic congregations or communities. Islam within them has different orientations and interpretive traditions. This diversity is clearly noticeable in the form of, among other aspects, the presence of different mosques, each with its own sheikh or imam or, in rare cases, mufti.

As the Muslim community grew and its activities increased, so did community needs. This situation made it necessary for Muslim clergy to play an important and direct role. Thus, the role of the clergy grew in proportion to the increase in the migrant population. Initially, the key religious functions of Muslim clergy were to lead daily ritual prayers and the Friday congregational prayer, offer services for what may be collectively described as Muslim life-cycle rituals (birth, marriage and death), and give advice on religious matters to individuals within the local community framework.

Humphrey notes that each Muslim community or community organisation recruited its own Muslim scholar, often called an imam, from its respective country to carry out these functions.[21] In the absence of an effective umbrella organisation and the shura (consultative committee) or any other formal or centralised Muslim institution, the imam often emerged as an important figure in the Muslim settlement process. His role would extend beyond leading prayers and offering life-cycle services to include community-building in an ethno-parochial setting.

However, Muslim clergy in Australia has never been a homogenous group. Due to sectarian, jurisprudential, ethno-parochial and ideological differences and the formation and perpetuation of Muslim ethnic enclaves, Muslim religious leaders have always concentrated on their own ethno-parochial communities and have remained disengaged from bridging the divides between communities and building a more cohesive and inclusive ummah.

The organisation and politics of Sunni and Shi'a Muslim communities around the world have always been influenced by competition for leadership based on village community organisations. In the case of Sunni Muslims, the range of Sunni immigrant organisations was not simply a reflection of internal community fragmentation but also, more importantly, the absence of a centralised Islamic institution to amalgamate Muslim immigrant organisations into a large, united, single entity. A centralised Islamic institution would have produced not only quite different politics and organisation but very different leadership in Muslim communities. This was seen quite clearly with Christian Maronite immigrants, where the church was the dominant organisation. In contrast, among both Sunni and Shi'a Muslims there was a range of community associations that became vehicles for leadership competition in the two communities.[22] Based on kin ties and temporary in nature, and usually produced by an election or politically significant event, these organisations were small in size with a single vision and purpose.

In the past ten to fifteen years, the role of Muslim clergy has changed sharply in Australia to become very diverse and complex. While a vast majority of clerics still restrict their role to religious duties within the confines of their specific ethno-parochial community setting, some now run what may be descriptively equivalent to madrasas—for example, the Daar Aisha Shariah College in the Sydney suburb of Lakemba, founded by a Tunisian-born scholar, Sheikh Abdul Moez Nafti al Idrisi Al-Hasany; and AlKauthar Institute, also in Lakemba, currently chaired by UK-born Sheikh Sajid Umar. Others teach in Australian universities—for example, Professor Mohamad Abdalla,[23] an eminent sheikh who is the founding director of the Griffith Islamic Research Unit and director of the Queensland node of the National Centre of Excellence for Islamic Studies. Yet others move between roles.

The diverse and complex roles of Muslim clergy can be better understood in the context of Muslims constituting a minority community in

Australia. The most important characteristic of this community is its observance of customs and unofficial religious laws that are seen to be in conflict with those of the dominant Australian community, as discussed in Chapter 6. It is common knowledge that sharia, for example, exists as an unofficial law among Muslims in Australia; studies have shown that it exists in other Western countries too.[24] The existence of sharia in Australia is behind the demands of Muslims to govern themselves by the personal laws of their own religion. However, a critical question is whether it is possible to make room for Islam within the Australian legal system given the secular nature of Australian laws and their uniform application across national, ethnic and religious divides. A few concessions are granted to Muslims in Australia—for instance, slaughtering animals and burying the dead according to Islamic precepts.

There is no doubt that Muslim clergy plays an important role in the unofficial application of sharia in Australia. Muslims consult their imams on legal matters all the time: matters such as how to distribute inheritances among children, how to calculate zakat, how to perform ghusl (major canonical ablution or ritual bath), the obligations of husband and wife in a marriage, rules of animal slaughtering, and rulings on mortgages. Although not binding or officially recognised in Australia, many imams of mosques and sharia experts in other Muslim organisations and institutions act in the capacity of juridical courts to apply Islamic family law to cases brought to them by individual Muslims.

In Muslim history we can find ample evidence of the governance of Muslim clergy in minority contexts. Bustami Khir notes that in Sunni circles the governance of Muslim clergy or the principle of delegation of authority had become quite a common practice by the eighth century.[25] Kamal al-Dın Ibn al-Humam, a leading Egyptian Hanafi jurist, asserts that:

> When there is no *sulān* or an authorised acting person in his [the sultan's] place, as it is the case now in some Muslim lands, such as Cordoba, Valencia and Abyssinia where the reins of power are in the hands of non-Muslims, the Muslims, who have resided there under a pact to pay a tax, are responsible to choose a person to lead them. The chosen person is to carry out the responsibility of a governor (*walī*). He should either act as a judge or appoint another person to be a judge in order to settle the legal disputes among the Muslims.[26]

In Australia since the 1970s, the task of representing Islam and Muslims has fallen on the shoulders of the mufti. This role has been more symbolic than real, as not all Australian Muslims or Muslim communities swore allegiance to such a figure. However, this changed in the first decade of the twenty-first century: instead of a particular individual representing Islam and Muslims in Australia, some members of the Australian Muslim clergy resolved to allocate the role to an institution. Thus, the Australian National Imams Council (ANIC) emerged as an important umbrella organisation to represent Islam and Muslims in Australia, to provide Australian Muslims with broad-ranging legal services, and to adjudicate on issues and cases brought to it by individual Muslims.

Established in late 2006, ANIC is a non-governmental organisation made up of a council of imams representing Australia's six states and two territories. Its central focus is to streamline the activities of Muslim clerics in Australia by bringing together the council of imams in each state and territory under a single unified umbrella organisation. ANIC can be viewed in a much broader Western context where there is a growing trend for sheikhs and imams to seek to professionalise their role in the community.[27] As a central Muslim organisation, ANIC claims to hold key representation of Muslim clergy from the whole of Australia. However, Ryan Edwards is not sure, stating: 'It is difficult to determine how truly representative of Australia's imams ANIC is given there exists no formal process for monitoring the number of Muslim religious professionals in Australia.'[28]

Governed by a general assembly, ANIC has a seventeen-member executive board, each of whom is elected for a four-year term by ANIC's members. The current president is Sheikh Shady Alsuleiman. ANIC is responsible for appointing the Mufti of Australia and has a Council of Fatwa consisting of seven imams.

ANIC aims to be the leading organisation representing mainstream Islam in Australia through using the skills, qualifications and expertise of imams and Muslim clergy generally to achieve improvement and cohesion in Muslim communities and to develop enhanced and more harmonious relationships with wider Australian society. Its mission is to offer religious leadership, legal rulings and Islamic services to Muslim communities in Australia by developing educational services, supporting local Muslim organisations and providing social and outreach programs; and to promote interfaith interaction and cooperation with wider Australian society. From this it can be deduced that there is 'a clear undertone that can be described as being reflective of [ANIC's] positioning as "moderate" imams: emphasis on building relationships with wider society, interfaith dialogue and promoting Australian values.'[29]

Membership of ANIC is open to all qualified imams who are actively involved in the affairs of their respective Muslim communities. It claims to have over 150 imams registered with it as active members.[30]

In the Australian Muslim-minority context, the existence of an organisation such as ANIC is useful and important. It fills the vacuum of Islamic rule created by secularism and acts as a conduit between individual Muslims and Muslim clergy and organisations. In Australia, where state structures don't cater for specific religious needs, and where religious education and the design, development and implementation of religious laws are left to individuals and communities to manage, ANIC finds itself in an enviable position. Having large intellectual resources at its disposal, it can realistically represent Islam and Muslims in Australia, give Australian Muslims a single unified voice, and revolutionise the development and implementation of sharia in a secular Muslim-minority context. This demonstrates that there is both a theoretical and a practical basis for ANIC to exist. However, although it is an important organisation for the Muslim community, particularly in conflict resolution in the context of family and marriage, it has not exercised enough influence over large sections of the community, and its role and ability to interact and negotiate with broader state structures on behalf of Muslim communities have been marginal at best.

ANIC has been in existence for fourteen years but not much is known about it in the Muslim community or wider Australian society. It is a well-known fact that Muslim community organisations, mosque committees and non-government organisations in Australia have a very poor record regarding community consultation and community engagement at grassroots level, and ANIC is no exception. While membership is open to any mufti, sheikh or imam, the council doesn't articulate how it assesses and determines the qualifications and authenticity of Muslim clergy and if members' qualifications and experiences are adequate and suitable for the Australian context. Nor is it known if Muslim clerics have training in Islamic law and fiqh or how their conduct is monitored. Importantly, the general public and the Muslim community in particular have no way of knowing the effectiveness and success of ANIC. There is no public forum in which ordinary members of the Muslim community can take part and no official report exists to gauge the council's performance.

Overall, there is not enough evidence to state that the establishment of ANIC in 2006 has made a major impact on Muslim communities in Australia in terms of overcoming ethnic, parochial and sectarian divisions; improving the level of understanding and application of sharia in Muslim everyday living; or being representative of Australian Muslim clergy and the Australian Muslim population. It is safe to suggest that ANIC has not been able to work out ways to reach Muslims at the grassroots level. In the age of modern technologies and means of fast communication such as the internet, SMS and social media platforms, it has failed to compete with other individual and organisational voices that claim to represent Islam and Muslims in Australia.

When it comes to the question of religious leadership and representation of Islam and Muslims in Australia, three points need highlighting: concerns around the nature of qualification and training of Muslim theologians; the level of professionalism in the work of Muslim clergy; and the competition that exists between Muslim clerics and the alternative voices who claim to speak for Islam and Muslims in Australia.

Clerical qualification and training

Muslim clergy has an important role to play within Australian Muslim communities and even internationally in terms of providing religious leadership, education in various capacities, assistance in personal and social matters, instructions for compliance with religious obligations, and edicts on what is and is not permissible based on the principles of sharia. For this, members of Muslim clergy require proper and adequate education and training in order to impart the knowledge they have acquired. Usually they go through years of training, including memorisation of the Qur'an and learning Arabic and prophetic tradition.

However, a worrying trend is emerging in Australia where individuals claim to be sheikhs or imams without having any or proper qualifications. The founder of the Forum on Australian Islamic Relations, Kuranda Seyit, describes such individuals as 'fake sheikhs', while the former president of ANIC, Sheikh Abdul Azim, calls them 'Sheikh Google' or 'Imam YouTube'.[31] The director of the Islamic Sciences & Research Academy at Charles Sturt University, Associate Professor Mehmet Ozalp, explains how this is occurring: 'At the moment if somebody grows a beard, dons religious attire and is able to quote verses from the Koran, people can fool anyone that they are qualified to be Sheikh. People have no way of checking.'[32]

Another important concern often raised more generally is that sheikhs and imams in the contemporary period usually acquire their qualifications and religious training, which essentially involves textual studies, from madrasas and 'Muslim' universities in underdeveloped countries where the focus is often on teaching the Qur'an, the recorded sayings of the Prophet Mohammed, sharia, and various other Islamic subjects,[33] and where there is a disjuncture between religious and worldly education.[34] Some of these sheikhs and imam—often called 'import-imams' or 'import-sheikhs'—end up working in Muslim diasporas such as Australia.

Australian Muslim clergy needs to address this in a systematic fashion and find solutions so the confidence of the Muslim population can be secured and Australian state and key institutions can have certainty in dealing with Muslim clergy.

Clerical professionalism

Apart from offering religious services to their communities, members of Muslim clergy in Australia take up various 'worldly' duties, such as family dispute mediation and arbitration, marital counselling, and divorce settlement. These tasks require specialist knowledge and professional skills. Since Muslim clerics are usually qualified theologians, carrying out these duties without other appropriate qualifications and skills can prove difficult and even problematic. Take, for example, divorce in Australia. A husband and wife can apply to the Family Court for orders to settle their property share, and according to section 79(1) of the Family Law Act 1975 (Cth), extensive discretion is accorded to the court, which may make any decision it considers appropriate and thereby change the interests of the husband and wife in the property. In Islam, however, the principles of property settlement are applied according to sharia and the sheikh or imam has to advise the couple accordingly because mahr is involved. On the part of the sheikh or imam, this requires not only an understanding of Australia's common law rules but also skills in counselling Muslim couples appropriately and adequately in the matter of Islamic law and in relation to Australian common law principles and modern secular social norms and values.

Ghena Krayem, an associate professor of Islamic law at the University of Sydney, observes that despite attempts by sheikhs and imams to resolve, for instance, divorce cases as best they can, Muslim community members often appear to be frustrated by the ad hoc nature of the process, which leaves the 'professionalism' of sheikhs and imams open to question. She also found that while sheikhs and imams possess religious knowledge, that knowledge is not matched by the skills and know-how required to deal with many problems in a practical manner. Furthermore, she says that Muslim community members question whether the sheikhs and imams really have all the skills and professional etiquette needed to resolve family law conflicts and other matters, and if mosque committees have strategies in place to systematically review the qualifications, level of professionalism and skill sets of the clergy under their management.[35]

Muslim clerics and alternative voices

With the arrival of Muslims in Australia from numerous parts of the world and the proliferation of Muslim ethnic enclaves in cities such as Sydney and Melbourne, Muslims are not a homogeneous religious community and Islam as a way of life is an extremely diverse practice. Thus, Islam and Muslims are represented not by a single individual or entity but by competing forces. In Australia and even globally, alternative voices represent and speak for them.

Muslim clerics might think they have the authority and qualifications to represent and speak for Muslims and Islam, but in light of the above discussion and the facts that Muslim clerics are themselves internally divided, many cannot speak English or communicate in English effectively, and many do not socialise with their congregations regularly and informally to build social bonds, alternative voices with more in-depth community knowledge and social ties, better understanding of Australian norms and values, strong connections with mainstream social and cultural institutions, and good command of the English language have emerged to fulfil the role. For example, Australia's designated Grand Mufti, Dr Ibrahim Abu Mohamed, cannot speak English yet claims to represent the Australian Muslim community whose members largely speak English,[36] especially the fast-growing number of those born in Australia.

The issue seems to be that Muslim clerics lack the relevant knowledge and skills to enable them to competently meet the requirements of their complex and dynamic role in a very diverse Muslim population. They need to acquire qualifications and training in alignment with their roles and responsibilities. Apparently this deficiency has been aptly and promptly recognised by various Muslim CSOs and numerous 'celebrity' clerics whose particularly online advice and fatwas have proven popular among young Muslims. ANIC and the broader Muslim clergy have failed to understand the psychological ontology of Muslims and the sociological reality of modern secular Australia, and have evidently steered away from active Muslim community-building and participation in Australian politics, national development and public policy. Where ANIC and the Muslim clergy have failed Muslim CSOs, individual Muslim activists and celebrity clerics have succeeded: they have recognised not just the religious needs of the community and the importance of participating in politics, national development and policy development, but also the need to meet the social, economic, cultural, recreational, welfare, health, educational and intellectual demands of their communities.[37] Whenever an opportunity presents itself, they capitalise on it by projecting their voices and making their presence felt.

There is no doubt that Muslim clergy plays an important role in disparate Muslim communities in Australia. However, its role is neither simple nor constant. It operates in a difficult context, in which Australian Muslims live in enclaves as minorities among a majority non-Muslim multicultural population. As religious scholars, Muslim clerics have the authority to interpret holy texts and religious sources, issue fatwas, provide directions and lead the community, and by virtue of this they are appropriately placed to represent Muslims and Islam. However, their social lives and religious authority have been seriously affected by local and international sociopolitical issues and events, particularly over the past two decades. Under community and public scrutiny, they have had to repeatedly articulate their role but have done so in conflicting ways, leaving their role very much undefined. Where it has been clearly defined, it has not been satisfactorily or successfully executed due to myriad factors.

At the local grassroots level, the Muslim clergy class in Australia has remained aloof from social networking, intercommunity engagement, and participation or involvement in Australian politics, national development and policy design. The structure of the clerical network has always been internally weak, and the ability of the clergy to play an active role in mobilising Muslims and challenging the authorities for greater religious recognition has never been demonstrated, as exemplified by ANIC. With this, the overall importance and status of the clergy in Australian Muslim communities is often loaded with confusion and ambiguity and risks becoming obsolete as competing alternative forces assume more prominent leadership roles.

Part 4

Islamic education in Australia

Chapter 8

Origins and development of Muslim schools

In the last fifty years Australia has seen a gradual growth in the number of Muslim schools, mainly in the capital cities of Sydney, Melbourne and Brisbane. Their setting-up has been in response to the dominant secular nature of education in the country.

Generally speaking, three types of schools exist in Australia: government schools, which are secular in nature, operate within an integrated governance framework and are funded by territory, state and federal governments; independent non-government schools (including faith-based schools) that are partially funded by government; and schools based on distinct educational philosophies such as Montessori or Steiner. All schools are required by law to be registered with the state or territory education department and must comply with government infrastructure and teacher registration requirements.

As a minority religious group in Australia, Muslims have from the very beginning of their arrival been concerned about the education of their children. As new arrivals, Muslims immersed themselves in securing employment as a priority, but at the same time held grave concerns about the preservation of their religious identity and culture. The project of building Muslim schools in Australia was driven by the enthusiasm of concerned parents and community leaders for a refined religious identity of all Muslims, including young individuals, and for the preservation of Islamic cultural tradition in a liberal secular plural society. The philosophical underpinnings of such a nascent approach were to make Muslim schools places for Islamic practices, nurturing of Islamic ethos, inculcation of Islamic moral and ethical behaviour, preservation of Islamic culture, Islamisation of knowledge, and the production of 'good' Muslims in whom rested the representation and future of Islam and Muslims in Australia.

Thus, the schools were established with a certain ideal in mind—to educate young minds in the Islamic framework within an Islamic ethos—and, at the same time, derive full benefits from the secular education of the country. Muslim schools are not madrasas where only Islamic curriculum is taught to produce specialists in Islamic sciences. (Madrasas play a totally different role, and their functions are discussed in some depth in Chapter 9.) Muslim schools are distinct in that they offer two added features to those of government and independent non-government schools: an Islamic studies program (Arabic, Qur'an, Islamic Creed, and Life of the Prophet) and an Islamic environment (Muslim students, majority Muslim teachers, halal canteen, time to pray, prayer facility, Islamic dress code and gender segregation).

The development of Muslim schools in Australia is an important sociological phenomenon that underscores Muslim dissatisfaction with the perceived shortcomings of the state education sector or with a national education system built upon secular principles and Judeo-Christian values. Muslims have serious concerns about certain subjects, such as sex education and Darwin's theory of evolution, that are taught as part of the standard Australian curriculum. Additionally, there is a perception among some Muslims that the Australian mainstream education system is insensitive to the centrality of Islam in the lives of Muslim pupils.

This chapter probes and offers a snapshot of the origins and development of Muslim schools in Australia. It seeks to show that Muslim schools are considered to be spaces where Islamic values are respected and promoted, self-confidence of students as Muslims is strengthened, an Islamic studies program is produced to educate students in the basics of Islam, and Muslim identity is cultivated and refined. The overall aim of Muslim schools is to provide the best way of creating and preserving Muslim identity and Islamising knowledge, while at the same time giving students the benefits of a modern education where they can learn English, mathematics, society and the environment, science, arts, technology, health and physical education. Muslims believe that a combination of these two aspects enables students to learn new knowledge and develop important life skills that can then be used to build a stronger Muslim community and contribute to a better Australia, in which Muslims have a say and their contributions are acknowledged and welcomed. The chapter doesn't measure or test the actual outcomes of education acquired from Muslim schools: it simply examines the discussions around the importance of Muslim schools in Australia from Muslim perspectives.

Muslim schools in Australia: A brief background

Despite sharing the same faith in one single God—Allah—and the Prophethood of Mohammed, Australian Muslims are a culturally and linguistically diverse community.[1] This diversity reflects in the way Muslims practise their faith and go about organising and managing the affairs of their individual communities. Peter Jones remarks that 'The ethnic diversity within the Islamic community in Australia prevents it from being a homogenous community, and to this day this is reflected in the diversity of the organisations, let alone the individuals, who started each [Muslim] school.'[2] The secular nature of the Australian state also impacts on this process as it relates to the question of social integration of Muslim immigrant communities and the notions of citizenship and belonging discussed in chapters 4 and 5. Furthermore, in the early 1980s, Australian Muslim communities did not have certain provisions for their children that existed in other Western countries with Muslim-minority communities—for instance, the United Kingdom, where provisions existed for Muslim children to receive education about their faith after school or at weekends in addition to their normal weekday schooling.[3]

Chris Hewer identifies four areas of concern that motivate Muslims to establish Muslim schools:
1. to provide a 'safe' and gender-appropriate environment, particularly for adolescent girls
2. to provide an integrated faith-based education in an Islamic environment to cultivate the total personality, the complete person
3. to offer specialist training in Islamic sciences alongside worldly sciences in an attempt especially to prepare boys to serve and lead their community
4. the desire to set high moral standards, inculcate discipline in pupils and strive for academic excellence.[4]

The emergence of Muslim schools in Australia thus grew out of concerns around Muslim identity, citizenship and belongingness, and the desire to educate Muslim children about their religious and cultural traditions.[5] Sadaf Rizvi says that:

> My research has shown that the emergence of Muslim faith schools is a result of dissatisfaction among Muslim parents. They felt local schools would not meet their children's educational needs or provide structures and facilities to enable them to meet their religious obligations.[6]

Many Muslims felt that character-building was pivotal and that in order to preserve a Muslim identity and Islamic culture, and at the same time feel a sense of belonging to broader Australian society as full citizens, they had to create an environment, especially for their children—the future representatives of Islam and their community—in which these could be properly and effectively nurtured.[7]

In Australia, the first Muslim school started in 1983:[8] King Khalid Islamic College, now called Australian International Academy, in Coburg, Melbourne. In New South Wales, Al-Noori Muslim School (formerly known as Al Noori Muslim Primary School) was unofficially started in 1983 in the Sydney suburb of Lakemba, in a house next door to Imam Ali Mosque, rented from the Lebanese Muslim Association;[9] the school was relocated to the suburb of Greenacre in 1987. Its origin is rooted in the vision of its husband-and-wife founders, Siddiq and Silma Buckley. When their daughter was turned away from Presbyterian Ladies' College in Croydon in Sydney's inner west in the early 1980s for wearing hijab, the Buckleys were given the impetus to realise their vision for a Muslim school.

Since the establishment of these first two Muslim schools in Australia, the number of Muslim schools has grown tenfold: it is estimated that in 2014 (the latest data available) there were thirty-eight.[10] The demand for schools that provide for the educational needs of the young Muslim population of Australia is the cause for the rapid increase. Jones reports that by 2008 'a total of 15, 938 students attended Islamic schools'[11] across major cities. This increased to over 28,000 students in 2014.[12] It is important to note, however, that this number constitutes a very small percentage of Muslim students overall. Due to a variety of social, educational and political factors, the vast majority of Muslim students attend non-Muslim schools—81 per cent in primary schools and 87 per cent in secondary schools.[13]

Muslim schools in Australia are independent, not-for-profit, faith-based schools that offer Islamic studies, Arabic-language and Qur'anic lessons[14] in conjunction with the 'normal curriculum'[15] set by the Curriculum Council in each Australian state and territory. The additional lessons constitute only 'six hours a week'[16] of the total curriculum; in the broader scheme of teaching, this is a meagre percentage.

According to Mah,[17] in 2012 Muslim schools were represented in all states and territories except Tasmania and the Northern Territory. There were nineteen in Australia's most populated state, New South Wales; nine in Victoria; three in Western Australia; two in Queensland; one in South Australia; and one in the Australian Capital Territory. A vast majority of these schools are providers of both primary and secondary schooling, with a small number registered as just primary schools. The teachers in the schools come from a variety of backgrounds: 'While a few schools have wholly Muslim staff, most have around 50 per cent non-Muslim staff.'[18]

A vast majority of Muslim schools are co-educational, with rare exceptions where only girls are enrolled at the secondary level, such as Al Zahra College in New South Wales and the Australian Islamic College in Western Australia.[19] While many have the inclination to segregate girls and boys at secondary school level,[20] not all practise gender segregation, and when gender segregation is practised it differs from school to school, with some just seating girls and boys separately in the same classroom.[21]

Opting for Islamic education: Muslim parents' choice

It is an established fact that parents have the right to have their children educated; governments, policymakers and community leaders acknowledge this. Providing schooling or education for children not just as citizens but also as human beings and members of cultural communities is vital, and therefore parents and cultural communities naturally have a strong interest in children's education. The state also has the right to educate children as future citizens; however, this does not always fit well with the rights of parents to educate their children, particularly when they want to bring them up in accordance with religious and moral principles and retain a religious heritage. This can result in serious conflict. In an attempt to preserve religious heritage, many Muslim parents have a heightened engagement with the Muslimness of their children—that is, the building of a distinct Muslim identity—and parents expect Muslim schools to develop and foster the Muslimness of their students. Muslim parents' views regarding the educational needs of their children in hostile secular societies are shaped by perceived internal and external threats that then form the basis for such expectations.

There are numerous reasons for Muslim parents to select Muslim schools for the education of their children. In this section I explore some of these reasons in an attempt to understand Australia's broader schooling context. In Australia, state/government-run schools do not offer a formal religious curriculum. Religiously inclined Muslim parents and pupils have limited or, in some cases, no access to learning about the Islamic faith in public schools, which opens up a gap between secular schooling and faith-based education. In an endeavour to close this gap in Muslim students' education, Muslim parents often opt for Muslim schools for their children. Many Australian Muslim parents express concerns that public schools do not provide religious education and religion is 'left out of the syllabus',[22] which produces an environment in which Islamic values and ethos, Muslim identity and Islamic social ethics are not constantly cultivated and maintained. Mah notes that Muslim parents fear '"losing" their children and future generations to an open, predominantly Christian, but increasingly secular, society'[23] through the public schooling system. Irene Donohoue Clyne observes that a large number of Australian Muslim parents expect their children to attend Muslim schools in contrast to state schools so the children are kept away from secular influence and an identity crisis, and at the same time are taught Islamic cultural and moral values. She says that Australian Muslim parents opt to send their children to 'Islamic schools, outside the existing state-controlled system, to provide an education which reflects Islamic values and practices'.[24] One journalist quoted Clyne, saying:

> Muslim parents choose Islamic schools because the secular education system is underpinned by Judeo-Christian values that either ignore Islam or present it in a biased manner. Like other Australian parents, Muslims believe private schools deliver high academic standards, discipline and a moral framework consistent with home values.[25]

Similarly, in his study in Scandinavian and Western European contexts, Mark Sedgwick[26] found that parents send their children to Muslim schools because these schools are vigilant about mixed-gender physical exercises and swimming classes, and stick to the Islamic dress code. He highlights that most parents he interviewed used the word 'we', indicating an alignment between themselves and Muslim schools regarding mutual values and religious understanding. Sedgwick also remarks that parents in his case study were not fazed by reports that identified a possible lower standard of education, regarding complaints about low performance or lack of teacher training as a minor price to pay for having their children enrolled and taught in an Islamic-friendly environment.

Ibrahima Diallo's research shows that Muslim parents in Australia have a strong connection and loyalty to Islamic studies in Muslim schools, and therefore opt to enrol their children in Muslim schools. Talking about Muslim parents, she says:

> They believe that it is important to develop their Islamic culture and faith and transmit them to their children, and that studying Islamic studies is crucial to the formation of their Islamic identities. Their Islamic identities are expressed and embodied through knowledge of the Quran and by developing both Quranic and Arabic literacies. In other words, for the participants in this study, their Muslim identities are intimately associated with the Islamic

studies offered in these Islamic community schools; in particular, learning the Quran and developing Qur'anic reading and writing skills and learning the Arabic language.[27]

Rizvi's Australian research reveals that parents prefer Muslim schools because of underachievement, the prevalence of racism, and obstacles to meeting religious obligations in government-run schools.[28] Janet Phillips comments that Australian Muslim parents send their children to Muslim schools because of 'children experiencing bullying and intimidation at school, with many parents saying that they feel that they are forced to send their children to Islamic schools, not necessarily for the education, but for their safety'.[29] Muslim schools are also considered by parents as havens not just in terms of safety but, as Michael Merry and Geert Driessen explain, because they protect students from 'moral permissiveness and lower academic achievement' and that it is necessary to shelter students from government-run schools that 'ignore the cultural and religious identities of Muslim children'.[30]

Although educational standards and academic outcomes may not be uniform across Muslim schools, Muhammad Musharraf and Fatima Nabeel observe that these factors are major attractions for Muslim parents: 'We have come across findings from many researchers and reporters suggesting outstanding academic and overall achievements of Islamic schools.'[31] Academic performance seems be an important contributing factor attracting parents to Muslim schools. Saied Ameli and his colleagues found this to be the case in their British study, pointing out that among the reasons for Muslim parents to send their children to Muslim schools were 'high academic achievements' and 'discipline'.[32] Scholars have found that Muslim school students generally do well academically:

> Islamic school children demonstrated higher achievement levels in mathematics and primary school final examinations [and there is] no difference in non-verbal intelligence, cognitive capacities, home learning climate, attitude towards work, social behaviour, language achievement levels, student well-being and confidence between students at Islamic and other schools.[33]

There is also a perception among many Muslim parents that public schools may have the potential to feed negatively biased or inaccurate understandings of Islam to their children, and to expose them to anti-Islamic textbooks and secular theories and values. As Jones notes, 'There were also reservations about some of the subjects taught in the normal Australian curriculum'[34] and fears of losing control over the assimilation process of Muslim students, who might adopt unorthodox customs and un-Islamic ways of thinking. Coupled with this, Muslim parents understand that public schools disregard common Islamic rules governing diet, dress, gender relations and fundamental pillars of Islam, and that there is an inadequate focus on discipline to keep children respectful and away from narcotics and alcohol. Muslim parents who want to see their children have the opportunities of integration, social mobility and success in both the worldly and religious arenas are therefore 'concerned about the overall impact of the secular curriculum with its emphasis on a Euro-centric syllabus and no faith teaching'.[35]

Against this backdrop, many Muslim parents opt to send their children to a Muslim school in search of an authentic Islamic education that encompasses both a secular and an Islamic curriculum. For these parents, an authentic Islamic education denotes 'a total Islamic education in which the values and ethos of Islam are incorporated into the entire school culture and curriculum',[36] in 'some kind of integrated education system whereby their children could not only learn about their faith, but learn about it in a school where Islamic values and practices permeated the whole curriculum'.[37]

For many Muslim parents, an Islam-friendly environment is seen to be critical to the production of an authentic Islamic education. They see a close correlation between an authentic Islamic education and the environment in which Islam is both taught and normalised. In this connection, Aminah Mah found that in Australia:

> Most participants referred to the Islamic studies and the actions of the adults at the Muslim schools as sources from which they drew to develop as a Muslim. Two parents' ... decision for keeping their children in the Muslim schools was essentially due to the all-Muslim environment these schools provided. Yet for other parents, a Muslim school was seen as the one-stop shop they relied upon to meet all of the academic, social and religious needs of their children.[38]

Muslim parents believe that in an authentic Islamic education system, Islamic culture is preserved, Muslim identity is inculcated, knowledge is Islamised, and science and technology are taught. They see that Muslim schools provide this and are an important means to transmit religious and spiritual knowledge and to teach and develop ways of behaviour that are consistent with Islamic teachings. Moreover, they see Muslim schools as developing and encouraging in their students certain qualities pivotal for the foundations of social cohesion in Australian multiculturalism—qualities such as care and kindness, compassion, patience, understanding, respect and responsibility. The parents believe these 'value-added' ideals are integrated in the overall philosophy of the schools and are exhibited through the social justice and community service projects and activities that encompass curricular or co-curricular activities in many Muslim schools. Therefore, they choose to send their children to Muslim schools because they would like them to learn not only Islamic values that reflect their own values and practices, but also the common Australian values that are integrated into the curriculum of many Muslim schools.

The role of Muslim schools in secular Australia

As noted above, Muslim schools are a growing phenomenon in Australia essentially because Australia, as a liberal secular nation-state, doesn't administer its citizens' religious needs. Secularism creates a gap between the state and religion, which means that all the contributions religion can make to the development processes in society become the responsibility of religious communities. Thus, the religious needs of Australian citizens are very much left to individuals to organise for themselves, or to religious communities. Islamic education as a Muslim religious need is paramount in the developmental process of young Muslims and their identity formation, and the responsibility falls on the shoulders of the Muslim community. It is for this reason that the vast majority of Muslim schools in Australia are established and operated by Muslim communities.

Muslim schools function to fulfil Australian society's various needs and do not operate in a vacuum. One of those needs is education—a vital social institution through which a society teaches its members the skills, knowledge, norms and values they need so they can become productive members of that society. It is also a basic human right and should be fulfilled by the state. However, it becomes problematic in minority religious cases because minority religious groups such as Muslims have added religious needs within the education process that need to be satisfied internally. Education in general has various functions, but three are worth discussing here briefly.

The most important function of education is student socialisation. Like students in general, Muslim students are Australian citizens; their socialisation is as important as anyone else's. Muslim schools provide them with Islamic knowledge and give them a platform on which to learn, among other things, the values, norms and transferable skills—such as teamwork, leadership, organisation and time management, active listening, written and verbal communication, and research and critical analysis—needed to function in society; such learning is made possible through the primary medium of education. Thus, socialisation and social interaction are primary media for such learning. These processes enable Muslim students to learn values of harmony and group belonging at school and to value their membership of the school, community and wider Australian society. Schools generally teach reading, writing and arithmetic, but they also teach many of society's norms—including equality, tolerance and values such as respect and freedom. Muslim schools are no exception, and therefore their role in Australian society is not insignificant.

Another educational function Muslim schools perform is social integration. For Australian society to function well, its citizens must subscribe to a common set of beliefs and values, which are acquired through education. Muslim schools engage their students in such a learning process and prepare them for life after school and in the workforce and integrate them into Australian life.

Social and cultural innovation is another function of education in schools, including Muslim schools. Muslim schools deploy significant resources to improve the academic performance of students in an attempt to produce intellectuals and scientists who can make important discoveries that will benefit not only Australia but the entire world. In a sense, then, Muslim schools make important intellectual contributions not only to Australia but to the entire globe.

Education also involves numerous latent functions that are often referred to as the by-products of attending school and receiving an education rather than direct outcomes of the education itself. Muslim schools are integral to this process. The establishment of peer relationships in Muslim schools is one example; another is that Muslim schools keep thousands of high school students out of the full-time labour force and effectively keep Australia's unemployment rate lower than if Muslims were out of school and working or looking for employment.

Hostility towards Muslims exists in Australia, particularly in the wake of the events of 11 September 2001 and subsequent terror-related bombings in various parts of the world, along with national and international media campaigns maligning Muslims. This hostility has added to the challenges for Muslims living in 'secular' Australia who are subjected to ill-treatment and experience hatred on a regular basis. Muslim schools are seen by many Muslims as cultivating Muslimness to counter such malignity and marginalisation. The gradual growth in Muslim schools across Australia might be reflective, to an extent, of an increase in the number of school-age Muslims, but it also reveals the seriousness of Muslim concerns and an increase in Muslims' consciousness about moulding their needs.

In the earlier section we saw that Muslims do not necessarily desire faith-based education but, rather, the incorporation of Islamic values and principles into an integrated education system in an endeavour to make the 'whole person'. This is made possible through education in an Islamic environment and is apparently not achievable in Australian public schools, according to Muslim parents. The public schools are not sensitive enough or can be insensitive to the centrality of Islam in the life of Muslim students; Muslim parents then are swayed directly or indirectly to opt for Muslim schools.

Scholars such as Clyne and Mah have argued that Australian Muslim parents are often faced with perceived threats to their cultural values and family structures.[39] Parents see the cultural practices in wider Australian society and in the mixed-sex environment in schools, for example, as intensifying these threats. This reveals two contrasting worldviews and what education entails in them. Asad Zaman explains the difference between what may be called Western education and Islamic education:

> Western education is secular in outlook, skirts around moral issues central to Islam, and denies the idea that God is an active agent in human history. It is also highly Eurocentric, taking the key events in human history to be the Industrial Revolution in England and the French revolution, for example. It is built on a materialistic philosophy, stressing the primacy of physical objects over intangibles such as values, ideals and morals.[40]

Muslim schools provide the desired alternative: a safe haven with Islamic values, moral code and sex segregation where Muslim students are expected to learn to be valuable members of their community and larger Australian society. The schools also assist in eliminating barriers to educational achievement and provide greater accommodation of religious and cultural values, which leads to improved academic achievement and provides a culturally and religiously coherent learning environment.[41] Unlike Muslim schools, state schools do not promote respect for Muslim identity as such, respect for for Islamic social and moral values and principles indispensable to Muslims' social structure, or improving understanding of Islamic teachings through the curriculum. Muslim schools fill this gap by providing knowledge of Islamic history, languages and civilisation and by educating students in Islamic values and tenets to encourage a sense of Muslim identity, particularly at a time of much Muslim malignity, economic marginalisation, political targeting and securitising, and social polarisation. Students develop a strong sense of identity and establish connections and support in the wider community that can be valuable resources for fighting discrimination, stereotyping and maltreatment. Saeeda Shah aptly summarises the situation:

> Islamic schools might prove to be one of those new ways [to re-forge human diversity into human solidarity] because of the

potential contribution they might make to the sense of belonging and identity that human beings rightly value in addition to educational achievement of the learners. In the case of Muslims, religious identity provides a flexible discourse for accommodating other identities as is reflected in the very heterogeneous nature of the Muslim *Ummah* itself.[42]

The origins and development of Muslim schools in Australia reveal that Islam and Muslims are permanent features of Australian society. They inform us that Muslims are coming of age and prove that schools make Muslims part of the mainstream of Australian society despite mainstream denial of this fact. Muslim schools don't operate in a sociocultural or economic vacuum and are an important part of the development not only of Muslim community but of mainstream community too.

In this way, two main social entities—state education and religions such as Islam—intersect. Despite the secular nature of Australian nation-state education, religion clearly plays an important role in society. Muslim students spend most of their weekdays at school, spend weeknights doing homework, and on weekends participate in extracurricular activities; many then pursue further studies at university. By understanding the place of education and religion in secular Australia, we are able to better understand the Australian society that is home to Muslims and non-Muslims and to people from multicultural and multi-faith backgrounds. In such an Australia, all Muslims want is to be able to pass on valuable cultural, linguistic and religious traditions to their children and preserve Islamic heritage through a fair and integrated educational process within the framework of Muslim schools.

Chapter 9

Islamic studies in Australia

Academic study of Islam in Western scholarship is not a new phenomenon. As a scholarly tradition it started almost two centuries ago, when Islam and Muslim societies were seen as exotic as well as associated with sociocultural, economic and political concerns of the time.[1] With the global expansion of Western Europe—commonly known as the historical phenomenon of colonialism—in the eighteenth and nineteenth centuries, important questions were raised regarding the management of Muslims living in newly established colonies such as British India, the Dutch East Indies and French Algeria.

In the last fifty or so years, the governance of Muslims has re-emerged as a critical issue, only this time in relation to controlling natural resources in the Middle East and in the context of Muslims as immigrants and citizens living in Europe and other countries in the West. More recently, concerns about managing Muslims both in the West and in other parts of the world have been connected to global security threats and the 'war on terror'. Not only Western intellectuals but scholars from other cultural traditions, including Muslims themselves, have emerged—one could say in droves—to take full advantage of this situation not only to pursue their scholarly interests but to make a living. Many have been successful in securing large amounts of funding to establish research and teaching centres, and in winning research grants. No doubt they have produced an impressive body of innovative and useful work and politicians, policymakers, journalists and non-government organisations have made valuable use of it. However, a small portion of this knowledge has been produced under dubious circumstances and thus its efficacy is questionable.

In Australia in the wake of the events of 9/11 and the subsequent bombings in Bali, Madrid and London, the number of organisations offering courses in the study of Islam and its adherents has grown sharply. Islamic studies have become popular in many Muslim religious centres and in organisations and universities across the country. Within the Muslim community, a plethora of new centres, institutes and organisations have emerged offering Islamic studies programs, especially from a theological perspective. In academia, new research and/or teaching centres have emerged and stand-alone university degrees at undergraduate and postgraduate levels, as well as short courses and programs, have been developed to study Islam and Muslims from a social-scientific perspective.

This chapter examines the growth and development of Islamic studies under an overarching process of Islamic education both in the Muslim community and in Australian academic contexts. There are two contrasting networks of Islamic studies in Australia. One is relatively traditional and explicitly focuses on *kalam* (Islamic scholastic theology) and Islamic theology (the total belief system) from an all-encompassing Islamic worldview; the other is rather modern, with a social-scientific focus (sociology, anthropology, media studies, political science, psychology and social history) on the study of Islam and Muslims particularly in the modern world, based on a Western secular liberal worldview. The two networks demonstrate in various complex ways the challenges faced by and transformations impacting on Islamic studies in Australia today.

I argue that Islamic studies in the two networks have a non-aligned trajectory. The networks have different impacts on those who secure Islamic education from them, in terms of the understanding and implementation of Islamic knowledge. Despite the networks' disparity of character, the total effect is a further contribution to the heterogeneity of Islam in Australia and an ongoing, distinct making of an 'Aussie-Islam'.

Education in Islam

Religious knowledge is an integral part of Islam that is transmitted to Muslims through the process of education. The acquisition of knowledge is a key theme upon which the entire structure of the faith rests. It originates from Islam being a divinely revealed way of life that is focused on spreading God's teaching to the people. Muslims see the very process of revelation—where God speaks to the Prophet through the angel Gabriel and gives him instructions, explains Islamic doctrines and practices, sets out the law and offers guidance—as the first act of teaching the religion of Islam. The revelation in Islamic tradition is understood as informing the entire process of transmission of religious knowledge; therefore, memorisation of the Qur'an has played a central role from the very beginning.

From its very inception Islam placed a high value on education and as such it has a long and rich intellectual tradition. As it entered different territories it was embraced by people of diverse religious traditions and cultural practices who were able to do so through the process of education, which became an important channel for the transmission of *'ilm* (knowledge) as well as the creation of a broad-based and cohesive social order.

Islam as a way of life is based on the Qur'an, and for this reason the Qur'an occupies a special place in the hearts and minds of Muslims and is the foundation of the Islamic worldview. As Nidhal Guessoum says, 'The Qur'an plays a central role in defining the beliefs, the lifestyle, and the worldview of Muslims.'[2] Knowledge has always played a significant role in Islam and occupies premium status within it, as evidenced by over 800 references to it in the Qur'an.[3] From a Muslim perspective, the message of the Qur'an begins with the concepts of literacy, knowledge and channels of education. Learning is constantly exhorted and education is repeatedly emphasised, with frequent directives such as 'God will exalt those of you who believe and those who have knowledge to high degrees',[4] 'O my Lord! Increase me in knowledge',[5] 'As God has taught him, so let him write',[6] 'And Allah taught Adam all the names',[7] 'Are those who have knowledge equal to those who do not have knowledge?!'[8] and 'Read. Read in the name of thy Lord who created; [He] created the human being from blood clot. Read in the name of thy Lord who taught by the pen: [He] taught the human being what he did not know'.[9]

The Qur'an also pays particular attention to science, as this quote shows:

> In the creation of the heavens and the earth the alternation of the night and the day, in the ships that sail in the sea with their load ... in the rain which Allah sends down from the sky and thus revives the earth after its death; and then He spread in all kinds of animals; in the changing of the winds: in the clouds which have been left suspending between the heaven and the earth—in all these are clear signs for the people who understand.[10]

The importance of education is similarly emphasised in Hadith (the sayings and traditions of the Prophet Mohammed): for example, 'Seeking knowledge is obligatory upon every Muslim.'[11]

Such Qur'anic verses and Prophetic traditions are evidence of the importance placed on learning and teaching in Islam and provide a powerful impetus for Muslims to secure education. Education in Islam drives its significance largely, first, from the centrality of the Qur'an, its memorisation and study, and, second, from learning the Prophetic traditions. Robert Hefner and Muhammad Zaman note that Islamic education historically has been premised on the

Qur'an and Hadith as the two primary sources of the revealed way of life. They serve as a guide to human conduct in this world, and therefore transmission of knowledge derived from them across generations is deemed an act of worship that produces virtuous citizens.[12]

Muslim educational activity began in the eighth century in entirely informal educational settings—in the homes of teachers and in traditional elementary schools called *maktabs*, often attached to a mosque—principally to disseminate the teaching of the Qur'an and the Sunna (traditions and practices of the Prophet Mohammed). Education would begin at a young age with study of Arabic and the Qur'an. Young boys, and sometimes young girls in a separate group, would learn how to read and write in Arabic, learn Arabic grammar and *qira'at* (Qur'anic recitation) and receive training in other practical and theoretical subjects such as theology, medicine and mathematics.[13] Maktabs were the only means of mass education in the Muslim world. Some students would then proceed to training in *tafsir* (Qur'anic exegesis), sharia and fiqh.

In the eleventh and twelfth centuries Muslim states in cooperation with the Muslim bourgeoisie and nobility started to establish institutions of higher religious learning called madrasas, where the *ulama* (religious scholars; singular is *alim*) were based.[14] The ulama controlled the religious knowledge and its application and emerged as a professional class widely supported by state patronage. As religious specialists they operated as imams, muftis, qadis and *qaris* (reciters of the Qur'an).[15]

As Islam expanded into new territories and the Muslim population grew, madrasas multiplied throughout the Muslim world. Despite lacking a standardised curriculum or institutionalised system of certification, they helped the spread of Islamic learning not only in urban centres but in remote areas, uniting diverse Muslim communities in a shared cultural venture. In the madrasa system, the relationship between students and their teacher was close. Ebrahim Moosa explains the significance of the teacher–student dynamic as a transmission from 'heart to heart', which makes the knowledge easily digestible and also plausible:[16] 'Islamic teaching for a long time had followed the format of a private meeting between a knowledgeable person, a prayer leader or scholar, and students gathering in a circle at the local mosque after prayer.'[17] When the study was completed, the student would be issued with an *ijaza* (a licence to transmit a certain text or subject) not by the institution but by a particular scholar from the genealogy of scholars, who were the only recognised authority in the educational system.[18] This group of scholars claimed religious authority based on an authenticated, uninterrupted chain of scholarship extending from their teachers to the Prophet Mohammed.[19]

Madrasas such as the House of Wisdom in Baghdad were principally designed to concentrate on the development of religious knowledge such as sharia, fiqh and tafsir but were opened to the study of other subjects, such as astronomy, medicine and mathematics.[20] For Muslim scholars and from the Qur'anic perspective, knowledge and religion were intertwined and operated in tandem with each other to assist humans to solve their sociocultural, economic and political problems. Due to madrasas' openness to education, sciences flourished for several centuries and constituted the educational framework in classical and medieval Islam. The madrasa campus usually comprised a mosque, a library and a boarding house and was funded by a *waqf* (charitable endowment) that covered the servicing and maintenance of the campus and paid the salaries of ulama and the stipends of students.[21]

The University of al-Qarawiyyin, founded in 859 CE in Fez, Morocco, is the world's oldest existing degree-granting continually operating university. The next oldest is Al-Azhar University, associated with Al-Azhar Mosque in Cairo, which was founded in 970 CE by the Fatimid Caliphate.[22] Since Islam is considered to be a complete way of life, many scholars preached the indivisibility of knowledge. Therefore, in these and other institutions Islamic education encompassed the dissemination of both sacred and profane knowledge. Worldly knowledge such as geometry, algebra and the philosophy of the ancient Greeks was incorporated into the religious curriculum.[23] Historically, the ulama never restricted their learning and teaching to the revealed sciences and were aware, as God's vicegerents on earth, that the purpose of understanding the natural and physical sciences was to effectively render service to God's creations.

The function of knowledge in Islam is all-encompassing and thus education and knowledge are about more than simply securing a stable income. In fact, they are about the pursuit of truth for its own sake and its benefit to all of humanity. Gerhard Bowering asserts that:

> By transforming the world during the ascendancy of the Abbasid Empire (750–1258), Islam created a splendid cosmopolitan civilization built on the Arabic language; the message of its scripture, tradition, and law (Qur'an, hadith and sharia); and the wisdom and science of the cultures newly incorporated during its expansion over three continents. The practice of philosophy, medicine, and the sciences within the Islamic empire was at a level of sophistication unmatched by any other civilization; it secured pride of place in such diverse fields as architecture, philosophy, maritime navigation and trade, and commerce by land and sea, and saw the founding of the world's first universities.[24]

Until recently, Islamic education was approached from an all-inclusive perspective: any intellectual endeavour considered as arousing the recognition of the Creator was deemed to be beneficial and from Allah. Other functions performed by religious education in Islam included preaching the faith, building character, developing a moral compass, strengthening the ummah and Islamic identity, preserving Islamic tradition, and mobilising the faithful.

The essence of Islam is to impart God's message and, in the process, win over adherents. Winning over new adherents has been the catalyst for the formation of a system of transfer of Islamic knowledge. In a sense, then, Islamic education is synonymous with preaching. Transforming the world into *dar al-Islam* (the abode of Islam) through the teaching of the 'true' and 'perfect' religion—Islam—has been the aim of the ulama and Islam. Following from this, Islamic educational institutions have always seen their primary duty as spreading the Islamic 'truth' of preaching. Based on this supposition, every student and teacher is obliged to see their acquired knowledge as to be shared and not hoarded; therefore, they must go out into the world and preach *tawhid* (unity of God) and spread Islam.

Islamic studies in Australia

As stated earlier, the events of 9/11, the Bali, Madrid and London bombings, and various other terror-related incidents in different parts of the world have drawn intense focus onto Islam and Muslims, particularly in the West and including Australia. Since these events Islam and Muslims have increasingly been equated with terrorism, and vilification of the religion and its adherents has been on the rise.[25] In Australia and in various other countries of the West, Islam and Muslims have come to be negatively viewed and their complicity in these events has been alleged. This is an exaggeration and misunderstanding. Islamic and Muslim reality has been deeply distorted by the popular construction of Islam as a monolith and Muslims as a homogeneous people such that both are now associated with acts of terrorism and political violence.[26]

For Australia, one of the most pressing concerns has been the presence so close to its soil of the militant group Jemaah Islamiah (JI) in Indonesia. Whether or not JI or, for that matter, Indonesia as the world's largest Muslim country poses a 'real' or perceived threat of terrorism or undermining of secular liberal democracy, Australia nevertheless remains concerned and has taken the matter seriously. It has cast its focus on Indonesia and South-East Asia generally to better understand Islam and the internal dynamics of the Muslim population in Muslim-majority countries and in diaspora Muslim communities. Shahram Akbarzadeh and his colleagues assert that:

There has been an acknowledgment in the Australian policy-making circles of the increasing relevance of scholarly research into our region. The importance of research into Islam in South East Asia and its implications for Australian security have become even more salient in the wake of the September 11, 2001, attack in New York and the October 2002 attack in Bali.[27]

Mohammad Kamali and Zarina Nalla note that:

> Compared to Europe, Australia and New Zealand are relative newcomers to Islamic studies and the burgeoning interest that is seen in starting programs of study and research on Islam which is also informed in recent years by the rise of extremism and violence.[28]

Behind this background and the fact that the Muslim population is fast growing in Australia, both academic and Muslim religio-spiritual interest in Islam is growing speedily. The increased academic research and teaching interest in Islam is noted by Akbarzadeh and his colleagues, who say, 'Studies of Islam and Muslim societies constitute a relatively new, but growing, field of research in Australia.'[29] Australian Muslim religio-spiritual interest in Islam is evident in the emergence and growth of a plethora of new Muslim centres, institutes and CSOs offering religious-based Islamic studies programs.

As mentioned above, in Australia there are two contrasting networks of Islamic studies. The one I characterise as being based on *traditional religious science* involves Muslim centres, institutes and CSOs offering students (children, adolescents and adults) the opportunity and space to study Islam using revealed science—for instance, science of the Qur'an, science of Hadith, Qur'anic exegesis, Islamic law and Islamic jurisprudence. Here, 'Islamic studies' denotes Islamic theology, or teaching and learning Islam. The other, based on *modern science*, allows students from both Muslim and non-Muslim backgrounds to formally enrol in a university course or subject to study existential Islam and Muslim communalism. Here, the students learn scientific research methods, and apply sociological, anthropological, historical and philosophical principles to better understand different aspects of Islam, the role of Islamic civilisation in global history, and contemporary Muslim peoples. Therefore, a growing trend in research activity and a heightened interest in various aspects of Islam, particularly its sociocultural and political role in a globalised world, are penetrating academia with great force.

It is critical to understand that the growing effects of globalisation and the post-9/11 world order have important ramifications for Muslim residents in Australia. Issues of Muslim citizenship in relation to their ability to access the labour market and participate fully in civic life, as well as the growth of the phenomenon of Islamic revivalism and its impact on governance in numerous Muslim states, are also important considerations in better understanding the role of Islam today. This can be made possible through academic research and formal and comprehensive Islamic studies programs.

While the 'traditional religious science' institutions may be seen as religious, the 'modern science' ones are usually recognised as secular. Moreover, the former may be considered as Muslims-only spaces to study their own religion, its sacred texts and religious law, while the latter are understood as spaces for anyone keen to learn about diverse aspects of Islam and develop a critical and 'rational' understanding of Islam and Muslims and their place in modernity. Consequently, in describing both forms of Islamic studies we find several dichotomies: distinct and analogous, religious and secular, imitational and analytical, doctrinal and rational, and sacred and profane. However, one of the arguments of this chapter is that both forms are useful and even necessary in multicultural Australia, and that although at the moment they generally operate independently and in isolation from each other, there is a fast-growing need for interaction and collaboration between them and the promotion of inter-community relationships.

It is not possible to distinctly articulate the direct outcomes of the two networks, because to date no empirical research has been conducted that has studied both networks in tandem and measured their effects on Islam and Muslims in Australia. However, there is no doubt that Islamic studies is an empirical phenomenon in Australia and that its overall impact, particularly on Muslim everyday living, is inevitable. As a learning process, Islamic studies serve as a means through which the aims and habits of Muslims are transmitted from individual to individual, group to group, and generation to generation. Islamic studies as an educational process is when both educators and students deliberately transmit Islamic and Muslim accumulated knowledge, skills, customs and values across time and space. Islamic studies put in motion socialisation, which sociologists claim inevitably impacts on human beings directly or indirectly:

> Socialization is the multifaceted process through which individuals learn and internalize cultural norms, codes, and values. This process enables entry into and sustained membership in one or more social groups. Individuals develop social and cultural competencies through (1) interaction with other individuals and social institutions and (2) response to their macro- and micro-sociocultural contexts. Socialization does not occur in a vacuum: this process operates in

social locations that both afford and constrain interaction and opportunity ... Socialization facilitates processes of inclusion and participation of diverse individuals and groups in society. At the same time, socialization contributes to the stabilization of social order, which can include reproduction of existing stratification by race, gender, and social class. Processes of socialization continue to shape generational cohorts and intergenerational dynamics as well as across various social institutions.[30]

In light of this and the fact that research conducted on Islamic studies in various other Western countries reveals that Islamic studies have a significant impact on Muslims,[31] there is no reason to believe the same is not true about their impact on Australian Muslims and the shaping of their identity. Therefore, the two networks of Islamic studies are crucial in understanding Islam and Muslims in Australia. They contribute to the shaping and making of a distinct Australian Islam, one with distinct Australian characteristics—that is, an 'Aussie-Islam', an Islam emanating from and for the Australian multicultural context. An Aussie-Islam allows for Muslims to maintain their Islamic heritage and character but at the same time participate in the social and cultural life of multicultural Australia. An Aussie-Islam is a project in the making that involves Australian-born Muslims and young migrants and seeks to weed out ethnic and parochial accretions from scriptural and rational Islam through the educational process. In this way, it can share values such as pluralism and tolerance with Australia and coexist in a political system where there is separation of church and state.

An Aussie-Islam is gradually becoming Australianised and can be considered an Australian religion. However, its slow progress is largely due to the two networks of Islamic studies operating in isolation from one another and having different trajectories. To demonstrate the difference between them, two examples of educational models should suffice. What follows is a brief description of some of the courses, programs (major and/or minor) and subjects offered by Muslim community organisations and by universities. I have chosen Daar Aisha Shari'ah College and its affiliate, Daar Ibn Abbas, to show the kinds of courses and subjects offered by Muslim CSOs. They are typical Muslim centres organised and operated around the idea of Islamic education as traditional religious science.

Daar Aisha College was established in 2003 by a Tunisian-born scholar, Sheikh Abdul Moez Nafti al Idrisi Al-Hasany. He was keen to impart knowledge derived from the Qur'an and established the college with a mission to enlighten Muslims with sacred knowledge for the purpose of gaining God's blessings. He moved to expand his mission and religious project by establishing

Daar Ibn Abbas in 2010 to concentrate on imparting Islamic knowledge to male Muslims in particular. In the sheikh's vision, Daar Ibn Abbas is a vehicle to facilitate, revive and implement authentic Islamic education in a mosque that expands to a multifunctional community centre in the centre of south-west Sydney. Tables 8 and 9 show the courses and subjects offered at the two colleges.

Table 8: Islamic studies at Daar Aisha Shari'ah College, 2020

Sharia course subjects	Qur'an course subjects	Women's course subjects
Islamic Theology	Introduction to Tajweed	Raising Muslim Children
Sciences of the Qur'an	Applied Tajweed	Islam for Beginners
Sciences of Hadith	Tahfiz Memorisation	Classic Arabic Language
Hadith	Learn to Read the Qur'an	On Death & Dying: The Journey of the Soul
Purification of the Heart		Al Shama'il al Muhammadeyyah (In the Footsteps of the Prophet)
Tafsir (exegesis)		
Seerah (Prophetic biography)		
Islamic Law		
Islamic Creed		
Tajweed and Tahfiz (recitation and memorisation of the Qur'an)		

Source: Daar Aisha Shari'ah College website (https://www.daaraisha.org/courses/catalog)

Table 9: Islamic studies at Daar Ibn Abbas, 2020

Boys' Islamic Studies course (7–17 years) subjects	Part-time Tajwid and Tahfiz course subjects	Men's Essentials of Islam course subjects
Islamic Studies	Tajwid (recitation of the Qur'an)	Fiqh (Jurisprudence)
Qur'an	Tahfiz (memorisation)	Aqeedah (Belief)
Duas (invocation) & Athkaar (remembrance)		Tarbiyah (Purification of the Heart)
Mastery Subject: Tahara & Salah		

Source: Daar Ibn Abbas website (https://ibnabbas.org.au/courses)

Table 10, although by no means exhaustive, contains a list of Islamic studies courses and subjects offered by certain universities in Australia at undergraduate and postgraduate levels. It shows the great diversity of units available to students in Australian academia. In some instances universities offer distinct subjects; in others there is overlap between subjects across institutions. Most of the universities that offer Islamic studies offer only a small number of subjects as electives that can be counted towards a degree such as Bachelor of Arts. Some, such as Western Sydney University, offer students this option as well as the opportunity to take up an entire Islamic studies program by doing a major or sub-major in Islamic studies while pursuing a Bachelor of Arts or BA (Pathway to Teaching Primary) or BA (Pathway to Teaching Secondary). A handful of universities offer a complete undergraduate and/or postgraduate degree in Islamic studies.

In contrast to Muslim community-based religious centres such as Daar Ibn Abbas, Australian universities provide more robust and formal Islamic studies programs and courses with a strong focus on analysis and theorising. For example, at Western Sydney University a theoretical foundation is laid down in the first year of study, and students are then able to gradually progress to topics and disciplines critical to understanding Islam. The field of study considers text and context, historical and modern Islamic studies, and research methods. There is an emphasis on the relevance of Islamic studies to the modern world through developing a solid understanding of past traditions in Islamic scholarship and their social and historical contexts. Preparation for graduate study is another important aim of Islamic studies at Western Sydney University, with strong attention paid to developing analytical and interdisciplinary research skills by combining several approaches.

Table 10: Universities teaching Islamic studies in Australia, 2020

Institution	State	Unit name	Course level
University of Melbourne National Centre of Excellence for Islamic Studies Australia and Graduate School of Humanities and Social Sciences	VIC	110-113: Understanding Islam and Muslim Societies 110-211: Great Texts of Islam: Qur'an and Hadith 110-253: Islam in Southeast Asia 110-114: Islam in the Modern World 110-250: Islam, Media and Conflict 110-254: Islamic Banking and Finance 110-252: Islamic Law in a Changing World 110-210: Ethical Traditions in Islam 131-046: Great Empires of Islamic Civilisation 110-223: Islam and the West 110-251: Islam and the Making of Europe	Undergraduate
		ISLM40003: Methodologies of Hadith ISLM40005: Muslim Philosophical Traditions ISLM90008: Islam and Politics ISLM40002: The Qur'an and Its Interpretation ISLM90009: Special Seminar in Islamic Studies ISLM40004: Islamic Theology: Schools and Methods ISLM40001: Topics in Arabic & Islamic Studies ISLM40007: Methods of Islamic Law ISLM90005: Islam and Questioning of Modernity	Postgraduate (Master of Islamic Studies)
Western Sydney University School of Humanities and Communication Arts	NSW	101462: Understanding Islam and Muslim Societies 102296: Hadith; The Prophetic Tradition 101911: The Qur'an: An Introduction 101467: Islam in Southeast Asia 102294: Islam in the Modern World 101468: Islam, Media and Conflict 101879: Women with Muslim Identity 101465: Islamic Law in a Changing World 101466: Ethical Traditions in Islam 101822: Islam and the West 102297: Islamic Revivalism in the Globalised World	Undergraduate

Institution	State	Unit name	Course level
Charles Sturt University and Islamic Sciences & Research Academy of Australia	NSW	Core subjects ISL100 Islamic Worldview and Faith Essentials ISL110 Fiqh (Islamic Law) of the Five Pillars ISL170 Ihsan (Spirituality) Essentials ISL181 Sirah (Life of Prophet Mohammed) ISL202 Usul al-Din (Foundational Islamic Theology) ISL211 Usul al-Fiqh (Methodology of Islamic Law) ISL230 Usul al-Tafsir (Methodology of Qur'anic Exegesis) ISL232 Usul al-Hadith (Methodology of Prophetic Traditions) ISL331 Advanced Study of Tafsir (Qur'anic Exegesis) Literature ISL333 Advanced Study of Hadith Literature Arabic electives ISL441 Arabic Skills 1 ISL442 Arabic Skills 2 ISL443 Arabic Skills 3 ISL460 Introduction to Arabic Reading ISL461 Beginner Arabic Language 1 ISL462 Beginner Arabic Language 2 ISL463 Intermediate Arabic Grammar 1 ISL464 Intermediate Arabic Grammar 2 ISL465 Advanced Arabic Grammar Islamic Studies electives ISL101 Mantiq (Logic) and Critical Reasoning ISL151 Islam in the Modern World ISL171 Akhlaq (Morality) and Adab (Manners) in Islam ISL271 Purification of the Heart ISL282 History of Prophets: Adam to Jesus ISL312 Religious Service and Community Leadership ISL313 Islamic Family Law ISL353 World Religions in Australia ISL355 Women in Islam and Islamic Cultures ISL383 Islamic History and Civilisations ISL399 Guided Research	Undergraduate

Institution	State	Unit name	Course level
		Core subjects ISL400 Islamic Worldview and Theology ISL411 Methodology of Islamic Law (Usul al-Fiqh) ISL430 Methodology of Qur'anic Exegesis (Usul al-Tafsir) ISL432 Methodology of Prophetic Traditions (Usul al-Hadith) Electives ISL410 Islamic Jurisprudence of Five Pillars ISL413 Islamic Family Law and Society ISL451 Islam in the Modern World ISL455 Women in Islam, Civilisations and Cultures ISL470 Essentials of Islamic Spirituality ISL471 Islam: Morality and Etiquette in Daily Life ISL481 Philosophy of Prophet Mohammed's Life (Sirah) ISL483 Islamic History and Civilisations ISL484 Modern History of the Muslim World ISL441 Arabic Skills 1 ISL442 Arabic Skills 2 ISL443 Arabic Skills 3 ISL460 Introduction to Arabic Reading ISL461 Beginner Arabic Language 1 ISL462 Beginner Arabic Language 2 ISL463 Intermediate Arabic Grammar 1 ISL464 Intermediate Arabic Grammar 2 ISL465 Advanced Arabic Grammar Electives ISL591 Interpreting Islamic Sacred Texts ISL593 Islamic Theology: Classical to Contemporary Thought ISL550 Islam and Science: Contemporary Ethical Issues ISL555 Contemporary Islamic Movements ISL556 Islamic Economy, Banking and Finance PLUS ISL599 Guided Research OR ISL596 Islamic Studies Project	Postgraduate (Master of Islamic Studies)

Source: Relevant university websites.

Generally speaking, research into Islam and Muslim societies and formal Islamic studies programs have important benefits. As can be ascertained from Table 10 and as discussed above, the courses allow students to structure a career or professional path such as primary or secondary school teaching. Another important benefit is that individuals gain a better appreciation of lived Islam and learn more about Muslim societies and Muslim diaspora communities. Islamic studies programs help students to focus on various aspects of Islam but at the same time gain more specific knowledge of the religion as a cultural and belief system: this is important in understanding Islam's contribution to the multicultural and multi-faith nature of contemporary Australia. It also enhances researchers' and students' knowledge of different Islamic values, rituals and practices and thereby dispels some of the myths and misconceptions propagated by the media—for example, it defuses the threat wrongly ascribed to Islam in the age of terror.

Islamic studies are undeniably a fast-growing phenomenon in Australia. People from different religious and ideological backgrounds and Muslims themselves seek to study Islam in order to gain a better appreciation of an important world religion that shares its tradition in a fundamental way with Christianity and Judaism. Islam is a complex phenomenon and studying it can mean a variety of things, including exploring its holy texts (the Qur'an and Hadith), laws and artefacts and analysing its sociocultural, economic and political impact not only in Australia but around the globe. It can also mean investigating the internal and external factors behind Islam's internal religious dynamism and, in the age of the 'war on terror', the rise, causes and consequences of Islamism and Muslim radicalism and terrorism.

It is important to appreciate that Islamic studies are not about the study of the religion alone, but also about Islam's adherents. In other words, Islamic studies in a Muslim community context is about Muslims learning the fundamentals of their religion, its language and texts, and in a university context it is about social-scientific exploration of the ways in which Muslims describe and pursue their everyday religious life. In both contexts, Islamic studies are also about how Muslims in Australia go about constructing their identity. Since Islam is being interpreted and practised by its followers in a variety of ways, understanding this dimension of Muslim everyday living is critical, particularly through the higher learning that is made possible in Muslim community settings and universities.

Part 5

Australia in the era of global terrorism

Chapter 10

Radicalised Muslim 'Other' and countering violent extremism

In the post-9/11 'war on terror' era, 'radicalisation' has been linked to Islam and Muslims and therefore has inevitably been rendered an Islamic and a Muslim phenomenon. As such, 'radicalisation' has found fame in the field of countering violent extremism (CVE), particularly among policymakers, politicians, journalists and some academics. Even in the public discourse, the concept of radicalisation is often passionately debated.

Radicalisation (a process by which an individual or a group adopts radical views in opposition to prevailing normative views) and theories linked to it seeking an explanation of the processes and causes of radicalism (radical ideas as an expression of legitimate thought or views that lead to radicalisation) have become a critical analytical tool for understanding issues of 'homegrown' violent extremism, particularly in the West.[1] To understand these factors and issues and the actual process of radicalisation, a theoretical model is necessary. However, there is no single theory that can provide a universal understanding of the causes of radicalisation. This is because radicalism is a constantly changing, dynamic and heterogeneous phenomenon.

Over the years scholars have tried to explain radicalisation using a variety of theoretical frameworks, including 'conflict theory', 'socialisation theory', 'social identity theory' and 'social categorisation theory'. For example, the social categorisation theory relates to the cognitive process through which individuals reinforce their social identity by underscoring intra-group closeness and interconnectedness, and intergroup differences. Individuals are grouped into similar or different people based on social, cultural, economic and political distinctions. Such distinctions demarcate the world into 'us' and 'them', creating sharp group boundaries; in addition, the systems of meaning integral to the group eventually pave the way for a set of behaviours distinct from members of the larger society.

Explaining the process of radicalisation requires the use of multiple theoretical models in conjunction with, not in isolation from, each other. Hence, one could use conflict theory—which argues that social structures are produced from conflict situations between people with incongruent interests and resources where individuals and resources, in turn, affect these structures—in conjunction with social identity theory, which posits that certain parts of an individual's self-concept originate from perceived or real membership in a particular social group, and that membership influences intergroup behaviour to explain the process of radicalisation.

Ostensibly, the growing problem of narrow-minded extremist ideas and actions, especially among young Muslims in Australia and other countries of the West, is being understood and interpreted through the popular discourse of radicalisation. Radicalisation is generally defined, at least in theory, as a process through which an individual is gradually socialised into 'extreme' ideas and stances that potentially pave the way for political action, often of a destructive or violent nature. In this sense, radicalisation poses a great threat to national security and therefore gives authorities the legitimacy and reason to identify and deal with perpetrators accordingly. Hence, the radicalisation discussion comfortably fits with neoliberal notions of governmentality[2] and risk management[3] and renders radicalisation a political football.

No doubt Muslim radicalisation takes place in society and warrants a national strategy for prevention and countering violent extremism and terrorism. Some Muslims have a very superficial understanding of their religion and are susceptible to extreme views and ideas that are promoted and promulgated by a select few overzealous, ill-informed, manipulative sheikhs and imams. Risk management of such Muslims may be necessary. However, what is not warranted are government strategies that are poorly, impetuously and expediently developed and consequently, instead of targeting perpetrators, target Muslims in general. One of the serious unintended consequences of this is that Muslims end up experiencing enhanced discrimination and marginalisation through the imposition of a complex web of social, cultural, economic and political barriers in their everyday living. Muslim net experience, particularly in relation to their participation in social processes, becomes a socio-spatial challenge and an experience of social exclusion and 'Othering'.

This chapter looks at the process of Muslim radicalisation and the Australian Government's response to it in terms of CVE, and the consequences of such a response for Muslims in Australia. I argue that the government's strategy specifically indiscriminately targets Muslims, which results in the construction of Australian Muslims as a radicalised 'Other'. Importantly, the inability of the strategy's internal mechanisms to clearly differentiate radicalised Muslims from ordinary Muslims leads to targeting all Muslims, and hence further enhances their marginalisation in Australian society.

Politics of radicalism

The concept of Muslim radicalism in recent years in light of the events of 11 September 2001 has been grossly politicised, and the politics of Muslim radicalism are deeply embedded in the risk management paradigm. Risk management has become important in governmental planning documentation and processes, particularly in the wake of German sociologist Ulrich Beck's work on 'risk society'.[4] Social scientists have been quick in attempting to understand the remodelling of modernity using a macro-level sociological analysis of environmental risk, but some—particularly theorists of governmentality and the war on terror—have used such analysis to their own advantage.[5]

These Foucauldian analyses pay particular attention to the way risk management know-how is used for population management through refined conceptual factors that did not exist in the past. The burgeoning corpus of critical investigational technique designed initially by Beck to examine 'risk' in society is, in the age of terror, borrowed to study terrorism and used to manage it as a 'risk' phenomenon, although risk or objective threat is not necessarily clear or evident. In other words, there is an exploitative element in the process. If there is exploitation involved then it means that risk is being used expediently in studies, leaving an unanswered question about the real existence of threat: is there an objective threat, or is the threat a concoction? In this fast-rising critical scholarship, risk is understood to have a 'performative' function in that it not only describes a given reality but actively engages in the production of manipulating that reality. In connection to international relations and politics and the study of crime, critical risk studies employ the Foucauldian conceptualisation of risk as a productive method of governance that brings security into operation.[6]

Within the analysis of terrorism, counterterrorism (CT), radicalisation and deradicalisation, the critical scholarship underscores a new criminology of 'protective incarceration', the use of cyber-technology to chase after enemies, and the production of enemy populations through risk profiles based on 'people essentialising'.[7] Preventive strategies—for example, airline passenger monitoring and the unrestrained use of personal data systems in the investigation of the actions or communications of suspects—are used to expose the 'unknown'; without these strategies, such intelligence or information gathering is not possible. These preventive strategies or techniques of performative risk management are made exceptions on the grounds that they assist in the necessary process of intelligence gathering or of risk profiling by authorities.[8] In the end we learn that risk is not the objective threat: the existence of danger is merely a presupposition that becomes a vehicle through which the world is reorganised by those with authority and power.

Muslim radicalism: What is it?

In popular discourse, religious radicalism denotes extreme violence in the name of religion.[9] Radicals are understood to be ready to engage in violent acts in the service of God and show no mercy towards their victims because the victims are seen as the enemies of God and therefore their enemies too. Religious radicalism also inculcates the will to sacrifice oneself as a 'martyr' in the perceived service of God and as a means to eschew the horror of the Day of Judgement and earn rewards in the afterlife.

However, radicalism, whether religious or non-religious in nature, is not always and does not necessarily have to be about extreme acts of violence or terrorism. Religious radicalism is multifaceted and multidimensional and is often and in a majority of cases nonviolent. This is true for Muslim radicalism, as noted by Faisal Kutty: 'Far from being monolithic, the movement is composed of divergent groups ranging from the rejectionist and extremist minority to a mainstream committed to working peacefully within the existing order.'[10]

Religious radicalism is initially driven by a need to expand the religious law of a particular radical group or faith community. For example, Jewish religious radicals aspire for the supremacy of the Halakah, and Muslim radicals work towards the dominance of sharia.[11] Since radicals are critical of what they consider to be inappropriate and inefficient—the status quo, the role of key civil institutions, and the secular state—they strive towards the imposition of their own programs and the rebuilding of society. Another driving force is the attitude of radicals towards members of the society who don't share their views and laws. Radicals, depending on the circumstance, either apply great efforts to converting other members of the society or steer away from them. The final driving force is the removal, by radicals, of foreign values and norms from their religion and infusing it with what they refer to as its pure tenets, principles and ideals. Thus, radicals protect their members and supporters by keeping them away from the common pattern of living of mainstream society and engaging them in what the radicals consider to be a religiously sanctioned way of life.

Religious radicalism has existed for hundreds of years. Contrary to popular belief, it is neither a new phenomenon nor unique to Muslims.[12]

Religious radicals believe that their society is in crisis, and seek remedies. They strive to introduce change and bring about development based on their understanding of religious teachings and ideals. The aim is to transition society, preferably nonviolently, for universal benefit by restructuring education and communication systems, recovering interpersonal relations, restoring traditional family structures, and reforming the social and political order. Rem Korteweg and his colleagues note that 'radicalization is the quest to drastically alter society, possibly through the use of unorthodox *but not necessarily violent* means' [emphasis added].[13]

This is exactly the goal of Muslim radicals. They intend to make the Islamic lifestyle pervasive throughout the modern world and Islam the dominant global system. The strategy they have adopted is setting up boundaries of difference, identifying the enemy, seeking out converts, creating and maintaining institutions and, finally, working towards the establishment of a caliphate (Islamic state) with sharia as its constitution in an attempt to comprehensively recreate society. Often driven by anti-materialist ideology, Muslim radicals seek to reconstruct an indigenous global Islamic culture in a modern caliphate that will itself be Islamic, and in which Muslims will emancipate themselves.[14] Muslim radicalism is intended as a solution to the 'crisis of modernity'—the increasing gap between rich and poor; the constant growth of urban slums; unmanageable urban growth; urban transportation, housing and infrastructure crises; homelessness; unemployment; poverty; under-education; limited social mobility; discrimination and prejudice; injustice; disenfranchisement; intensification of class divisions; unfair spread of and failure to generate prosperity; political discontent; debt-driven 'growth'; and weakening of faith in reason's ability to validate its (reason's) supreme aims—or as an answer to the dilemmas posed by modernity and a positive reaction to modernity's challenges.

Muslim radicalism, therefore, is not anti-modernity, nor does it pursue modernity's destruction. Instead, it 'seek[s] peaceful and democratic change'.[15] It strives to eliminate secularism and Westernism from modernity and harmoniously blend modernity's impartial sensibilities and corpus of knowledge with traditional religious attachments and norms. George Joffé posits that:

> The challenge embodied in radicalisation is a process of contention designed to alter order and discourse but does not necessarily seek to destroy or replace the structures through which they are articulated ... [And] ... for the radical, the state can, initially at least, be challenged in order to modify its hegemonic discourse ...[16]

However, in the wake of the 9/11 terrorist bombings in the United States and subsequent bombings elsewhere, Western political discourse about Muslim radicalism has become extraordinarily compelling and the only legitimate framework to explain violent extremism and terrorism in the era of the 'war on terror'. Muslim radicalism in this framework is understood to pose a great threat to national security and therefore gives authorities the legitimacy to deal punitively with perpetrators. Can it then be said with certainty that Muslim radicalism necessarily leads to or results in acts of violence and terrorism?

The ideology and inspirations of Muslim militants or Islamists do not on their own radicalise individual Muslims. However, a complex set of pathways and series of catalysts do operate that lead to radicalisation, and sometimes this radicalisation paves the way for acts of violence and terrorism. Tahir Abbas notes that 'it is also palpably clear that questions in relation to what drives radicalisation and how to engage with radicalised young people remain difficult to answer'.[17]

It is almost common knowledge that Muslim radicalism has a range of explanations, and that in political discourse and policy formulation there is a variety of responses to it. This confusion regarding Muslim radicalism exhibits the problematic nature of the term. Muslim radicalism is taken to refer to a phenomenon in which the process of socialisation enables individuals to engage in acts of terrorism. This idea forms the core of the explanation of terrorist activities through ideology. However, it is worth noting that rendering socialisation in this manner is misleading because it promotes the assumption that the process of socialisation results in violent behaviour or involvement in acts of terrorism when in fact this does not always happen or necessarily have to be the case. The fact of the matter is that there are individuals who may adopt beliefs and show support that is construed as 'radical' but they may not become 'violent' or engage in violence or seek violent outcomes. In his work on Islamic radicalisation in Nigeria, Abiodun Alao notes that:

> There seem to be categories in radicalisation ... those who are genuinely committed to the religion and feel concerned about whatever they see as a desecration of the religion; those who may be described as ad hoc radicals who only follow instructions to go on the rampage once there is an instruction to that effect from 'spiritual' leaders and revert ... to their 'ordinary' ways of life afterwards; and those who may be described as 'opportunistic radicals', who only seize the opportunity of the moment to loot and vandalise, after which they wait anxiously for another opportunity ... in the process of militant activities, it is difficult to identify who belongs to what among these individuals.[18]

Thus, to distinguish between nonviolent radicals and those actually involved in acts of political agitation and violence is not a simple task, and this must be clearly recognised. Importantly, those within the camp of Muslim radicalism who opt to engage in acts of violence and terrorism are minute in number but this is not particularly acknowledged in Western political discourse or public policy. Instead, Muslim radicalism is essentialised, communitarianised and homogeneously demonised, and its threat is expediently inflated.

Australian Muslims as the 'Other'

In the age of the 'war on terror', homogeneous notions of Muslims in the West[19] see all Muslims as a single family of people and label them as the Other and potential risks to society who then end up being viewed as terrorists. Due to the actions of a few, the entire Muslim population is blamed. The homogenised concept of 'the Muslim' is situated in the worldwide resurgence of Islam and exhibits the return of the suppressed. Muslims are not the first to be constructed as the terrorist Other: this kind of functional Othering[20] has a long history and has affected groups in the past such as the Irish Republican Army.[21] Notions of 'Otherness' play a critical role in the construction of the narrative of 'us' and 'them' and are central to ways in which 'danger', 'threat' and 'risk' are conceptualised.[22] The Other is unlike and the opposite of the Self, of Us, of the Same, and of the collective Self. The Other is the state of being dissimilar and alien to the social identity of a person and to the identity of the Self, and therefore the Other is peculiar.

Othering categorises and refers to characteristics of the Other (who and what is the Other?) that are different and detached from the representational order of things, from the genuine (the authentic and fixed), from social rules and social identity, and from the Self. Cultural geographer Mike Crang says that Othering is 'a process ... through which identities are set up in an unequal relationship'.[23] The word 'Othering' depicts the reductive action of identifying an individual as someone who is part of a subordinate social category described as the Other, as explained by Lajos Brons:

> Othering is the simultaneous construction of the self or in-group and the other or out-group in mutual and unequal opposition through identification of some desirable characteristic that the self/in-group has and the other/out-group lacks and/or some undesirable characteristic that the other/out-group has and the self/in-group lacks. Othering thus sets up a superior self/in-group in contrast to an inferior other/out-group, but this superiority/ inferiority is nearly always left implicit.[24]

The operational function of Othering is to exclude people who do not fit in or adhere to the norms of the social group, which is a reflection of the Self. The Other is conceptualised as fundamentally dissimilar to the Self and therefore a source of apprehension, concern and danger who threatens to obscure boundaries and surpass the Self. The Other becomes 'risky' for the society and deserves to be blamed for any dangerous conduct or activity.

In Australia and other Western countries, the community favours increased powers of the state to combat Muslim terrorism, notwithstanding that 'Australia has not experienced Islamic terrorism on its soil'[25] and has an anti-terror discourse that takes into consideration the threat posed by the stranger—that is, the 'homegrown terrorist' who breaches the norms and security of the world of 'the Self' and who is ironically both 'of us' and 'not of us'. Contemporary fear of breaching the norms and security of the world of 'the Self' by the dangerous 'risky Other' who lives 'among us and with us' helps to strengthen religious and racial intolerance promoted in the popular media by the dominant social group. Fear of the Other produces anxiety in people and they start to coalesce. When they do amalgamate, 'anti-Other' movements emerge that often exhibit explicitly xenophobic tendencies.

The terrorist attacks in New York on 11 September 2001, which were undertaken by Muslims, had global consequences and gave impetus to the proliferation of anti-terror laws in many Western countries, including Australia. According to George Williams, Professor of Law at the University of New South Wales, since 9/11 Australia has passed sixty-one new anti-terror statutes.[26] He notes that between 2001 and 2007 under the Howard Government, forty-eight anti-terror statutes were enacted.[27] It was an extraordinary period of lawmaking that no other country in the world witnessed, even those countries facing a greater level of terrorism threat. Kent Roach describes this as Australia suffering from 'hyper-legislation … caught up in the 9/11 effect'.[28]

In Australia, there is no doubt that anti-terror laws were enacted to be aggressively enforced in order to keep Muslims under constant surveillance and to manage them as strictly as possible. Since the new laws came into being, only Muslims have been charged and prosecuted under them: 'Thirty-eight men, all but one of them Muslim, have been charged with terrorism offences in Australia to date.'[29] This in itself is telling and lends support to the claim that the laws indiscriminately target Australian Muslims. All Muslims are perceived to collectively constitute the source of the threat of terrorism. They are the target of anti-terror laws because they are seen as 'strangers'—Others who don't respect or value the Australian way of life and are bent on its destruction. Muslims are the terrorist Other. The popular support for the state to develop new anti-terror laws through which to secure powers to 'fight terrorism' is a reflection of a strong anti-terror discourse that draws on the threat of the Other breaching the norms and security of the world of 'the Self', which is the whole of Australia.

Countering violent extremism

In light of the perceived rise of Muslim radicalism that seeks to make the Islamic lifestyle pervasive throughout the modern world and establish global Islamic dominance, and the perceived fear of homegrown and imported terrorism in Australia as well as the parallel rise of politically motivated violent extremism in other parts of the Western world, Australia has passed numerous pieces of legislation and introduced policies[30] and developed a range of national and state programs to counter violent extremism.[31] Generally speaking, CVE is a collective effort and a partnership between state and local communities—mainly Muslim communities—and non-government organisations to develop strategies to combat the violent extremist narrative promulgated by extremists or radicals that can provoke terrorist acts. The strategies and programs often include identifying extremist or radicalised and at-risk individuals and providing them with appropriate services to undo the root causes of their extremism or radicalisation; empowering young people and religious, cultural and education leaders; and promoting social inclusion and cohesion.

The Australian Government and CVE

CVE in Australia is a shared government (federal, state and local) response to the threat of terrorism, 'which is the use of violence to create fear (i.e. terror; psychic fear), for political, religious or ideological reasons',[32] encompassing 'intervention programs'. The objective of the CVE program is to counter the threat posed by homegrown terrorism and to prevent citizens of Australia from travelling overseas to take part in state-vetoed religious or ideological conflicts. In the program, the expectation is that all levels of Australian government and communities, particularly those from Islamic backgrounds, will work together to build resistance to politically, religiously or racially motivated violent extremism. It is a government and community partnership comprising four complementary streams of activity:
1. building strength in diversity and social participation
2. targeted work with vulnerable communities and institutions
3. addressing terrorist propaganda online
4. diversion and deradicalisation.[33]

Australian CVE activities are organised and managed by the Attorney-General's Department, which in 2010 developed the Countering Violent

Extremism Taskforce/Unit.[34] The program, also launched in 2010 by the federal government, operated under an umbrella strategy known as Australia's Counter-Terrorism Machinery. It brought various agencies together to combat the threat of terrorism in Australia, and its overarching objective was to keep Australians safe and protected from terrorist attacks. Under this overarching objective, the Counter-Terrorism Machinery aimed to:
1. disrupt any activities or planning by individuals to launch an attack
2. undermine terrorist activities and support—which involves detecting and destroying when possible terrorist activity by:
   a. obstructing the flow of support, such as finances, commodities and people, to or from terrorists and their networks
   b. hampering the expansion of terrorist capability by targeting their tactical and operational security training in every practical way possible
   c. debasing ideological support for terrorist activities
3. promote community cohesion by building resilience to extremism and radicalisation.[35]

These activities can be seen in summary form in Figure 4.

Figure 4: The spectrum of Australian federal government CVE efforts

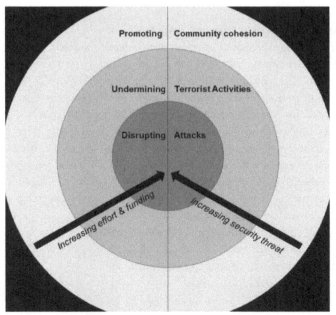

Department of the Prime Minister and Cabinet, *Review of Australia's Counter-Terrorism Machinery*, Commonwealth of Australia, Canberra, 2015, p. 2.

Since 11 September 2001, according to a review undertaken by the Department of the Prime Minister and Cabinet in January 2015, the Counter-Terrorism Machinery has been successful in achieving goals in all three categories.[36] In the 'disrupting' terrorist attacks category, it was able to achieve its aim by successfully prosecuting thirty-five cases and securing twenty-six convictions for terrorism-related offences.[37] In the 'undermining' terrorist support and activity category, it achieved success by seeing an exponential increase in the cancellation of passports and thereby curtailing the flow of Australians travelling overseas to fight with terrorist groups in Syria and Iraq and significantly weakening terrorism support. In this category it was also able to 'obstruct the flow of terrorist support' by successfully disrupting terrorist financing and recruitment through cooperation with other countries; this involved denying terrorists access to goods and materials and, since the start of the civil war in Syria, the Australian Transaction Reports and Analysis Centre (AUSTRAC) successfully preventing certain terrorist groups from accessing funds, including deregistering four international organisations suspected of transferring money to terrorist groups. In the same category, the Counter-Terrorism Machinery succeeded in 'hampering the expansion of terrorist capability' by identifying changes in the threat environment and confirming changes in terrorist methodological approaches. By mid-2012, the Australian Security and Intelligence Organisation (ASIO) was able to report that inter-communal violence in Australia resulting from the Syrian conflict was imminent, that it had identified Australians who had left for Syria to participate in the conflict there, and that it had warned of the development of terrorist capability associated with this travel. Importantly, success was noted in 'debasing ideological support for terrorist activities', evident in intelligence agencies engaging with individuals at different levels within communities to reduce support for violent extremist ideology. There was also serious focus on activities to combat violent extremism through education and training, skills-building, leadership and mentoring, and the development of counternarratives to combat violent extremist ideologies, coupled with various online media projects. In addition, the Commonwealth in cooperation with state and territory governments established a funding regime for a range of short-term initiatives to:

- support the rehabilitation of people imprisoned for terrorism-related offences
- prevent the radicalisation of other prisoners
- conduct joint research with academics to build Australia's understanding of violent extremism and the most effective ways of countering it.[38]

In the 'promoting community cohesion' category, agencies actively engaged and raised community awareness of:

- the legal consequences of travelling to fight in overseas conflicts
- the personal impact for those participating or supporting participation, and the impact on their families
- Australia's foreign policy position
- how the Australian Government is providing development assistance and humanitarian aid to those affected by the conflicts
- alternative options for communities to support those affected.[39]

Impact of CVE on Australian Muslims

The Commonwealth's CVE strategy under its Counter-Terrorism Machinery is designed to curtail the risk of homegrown terrorism by enhancing Australia's resilience to extremism and radicalisation and working with individuals, communities and non-government organisations to combat violent extremist influences and beliefs. This undertaking has been developed to manage the 'risk' and 'threat' posed by terrorism. In the CVE narrative, Australian society is presented as being at risk—that is, vulnerable to terrorist attacks by homegrown terrorists, who are mainly Muslims—and CVE is presented as a means to combat that risk.

According to the 2015 review of Australia's Counter-Terrorism Machinery:

> There has not been a large-scale terrorist attack in Australia this century. The attack by Numan Haider on two police officers in September 2014, and the Martin Place siege in December 2014 were the only successful terrorist attacks or incidents on Australian soil.[40]

Yet in the past two decades the Commonwealth has invested over half a billion dollars in national security activities that include addressing CT priorities. The justification for such a large sum is in the claim that Australia is at risk of being attacked by homegrown as well as foreign terrorists. According to the federal government, this risk needs to be managed and the CVE strategy is the appropriate risk management tool to ensure the protection of Australian citizens. However, if Australia is at such grave risk, why have there been only thirty-five successful prosecution cases and twenty-six convictions connected to terrorism-related offences in recent years?[41] And if the CVE strategy doesn't target Muslims, then why is it that:[42]

- in 2005, nine men in Sydney were arrested and charged with terrorism offences, all nine were convicted, and all nine were Muslims?
- in 2006, Australian national Faheem Lodhi, a Muslim, was convicted of planning terrorist attacks in Australia during 2003? Lodhi was working with Muslim French national Willie Brigitte, who had been sent to Australia by a senior member of Lashkar-e-Tayyiba (a Pakistan-based terrorist organisation). Brigitte was subsequently convicted on terrorism charges in France.
- in September 2008, a Muslim Sydney man was convicted of collecting or making documents likely to facilitate terrorist acts?
- in 2006, thirteen men in Melbourne, all Muslims, were arrested and charged with terrorism offences, and nine of them were convicted of being members of a terrorist organisation?

In addition to this, there are various problems associated with effective implementation of the CVE program. To understand the factors, issues and actual process of radicalisation, a theoretical model is necessary. However, as mentioned above, the problem with a theoretical model is that there is no single theory of radicalisation that can provide a universal understanding of the causes of radicalisation, because radicalism is a constantly changing, dynamic and heterogeneous phenomenon.

To counter radicalisation in Muslim communities the actual process of radicalisation and its causes need to be understood. We need to find out what triggers young Muslims to radicalise to the extent that they are prepared to engage in extreme physical violence and sometimes even sacrifice their own lives. Why do they actually do it? To understand why, we need to seriously and systematically look at the causal factors, both in isolation and in conjunction with one another. The need to identify and examine the 'direct' and 'indirect' factors and 'slow' and 'fast' factors is critical. It must be noted that these factors don't exist in a vacuum but emanate from the complex and often fast-changing sociocultural, economic and political environment in which potential radical Muslims live. The factors are sociological in nature, and identifying and critically examining them is important in any attempt to address the problem of radicalisation. It is also important to recognise that some of the factors are local in nature and some are global.

There is further difficulty in identifying an 'at risk' individual because there is no consensus as to what radicalism denotes; and because 'radicalisation' can occur very swiftly and monitoring such a process is not easy. At the Muslim community level, there are added challenges because if the government identifies a community as being 'at risk'—for instance, the Somali community—it can isolate and 'securitise' that community. Any attempt to do so will likely fail because the very community the authorities are trying to support and work with is the community being targeted for deradicalisation. The whole planning process can be derailed and efforts wasted if members of the targeted community realise they have been targeted and feel further marginalised by the CVE program. Also, identifying a particularly Muslim community implies that that community is producing extremist and radical individuals; this will have the opposite effect of the aims of the CVE program. Moreover, while the identification of a particular Muslim community may lead to it being offered funding to address extremism and radicalism, this might ignore deep-seated problems such as youth unemployment and alienation, poverty, and victimisation.

The following statement made by dozens of members of the Australian Muslim community in 2014 summarises the sentiments of many Muslims and community leaders about the federal government's CVE program:

> The Muslim community is being asked to sign off on laws and policies that have already been decided. Prime Minister Tony Abbott is merely seeking approval under the cover of consultation. He seeks that the Muslim community be on board because the policy entails the community policing itself. We refuse to provide such a rubber stamp on what is an unjust and hypocritical policy. We also reject government attempts to divide the Muslim community into 'radicals' and 'moderates' and to use the community for its agenda.
>
> It is evident that the 'war on terror' has been a failure. After thirteen long years, everyone can see that the world is not a safer place. Rather, violence and instability are noticeably more prevalent. The approach of continuously ramping up laws, lowering legal standards, spending more on defence and intelligence agencies is not working. Over $30 billion has been spent in Australia on this war yet the threat is 'as high as it has ever been' according to the Prime Minister.[43]

Muslim radicalisation seems to be an objection against perceived wrongdoing against fellow Muslims either locally or overseas. So-called radical Muslims identify the sources of their grievances and intense outrage as American and Israeli actions in the Middle East, the foreign policies of many Western nations, and the terrible conditions in which Muslims are understood to be living in Middle Eastern countries such as Palestine and Syria—conditions that are attributed to the actions of the West. Radicalised Muslims, then, in this sense don't have to be necessarily victims themselves but sympathisers who feel 'bad' for their fellow faithfuls.

Causes such as political discontent, a culture of alienation and humiliation, and the urge for revenge against acts of repression motivate radicalisation or radical Muslims to resort to socially unorthodox political tactics and actions. The sociocultural 'ordinariness' of radical Muslims in Australia and other parts of the Western world, combined with the assertion that their anger and frustration often seem to be a response to real or perceived situations in which they have no direct involvement and experience, begs critical questions about the complexity of the causal factors that contribute to the radicalisation process.

It is clear that the various sociocultural, economic and political processes that determine who will and who will not take a turn towards radicalisation are absolutely complex, and that the homegrown radicalisation phenomenon can only be understood with deep insights into the intricate interaction between contextual processes on the one hand and broader societal processes on the other.

There is no denying that there are some radical Muslims in Australia and that CVE programs and strategies are needed to address the problem and work out solutions. However, those CVE programs with a focus on community engagement and intervention have raised important concerns, particularly in the Muslim community. The overall CVE policy has disproportionately focused on Australian Muslim communities. In an environment where Muslims are viewed with suspicion and as bearing primary responsibility as both perpetrators and gatekeepers of terroristic ideologies, Muslims in Australia have been forced to make legitimate claims to their innocence and loyalty to this country. In order to do this, they are required to reaffirm their commitment to Australian values not just by speaking out against terrorism but also by participating in programs, such as CVE programs, that are based on false assumptions about the nature of Muslim citizenship in Australia and the premise that Muslim Australians are, both individually and collectively, opposed to such values. The CVE policies have been seen to potentially divide Muslim communities because they embrace questionable notions of what it means to be 'moderate' or 'radical', and denote moderate as 'good' and radical as 'bad'.

The CVE programs are problematic because they indicate that the government has 'securitised' the Muslim community and because they have the potential to force an extra layer of unwanted scrutiny upon a community that is predominantly made up of law-abiding citizens. The strategies either directly or indirectly affect the everyday lives of all Muslims, and eventually lead to them feeling not safe and secure but socially marginalised, with no sense of belongingness and being seen as the radicalised and unwanted 'Other'.

Chapter 11

Securitised Muslims and Islam in Australia

In the wake of the events of 11 September 2001 in America and the subsequent bombings in Bali (2002 and 2005), Madrid (2004) and London (2005)[1] and other incidents, many policymakers, politicians, journalists, security experts, academics and sections of the community have come to consider Islam and Muslims as a menacing phenomenon that threatens Australian security and has a real possibility of undermining political stability, social harmony, and the civil and state wellbeing of the Australian nation-state. Islam and Muslims have been characterised as a global phenomenon pervading and causing worldwide disturbances through violent destabilisation of almost all nation-states on the planet. Recent terror-related activities and the successful prosecution of numerous terrorists in various countries, including Australia, are testimonies to such a claim. Thus, fearing the potential growth of 'homegrown' extremism, the state has sought to counter narrow-minded Islamic ideology and Muslim radicalism by enacting a raft of austere anti-terror laws and material implementation of remarkable CT and CVE strategies, as discussed in Chapter 10. In pursuit of this, Islam and Muslims in Australia have been rendered the extremist radicalised enemy 'Other' and consequently objects of securitisation as a preventive measure to secure the 'home'.

This chapter argues that securitisation as a process involving the construction of social issues around security concerns has turned Muslims into a transnational category that denotes the characterisation of a risky and dangerous 'Other'. Australia is discursively constructed as an Anglo-Celtic community, a cultural and political entity with secular 'spaces' that need to be maintained and put under surveillance so intruders—that is, Muslims—don't occupy them in a manner considered to be 'un-Australian' or 'threatening'. In this endeavour, Australia emerges as a monocultural society that has the legitimacy to set up rules and rituals for occupying its internal spaces.

The project of securitisation

Some very specific local issues and events have intensified the debate about the place of Islam and Muslims in modern Australian society and how to manage the Muslim-minority population. They include the high proportion of Muslims among asylum seekers and the allegations of 'illegality' and 'queue jumping' that have been levelled against them;[2] the continuous increase in drug use and trafficking and violent crime among Lebanese Muslim criminal gangs; the gang rapes of Anglo-Celtic Australian women and teenage girls by a group of Lebanese-Australian youths in Sydney in 2000, led by Bilal Skaf; the Tampa crisis in 2001; the Cronulla riots in 2005; and the Haneef case in 2007. Coupled with the bombings on London transport in July 2005 that followed the Bali bombings of 2002 and the New York and Washington attacks of 2001, and other incidents, these local events have aided in questioning Muslim national identity and citizenship rights and in amplifying suspicions about Muslims in Australia, who have been made the target of intensified material implementation of remarkable CT and CVE strategies. Entities such as the Attorney-General's Department, the Australian Federal Police, ASIO and Australian Border Force have been given increased preventive powers by the federal government to bolster surveillance and manage latent threats brought into the open by specific local issues and international events connected to Muslims.[3]

Key to these CT and CVE strategies has been strict new anti-terror laws, as discussed in Chapter 10, which were purportedly designed and targeted at iconoclastic threats posed by terrorists but in fact are cryptogrammic instruments for the management of the so-called risky, dangerous Muslim enemy 'Other'. Michael Humphrey writes that:

> *Muslims* [emphasis added] have become a shared 'security' concern for Western governments and been made the object of suspicion and the focus of state intervention and political management. Their citizenship has become increasingly conditional on their 'performance' as citizens measured by active efforts to integrate on the one hand and their rejection of radical Islam on the other.[4]

Muslim immigrants and their descendants in the West have come to be problematised, inhabiting the site of the desperate, the racialised group of 'folk devils',[5] 'extremists' and 'fanatics',[6] the 'suspect other'[7] and 'Risky Others'.[8] They have been rendered the 'enemy within' and as a homogenous bunch of 'Arab terrorists' who are 'backward, unshaven, fanatic, robe-covered, oil-rich, lecherous, desert dwellers',[9] who make unreasonable religious, cultural and citizenship demands and refuse to integrate into mainstream society. Unlike the pre-9/11 caricature of Muslim immigrants as merely 'culturally incompatible', they are now considered as 'politically unfaithful' and even outright dangerous. The wider community in Australia and elsewhere in the West has been made to feel increasing levels of alarm and fear. The conceptualisation of Muslims as 'Risky Others' involves xenophobia or racial hatred: the mainstream society ostensibly under threat is ethically and religiously constructed, with the racialised Other as the corresponding dangerous enemy. In the West, Muslims are equated with terrorism, religious and cultural difference, extremism and 'high risk', resulting in them being pushed to the social margins and the limits of citizenship. Constant demands are placed on them to prove their political loyalty, demonstrate integration into mainstream society, and justify the claims over their citizenship through 'attitude tests', language competency and knowledge of national civic values.[10] With some exceptions, where some Muslims may not feel excluded, the general outcome of this is the demonisation of Islam and Muslims, which weakens Australian Muslims' sense of belonging and citizenship.

Against the backdrop of these prejudiced perceptions and descriptions of Muslims, political and public calls for more stringent management of Muslims are being engineered. Thus, diaspora Muslim communities and Islam have been made objects of 'securitisation' as a preventive measure to secure the 'home' through policies that seek to closely scrutinise and police Muslims and place demands on them for swift social and cultural integration. In the discourse of securitisation, ethnic and religious identity claims of Muslims and the difficulties associated with integrating into mainstream society as outcomes of existing structural problems of poverty, unemployment, discrimination, disenfranchisement, inequality, upward social mobility, xenophobia and racism are masked by focusing on the reasons for these difficulties. Ayhan Kaya states that:

> modern states tend to employ the discourse of securitization as a political technique that can integrate a society politically by staging a credible existential threat in the form of an internal, or even an external enemy that is fabricated by security agencies (like the police and the army) through categorising migration together with drug trafficking, human trafficking, criminality and terrorism.[11]

The principal logic of the discourse of securitisation appears to have shifted from protecting the state to protecting society—or, in the language of James Ferguson and Akhil Gupta, from 'verticality' to 'encompassment', where verticality refers to the state as an institution above society, and encompassment denotes the state conceptually merged with the nation encompassing its locality, covering family, the local community and the system of nation-states.[12] Thus, the protection of society against danger and any form of attack, whether from within or without, has become the heart of the discourse of securitisation in such a manner that the term 'security' has been propelled into all provinces of life. In the discourse of securitisation, there is a framing of the 'enemy other' where the enemy other is constituted as not only being violent, uncivilised and anti-modernity but posing a global and interconnected threat that covers the entire planet. These shifts are employed to justify the new defensive responses and attacks of preventive military action on the enemy overseas and the securitisation of state borders.

In the end, securitisation directly or indirectly impacts on many Australian Muslims and has far-reaching consequences, manifesting in Islamophobia and in Muslims' political alienation and socioeconomic marginalisation, with a cumulative effect of social exclusion. In terms of political alienation, for instance, a study commissioned by the Department of Immigration and Citizenship exploring attitudes of young Muslims in Sydney and Melbourne found them to have a profound sense of alienation from the Australian political system and the media.[13] This sense of alienation was reinforced particularly through the securitisation undertakings by the Howard Government.[14] Furthermore, 'Legal citizenship status grants individuals full civic, social and political rights and responsibilities, including the right and duty to vote and the entitlement to run for public office. Muslims remain, however, severely under-represented in political decision-making processes.'[15]

Another direct or indirect consequence of securitisation for many Muslims is socioeconomic marginalisation. Australian census data reveal a disturbing discrepancy between Muslims and non-Muslims regarding living standards and access to wealth. Using the census data, Riaz Hassan establishes that in 2006 Muslim households were grouped in the low-income band, with 2 per cent recording no income. This was double that of non-Muslim Australians.[16] Regarding home ownership, which is a measurement of financial security, only 14 per cent of Muslims owned their home compared to 32 per cent of non-Muslim Australians.[17]

The figures for employment rates for Muslims are worrying too, and reinforce what is discussed above. According to 2006 and 2011 data, Australia's unemployment rates were marginally over 5 per cent in each census but Muslim unemployment rates were two-and-a-half times more—13.4 per cent and 12.6 per cent, respectively.[18] From these figures it can be deduced that financial insecurity and poverty are major concerns for Muslims.

Securitisation of Muslims has also resulted in increased Islamophobia in Australia. For all Muslims, but particularly for young Australian Muslims, Islamophobia exposes them to socioeconomic marginalisation and consequently problematises their integration in Australian multiculturalism. For example, Hassan found that Muslim men were more likely than non-Muslim men to possess university qualifications (21 per cent and 15 per cent respectively), but their rates of unemployment were two to four times higher depending on age.[19] As a result, Muslims had considerably lower labour force participation rates than other Australians. Since more Muslim men possess university qualifications than non-Muslim men, Muslim men's unemployment rate should be lower because qualification leads to employment. This would seem to indicate that due to the prevalence of Islamophobia, employers don't want to give jobs to Muslim men even if those men have university qualifications.

While the experience of Islamophobia generates feelings of harm and disrespect, there are more practical consequences for Australian Muslims, particularly young locally born Muslims who expect their citizenship rights to be honoured. Patterns of discomfort and fear, distrust and exclusion among Australian Muslims emphasise in a general sense that their whole way of life is not only devalued but not to be accommodated. The pervasive sense of Islamophobia creates for Australian Muslims generally, and young Muslim Australians in particular, discomfort and fear[20] that affects their sense of belonging both to the nation[21] and to their neighbourhoods and spaces of everyday life.[22]

Securitisation is a regulatory tool or strategy premised on the rationale that the power vested in some of the core institutions of government, such as the national security intelligence organisation and police, can either restrict a person or allow them access to a 'space'—a place to be in. In other words, securitisation regulates spatial exclusion and inclusion by concentrating on the individual person's identity and socio-religious background to establish the person's spatial appropriateness. Spatially anchored national sovereignty and territoriality is not a new phenomenon: what is new in present securitisation is the national and transnational dimensions of state-based exercise of power, control and governance over the populace[23] and the effect transnational securitisation has on citizenship where citizenship itself is contingent upon the citizen's performability and loyalty. Securitisation is both a state-regulated policy and a manifestation of what James Ferguson and Akhil Gupta call transnational governmentality,[24] borrowing governmentality from Michel Foucault[25] to develop their concept.

Securitisation is 'a political technique of framing policy questions in logics of survival with a capacity to mobilise politics of fear in which social relations are structured on the basis of distrust'.[26] Its impact on migrant Muslims is the transportation of them as a social category within a distinct ethnic and racial structure and national mosaic to a wider transnational context of the West. Securitisation renders migrant Muslims as a transnational social category for the purposes of scrutiny, surveillance and policing, resulting in them being conceptually separated from their particular social, political and national settings. At the same time, it produces a discourse in which diverse Muslim communities are collectively considered as dangerous and a social and political threat.[27] As with the past conceptualisation of migrant Muslims as a category for global monitoring and surveillance in the West, the contemporary conceptualisation turns all Muslims, including locally born Muslims, into a transnational category denoting the risky and dangerous Other.[28] Securitisation means presenting Muslims as a minority group and as existentially threatening, and thereby forms the basis for extraordinary political measures. It is a strategy of social protection characterising political community at the national level, and a project of transnational governmentality.

The project of securitisation of Islam and Muslims in Western societies seeks to remould Islam as a moderate religion in a serious attempt to weaken or even eliminate the appeal of radical Islam. Thus, Islam has become a focus of governmentality, a project of governance whereby the state has moved into civil society in an attempt to regulate Muslims by restructuring and legitimating local religious institutions and generating a discussion on moderate Islam.[29] Securitisation denotes political control and regulation of Islam and Muslims because they are seen to represent a global threat through international migration and the formation of Muslim diasporas. Securitisation cancels out of the democratic process the voices of securitised Muslim minority communities and represents the dual strategies of exclusion and inclusion.

As in other Western nation-states, Muslims in Australia are conceptualised by their host state as a transnational category, which acts as a code for differentiating the 'good' and 'civilised' from the 'bad' and 'barbaric'. This means that in the age of the global 'war on terror', they are no longer considered as a minority migrant community through cultural essentialisation of Islam and the political construction of radical Islam as a localised phenomenon embedded in the local minority Muslim communities and non-threatening to the state, but as a universal enemy Other. Securitisation of Muslims and Islam is a manifestation of transnational governmentality involving monitoring, regulating and controlling a social category not only within state borders but beyond. Muslims have been progressively conceptualised as a transnational homogenised entity through the fusion of public policy and law.

All Muslim immigrants and their descendants in Australia are subjected to restructuring in the 'social exclusion' discourse in an attempt to make Australia secure. This is determined through politico-cultural categorisation of 'enemy Muslims' (radicals and terrorists) and 'extremist Islam' (radical Islam). Social exclusion, according to Dragana Avramov, is:

> a condition of deprivation, that is manifested through the generalized disadvantages facing individuals of social groups due to accumulated social handicaps ... Exclusion is as a rule associated with social stigmatization, blame and isolation, which translate[s] to low self-esteem, a feeling of not belonging and not having been given a chance to be included in society.[30]

Social exclusion, then, denotes a policy designed to keep Australia protected, and a policy directed at social and cultural removal. Social exclusion relating to Muslims addresses social incorporation and cultural harmonisation. It seeks to introduce cultural change through the de-domestication and de-nationalisation of radical Islam and the domestication and nationalisation of 'moderate Islam' by aligning it with Australian values and the Australian 'way of life'. This approach to domestication in the context of Australian multiculturalism recognises Muslims as a distinct ethnocultural category premised on the idea that 'religion is embedded in a culture, so if one is a Muslim one belongs to a different culture',[31] and implies that if Australian Muslims are not an embodiment of moderate Islam than they must be a part of 'bad' and 'extremist Islam' and therefore a radicalised enemy Other subject to securitisation.

The construction of Australian Muslims as a security threat is an outcome of the state's attempt to manage 'globalised Islam' and the Muslim diaspora in the age of the 'war on terror'. Australian securitisation policy is a discursive exercise of power expressed by categorising Muslims, differentiating between them and the rest of the population, and effectively creating regimes of truth that organise political practices in a particular way. In doing so, Muslims are rendered a distinct social category and their experiences of social exclusion are enhanced.

The global rise of Muslim terrorism has produced a state response in Australia and in many other parts of the West to counter the supposedly invisible threat allegedly embodied in Muslim radicalism and to promise national security through securitisation. Securitisation of Islam and Muslims is a strategy to minimise risk nationally and internationally. However, the way public safety wars are being fought against Islam and Muslims has neither tamed the invisible enemy nor removed the risk it poses: it has only aggravated the risk, proving the state's inability to desecuritise societal security.

Conclusion

Islam is a complete way of life—a code of life. Those who believe in this code of life and pursue it are called Muslims. However, there are various interpretations and understandings of the code, rendering Islam a heterogeneous religious tradition. Muslims variously apply the code in Muslim-majority countries and in countries where they are a minority group, such as Australia.

Islam, which was originally established by the Prophet Mohammed in 610 CE in the Arabian Peninsula, quickly spread to Iberia in the west and the Indus River in the east, and within a century after the death of the Prophet in 632 CE, Muslims had brought a large part of the world—from Spain across Central Asia to India—under a new Arab Muslim empire. The period of Islamic conquests and empire-building marks the initial phase of the expansion of the religion of Islam. The great variety of people from different racial and cultural backgrounds who embraced Islam not only in the early periods of Islamic expansion but even as recently as the last century have produced important internal distinctions.

Deep political and subsequently theological differences arose within the Muslim community after the death of the Prophet Mohammed, paving the way for the emergence of sectarian groups such as Sunnis and Shi'ites, subsects such as Kharijites and Murjites, and theological groups such as Mu'tazilites and Asharites. All these and many other sociocultural and political factors have made Islam an extremely heterogeneous religion. However, media depictions and popular discourse in the past several decades have distorted our image of Islamic history and culture, in Australia and many other parts of the world. Islam is stereotypically portrayed as a homogeneous, backward, hyper-patriarchal and fanatical religion, and Muslims are depicted as an uncivilised, intolerant, uncooperative and violent group of people. In fact, Islam encompasses a great diversity of theological, jurisprudential and puritanical practices, and Muslims embody great variations within and between cultural traditions.

Thus, Islam and Muslims in Australia—with a history that goes back to the fourteenth century and predates white British contact and settlement—are a heterogeneous phenomenon. Islam is internally a diverse religious tradition and Muslims in Australia are multiple communities made up of people from 183 different ethno-national backgrounds. Islam and Muslims in Australia are neither a new sociocultural reality nor a monolithic phenomenon. Yet in the pages of Australian history the early presence of Islam in Australia doesn't appear, and in political and popular discourse Islam continues to be depicted as a monolith. In addition, the adherents of Islam are considered as a single and unitary community when in reality they are vastly diverse.

The negation of misrepresentation and misunderstanding of Islam and Muslims in Australia is the subject of this book. I have examined the growing presence of Islam and Muslims in Australia and how the country is transforming, and being transformed by, social, cultural and religious spaces. Islam and Muslims are an important part of Australia's project of nation-building and the promotion of cultural diversity, and this book provides critical elucidations of the various processes involved and the roles played by different institutions in making this happen. I have attempted to investigate the complex reality of Islam and Muslims in Australia from a sociological perspective. Employing critical analysis and macrosociology, I have offered insights into their growth and development and illuminated how sociocultural, economic and political processes maintain and manage the ways in which Australian Muslims build their religious lives and identities and engage in the wider world while facing the inevitable effects of modernity. The basic contention of my argument is that Islam in Australia is more than just a religion, a cultural system or a social structure: it is existentially a complex composite of diverse institutional processes and functions, social routines and norms, and sacred rituals and practices responsible for shaping the lives of Muslims.

Despite such a long presence and being now the second-largest religion in Australia, Islam has always been seen as a foreign faith in contradistinction to the Judeo-Christian tradition. It is only in the last several decades that Islam, once invisible and marginal, has surfaced in Australia's national imagery. Awareness and appreciation of this changing reality are evolving slowly, and previous depictions and understandings of Islam and Muslims as 'foreign' are no longer sustainable. The challenges faced by Muslims over the years to gain recognition have been extraordinarily difficult. The long-held view of Islam as 'Other' must be overturned: it needs to be properly recognised and accepted as part of the fabric of Australian plural society, and Muslims must be accepted as fellow citizens. Australian Muslims need to be given equal importance and a rightful place in multicultural Australia.

Similar to the experiences of other immigrant religious and ethnic minority communities, Muslims have encountered difficulties in defining and determining their place in Australian society. They have been challenged with issues relating to identity, intermarriage, gender relations, worship and education, as well as civil engagements and citizenship rights. Some Muslims struggle to reconcile the life in their birth country with the experiences in their new adopted homeland. Some have opted to integrate into Australian society while others struggle and continue to 'live in the past' in a 'home away from home'—leading the life of the 'home country' in a little Lebanon or little Turkey, for instance.

The permanency of Islam and Muslims in Australia began with mass migration of Muslims from the late 1960s to the 1990s, as discussed in Part 1. Prior to the late 1960s, Muslim migration was on a small scale, governed by the White Australia policy. Under that policy, immigration was controlled by an official assimilation strategy that was basically driven by a labour need for the purposes of economic development and defence, and the country largely welcomed migrants from the Caucasian races, with British people being the most preferred group. Assimilationist thinking was premised on the superiority of Anglo-Australian institutions and values, which were to be kept unchanged.

In 1973, the Whitlam Labor government officially abandoned the last remnants of the racist White Australia policy and replaced it with multiculturalism. Multiculturalism officially made Australia a plural society in which ethnic diversity was celebrated and promoted within the framework of shared Australian core values—namely, the rule of law; principles of tolerance, harmony, cohesion and free speech; and the values of a 'fair go' for all. Its purpose was to promote cultural diversity and share different cultural traditions and values rather than excluding certain cultural groups and forcing them into isolated enclaves. Multiculturalism sought to elucidate that language, skin colour, mode of dressing and religious belief could no longer be a basis for exclusion of cultural groups, and that the historical exclusionary policies were to be abandoned.

With the official declaration of Australia as a multicultural society, the gates of migration were opened wide with preference given to skilled migrants. This led to a gradual influx of Muslims, first from Turkey and then Lebanon and subsequently from various other parts of the world. Muslims came from diverse social, cultural and national backgrounds, making them the most diverse religious group in Australia. Upon arrival they settled in different suburbs in the capital cities, especially Sydney and Melbourne. In Sydney, Lebanese settled in Lakemba and Pakistanis in Rooty Hill; in Melbourne, Turkish moved to Broadmeadows, Lebanese to Coburg, Brunswick and Epping, and Bosnians to Noble Park and Dandenong.

Despite the shared experience of Muslims in Australia, there are distinct differences among them, and their integration into society and attainment of equal rights have often been difficult. Due to this and other factors, Muslims in Australia are multiple communities concentrated in certain suburbs.

As the Muslim population grew so did its religious and cultural needs, and as a result community associations, de facto mosques and a national Muslim body, the Australian Federation of Islamic Councils, were established. Over the years Muslim community associations proliferated, new permanent mosques and Muslim schools emerged, and state councils and Muslim businesses and services were established, all assuming significant roles in the Muslim settlement process and the establishment of Islam. They have become spiritual centres for symbolising the existence of Islam and have brought Muslims together. Collectively, they form the basis upon which an emerging Australian Islam rests, and add to the multiculturalism of Australia.

Muslims in Australia, however, have always remained a diverse group. This is reflected in their community associations, which are differentiated by each congregation's ethnic and language background. For example, in Sydney one can find the United Arab Muslim Association, Suburban Islamic Association, Al-Zahra Muslim Association, Lebanese Muslim Association, Bangladesh Islamic Centre and many more.

Demographically, Islam is the fastest-growing religion in Australia. Muslims were a relatively invisible religious minority group a number of decades ago, but today they are easily visible in many suburbs and public spaces of almost all Australian capital cities. Their presence is reflected in the significant contributions they have made to reconfiguration of the geographical landscapes of cities and towns through mosque construction; the establishment of Islamic centres and Muslim schools, nursing homes and cemeteries; the wearing of Muslim attire; and the introduction of halal commodities to butchers' shops, takeaway stores and restaurants.

The influx of Muslim migrants and the rapid increase in the Muslim population have occasionally generated fear and prejudice among a small number of Australians, resulting in Muslim economic and social marginalisation and hardship, and bringing into question Muslim inclusion in mainstream society. Often Muslims are labelled as the 'Other' with allusions to them not being part of the broader society. Xenophobia and discrimination against Muslims have emerged because of various international factors, including the 1979 Iranian hostage crisis, the 1980 Salman Rushdie affair, the 1990–91 Gulf Wars, and of course the 9/11 attacks in 2001 and the resulting media discourse arousing 'stranger-fear'. This discourse is based on perceptions of Muslim immigrants as foreigners with an alien and 'strange' culture, and ignorance and fear leading to the belief that Muslims are a threat to the majority culture and to security.

The dominant Australian population prefer their 'own cultural kind', and it has been argued that discrimination against Muslims is a 'natural' reaction of self-preservation from the outsider—that is, the Muslim presence—that allegedly threatens the 'Australian way of life'. Australians form a bounded community and are a nation of people conscious of their differences from other cultural groups: hence the xenophobia towards Muslims. The overall impact of this, as discussed in Part 2, is Muslims being excluded from many aspects of mainstream sociocultural, economic and political processes, and difficulties in their endeavours to integrate.

Due to xenophobia and discrimination, Australian Muslims have often struggled to secure employment. Consequently, the unemployment rate among Muslims in Australia has been high with a multiplier effect. In this regard, Riaz Hassan asserts that 'Employment rates for Australian Muslims are significantly lower than for all Australians and unemployment rates are significantly higher. One third of Muslims were not in the labour force in 2016, compared with just over one quarter of all Australians.'[1] Xenophobia and discrimination have also produced significant social disadvantage for Australian Muslims. Based on the findings of various studies, Hassan notes that 'All these indicators suggest that a significant proportion of Muslim Australians occupy a relatively marginal position in Australian society, both socially and economically.'[2]

Despite all this, the vast majority of Australian Muslims have always tried to be law-abiding citizens and at the same time true to their faith, pursuing their lives in light of their religious teachings and law. For Australian Muslims and for Muslims in general, pursuit of an Islamic life is vitally important: it is not only the basis of their identity but forms the very essence of their being. Sharia is one of the central resources for this and plays a pivotal role in all aspects of a Muslim's life, as discussed in Part 3. Originating from the Qur'an, the Hadith and a combination of other sources, sharia for Muslims is a system of law and guidance that is considered to be divinely revealed and nurtures humanity.

Many Australians, including Muslims, have limited understanding of sharia; some misunderstand it. As a result they may associate sharia with the chopping-off of hands, death by stoning, lashes, and other primitive methods of carrying out punishment. They then see sharia as a draconian, archaic, barbaric and unjust legal system. Thus, when Australian Muslims call for the formal accommodation of sharia in Australia, they are met with resistance. However, as long as Muslims live in Australia sharia will remain their central resource. It is the essence of Muslim faith and a path to guide Muslims on how to live in this world and to prepare for the afterlife. Although sharia takes diverse forms of observance among Muslims, it remains the guiding beacon without which there is no Islam.

If sharia is the life source of Islam and Muslims' everyday living, why is it such a misunderstood concept in Australia? As we have seen, it is not only sharia that is misunderstood but Islam itself. To reverse this, Muslim clergy operating as theologians and assuming important legal functionary responsibilities can play a critical role. They have the intellectual resources and capabilities to elucidate the function and importance of sharia as a complete way of life. Their authority and power can be directed to productive use in educating both Muslims and non-Muslims about sharia and the Islamic way of living, particularly in a country like Australia where religion is a private affair. However, Muslim clergy in Australia is a self-regulated heterogeneous group whose Islamic understanding and teaching lacks consensus, and this potentially impacts negatively on popular understandings of sharia and Islam. As the custodians of sharia and representatives of Islam and Muslims, Muslim clerics do not have a broadly agreed upon legal framework that caters for all Muslims and that takes into consideration Muslims' migrant position and Islam's minority status in Australia. As a consequence, sharia and Islam remain much-misunderstood concepts and phenomena. One way to remedy this is education. Islamic schools and Islamic studies, as discussed in Part 4, play critical roles in the promulgation of understanding Australia's second-largest religion.

Islamic education is an important area for Muslims to gain a better and more 'formal' understanding of their own faith, and offers opportunities even for non-Muslims to take advantage of the resources available, particularly in Muslim communities, to learn about the religion. Islamic education is a combination of religious experience, spiritual development and Islamic learning with which the Australian government, social institutions and Muslim community organisations have extensive dealings. It shapes Muslims' spirituality, prepares them for an understanding of knowledge from an Islamic perspective, guides them in the provision of religious services and teaching, and trains them in preserving religious heritage, particularly in the context of Muslim schools. Islamic education is also the means by which Islamic practices, nurturing of an Islamic ethos, inculcation of Islamic moral and ethical behaviour, preservation of Islamic culture, Islamisation of knowledge, and the production of 'good' Muslims, in whom rest the representation and the future of Islam in Australia, are accomplished.

Apart from Muslim schools, the provision of Islamic education in Muslim community-based organisations, such as Daar Aisha Shariah College, and in

Australian universities is proving to be a popular and useful way for adolescent and adult Muslims and non-Muslims to learn about the Islamic faith and its people. In the Australian context this is an important and major development, particularly in the era of the 'war on terror' and in a period when Islam is pervading important public spaces and the Muslim population is fast growing. Australian citizens from Muslim and non-Muslim backgrounds now have the opportunity to study Islam in a formal setting rather than travelling overseas to acquire Islamic knowledge. They can choose to study Islam in Muslim community organisations, colleges and institutes with a theological approach or in Australian academia using social-scientific approaches. In the latter case, there is an opportunity for dynamic intellectual engagement in order to gain a much broader understanding of Islam and in order to learn to respond to the modern needs of Muslims' spiritual wellbeing. For Australian Muslims more specifically, Islamic education helps to fill the cultural gap—that is, it gives them a forum in which to discuss and learn about their own faith in which their identity is embedded. For students outside the fold of Islam, it is an opportunity to learn about a religion that is very different from the stereotypical representations articulated by ignorant politicians, biased public intellectuals and parts of the media.

Some might argue that Islamic education in Muslim community-based organisations and Australian universities runs counter to Australia's secular ethos and should be proscribed. However, in the wake of the 2001 terrorist attacks in America and the subsequent bombings of civilians in Madrid, London, Bali and other places, learning about Islam and Muslims is more urgent and necessary. Fearing the potential growth of 'homegrown' violent Muslim extremism and the rise of Muslim terrorism cannot be overlooked, as discussed in Part 5.

Violent Muslim extremism and Muslim terrorism, which I have discussed at some length in chapters 10 and 11, are important aspects of a more broad understanding of the focus of this book—that is, Islam and Muslims in Australia. In the era of the 'war on terror', 'homegrown' violent Muslim extremism and the rise of Muslim terrorism are real fears in Australia. In response, the federal government developed a 'Countering Violent Extremism' program. However, the response to homegrown violent Muslim extremism, Muslim radicalisation and Muslim terrorism has arguably been poorly, impetuously and expediently developed; as a result, instead of targeting the perpetrators only, ordinary innocent Muslims have frequently been targeted. One of the dangerous unintended results of this is that members of the general Muslim population become victims, and their experiences of discrimination and marginalisation are significantly aggravated by a complex web of social, cultural, economic and political barriers in their everyday living. The overall

Muslim experience and Muslims' participation in socioeconomic processes become challenging and even problematic with increased social exclusion and 'Othering'.

Another critical outcome of the government's response to homegrown violent Muslim extremism, Muslim radicalism and Muslim terrorism is the securitisation of the general Muslim population. In the Australian securitisation paradigm, Islam and Muslims are envisaged as an existential threat to the country's modern secular liberal democracy. The paradigm encompasses a multifaceted process in which the usual rule of law is suspended in favour of remarkable courses of action justified by concocting situations that imperil the existence of the social order, economic structure and political community. It operates outside the realm of 'normal politics' as it aims to respond to what is understood to be an existential threat posed by Muslims. In the process, all Muslims apparently become targets of securitisation. While securitisation attempts to keep one set of Australian citizens from harm and danger, it targets and leaves exposed another set—Muslim citizens. Australian multiculturalism is faced with a paradox: even though it seeks to facilitate the socioeconomic and political integration of Muslims, antiterrorism policies and security measures fuel a desire to compromise liberties and restrict Islam and Muslims from public spaces.

Islam and Muslims are a developing phenomenon in Australia, with profound internal complexities and dynamism. They are shaped by local and international factors and influence Islam's relations with state and civil society, inter- and intra-community interactions, and intergenerational dynamics. Islam and Muslims are part of the social fabric of Australian multiculturalism and are here to stay. For this reason, Australia needs to work out ways to accommodate them rather than simply wishing them away.

Acknowledgements

My deepest gratitude to Professor Michael Humphrey for writing a genuine and perspicacious forward, to Professors Mohamad Abdalla and Samina Yasmeen for their kind words, and Amirah Ali for assisting in preparing the index and various other aspects of the book.

Jan A Ali
28 September 2020

Notes

Introduction
1. David Waines, *An Introduction to Islam*, Cambridge University Press, Cambridge, 1995; Seyyed Naser, *Islam: Religion, History, and Civilization*, HarperSanFrancisco, San Francisco, 2002; Tamara Sonn, *A Brief History of Islam*, Polity Press, London, 2004; Gabriele Marranci, *The Anthropology of Islam*, Berg, London & New York, 2008; Gabriele Marranci, *Understanding Muslim Identity, Rethinking Fundamentalism*, Palgrave Macmillan, London & New York, 2009; Bryan Turner & Kamaludeen Nasir (eds), *The Sociology of Islam: Collected Essays of Bryan S. Turner (Contemporary Thought in the Islamic World)*, 1st edn, Routledge, London & New York, 2016.
2. Gabriele Marranci, 'Sociology and anthropology of Islam: A critical debate', in Bryan Turner (ed.), *The New Blackwell Companion to the Sociology of Religion*, Blackwell Publishing, Malden, 2010, p. 368.
3. Nahid Kabir, *Muslims in Australia: Immigration, Race Relations and Cultural History*, Routledge, New York, 2010; Peta Stephenson, *Islam Dreaming: Indigenous Muslims in Australia*, UNSW Press, Sydney, 2010; Mario Peucker, Joshua Roose & Shahram Akbarzadeh, 'Muslim active citizenship in Australia: Socioeconomic challenges and the emergence of a Muslim elite', *Australian Journal of Political Science*, 49(2), 2014, pp. 282–99; Jan Ali, 'A dual legal system in Australia: The formalization of *Shari'a*', *Democracy and Security*, 7(4), 2011, pp. 354–73; Mohamad Abdalla, Dylan Chown & Muhammad Abdullah (eds), *Islamic Schooling in the West: Pathway to Renewal*, Palgrave, London, 2018; Kevin Dunn et al., 'Can you use community policing for counter terrorism? Evidence from NSW, Australia', *Police Practice and Research*, 17(3), 2015, pp. 196–211.
4. Riaz Hassan, *Australian Muslims: A Demographic, Social and Economic Profile of Muslims in Australia*. International Centre for Muslim and non-Muslim Understanding, Adelaide, 2015.
5. Christian von Sikorski et al., '"Muslims are not terrorists": Islamic state coverage, journalistic differentiation between terrorism and Islam, fear reactions, and attitudes toward Muslims', *Journal of Mass Communication and Society*, 20(6), 2017, pp. 825–48.
6. Tufyal Choudhury & Helen Fenwick, *The Impact of Counter-Terrorism Measures on Muslim Communities*, Durham University, Manchester, 2011.
7. Agreement Jotia, 'Globalization and the nation-state: Sovereignty and state welfare in jeopardy', *US-China Education Review B 2*, 2011, pp. 243–50.

Chapter 1: History of Muslim settlement in Australia

1. Amanda Wise & Jan Ali, *Muslim-Australians and Local Government: Grassroots Strategies to Improve Relations Between Muslim and non-Muslim Australians*, Department of Immigration and Citizenship and the Centre for Research on Social Inclusion, Macquarie University, Sydney, 2008; Riaz Hassan, *Australian Muslims: A Demographic, Social and Economic Profile of Muslims in Australia*, International Centre for Muslim and Non-Muslim Understanding, University of South Australia, Adelaide, 2015.
2. Gary Bouma, *Mosques and Muslim Settlement in Australia*, Bureau of Immigration and Population Research/Australian Government Publishing Service, Canberra, 1994, p. 87.
3. Andrew Jakubowicz, 'Political Islam and the future of Australian multiculturalism', *National Identities*, 9(3), 2007, p. 266.
4. Nahid Kabir, *Muslims in Australia: Immigration, Race Relations and Cultural History*, Routledge, New York, 2010, p. 3.
5. Peta Stephenson, *Islam Dreaming: Indigenous Muslims in Australia*, UNSW Press, Sydney, 2010.
6. Regina Ganter, 'Muslim Australians: The deep histories of contact', *Journal of Australian Studies*, 32(4), 2008, p. 483.
7. Ibid., p. 482.
8. Ibid., p. 483.
9. John Mulvaney & Johan Kamminga, *Prehistory of Australia*, Smithsonian Institution Press, Washington, DC, 1999.
10. Anne Clarke, '"The Moormans Trowers": Aboriginal and Macassan interactions and the changing fabric of Indigenous social life', in Sue O'Connor & Peter Veth (eds), *East of Wallace's Line: Modern Quaternary Research in East Asia*, vol. 16, AA Balkema, Rotterdam, 2000, pp. 315–35.
11. Ian McIntosh, 'Islam and Australia's Aborigines? Perspective from north-east Arnhem Land', *Journal of Religious History*, 20(1), 1996, pp. 53–77.
12. Bilal Cleland, 'The history of Muslims in Australia', in Abdullah Saeed & Shahram Akbarzadeh (eds), *Muslim Communities in Australia*, UNSW Press, Sydney, 2001, pp. 12–32.
13. Stephenson, pp. 21–2.
14. Jakubowicz, p. 266.
15. Katy Nebhan, 'Identifications: Between nationalistic "cells" and an Australian Muslim ummah', *Australian Journal of Social Issues*, 34(4), 1999, pp. 371–85.
16. Abdallah Mograby, 'Muslim migration and settlement: The Australian experience', in *Islam in Australia*, Middle East Research and Information Section / NSW Anti-Discrimination Board, Sydney, 1985, pp. 25–35.
17. Pamela Rajkowski, *In the Tracks of the Camelmen*, Angus & Robertson, North Ryde, NSW, 1987, p. 167.
18. Shahram Akbarzadeh, 'Unity or fragmentation?', in Saeed & Akbarzadeh (eds), pp. 228–34.
19. Christine Stevens, *Tin Mosques & Ghantowns: A History of Afghan Cameldrivers in Australia*, Oxford University Press, Melbourne, 1989.
20. Qazi Ahmad, 'Islam and Muslims in Australia', in Hussin Mutalib & Taj ul-Islam Hashmi (eds), *Islam, Muslims and the Modern State: Case-Studies of Muslims in Thirteen Countries*, St Martins Press, New York, 1994, pp. 317–38.
21. Ibid.
22. Stephen Castles & Mark Miller, *The Age of Migration: International Population Movements in the Modern World*, Guilford Books, New York, 1993.
23. Harry Field, *Citizen or Resident? Australian Social Security Provision to Immigrants*,

doctoral dissertation, University of New South Wales, Sydney, 2000.
24 Anthony Johns & Abdullah Saeed, 'Muslims in Australia: The building of a community', in Yvonne Haddad & Jane Smith (eds), *Muslim Minorities in the West: Visible and Invisible*, AltaMira Press, Walnut Creek, CA, 2002, pp. 195–216.
25 Garry Trompf (ed.), *Cargo Cults and Millenarian Movements: Transoceanic Comparisons of New Religious Movements (Religion and Society)*, Mouton de Gruyter, Berlin & New York, 1990.
26 Michael Humphrey, 'An Australian Islam? Religion in the multicultural city', in Saeed & Akbarzadeh (eds), pp. 33–52.
27 Wafia Omar & Kirsty Allen, *The Muslims in Australia*, Australian Government Publishing Service, Canberra, 1997.
28 Karen Armstrong, *Islam: A Short History*, Modern Library, New York, 2000.
29 Ahmad, p. 318.
30 Omar & Allen. This might seem a substantial increase, but when the length of the period (twenty-four years) is taken into consideration, the average annual growth was only 930 people. A point to note is that this was a time when the White Australia policy was very much alive.
31 Commonwealth of Australia, *1991 Census of Population and Housing*, Catalogue No. 2722.0, Australian Bureau of Statistics, Canberra, 1991.
32 Commonwealth of Australia, *1996 Census of Population and Housing*, Catalogue No. 2901.0, Australian Bureau of Statistics, Canberra, 1997.
33 Commonwealth of Australia, *2001 Census of Population and Housing*, Catalogue No. 2015.0, Australian Bureau of Statistics, Canberra, 2002.
34 Commonwealth of Australia, *2006 Census of Population and Housing*, Catalogue No. 2068.0, Australian Bureau of Statistics, Canberra, 2007.
35 Commonwealth of Australia, *2011 Census of Population and Housing: Reflecting a Nation: Stories from the 2011 Census*, Catalogue No. 2071.0, Australian Bureau of Statistics, Canberra, 2012–13.
36 Commonwealth of Australia, *2016 Census of Population and Housing: Reflecting Australia: Stories from the 2016 Census*, Catalogue No. 2071.0, Australian Bureau of Statistics, Canberra, 2017.
37 Hassan.
38 Commonwealth of Australia, 2012–13.
39 Omar & Allen.
40 Hassan.
41 James Forrest, 'Suburbs "swamped" by Asians and Muslims? The data show a different story', *The Conversation*, 5 July 2017.
42 Jeff Diamant, *The Countries with the 10 Largest Christian Populations and the 10 Largest Muslim Populations*, Pew Research Centre, 1 April 2019. https://www.pewresearch.org/fact-tank/2019/04/01/the-countries-with-the-10-largest-christian-populations-and-the-10-largest-muslim-populations/
43 *Exhibition: Islam in Asia: Diversity in Past and Present: Muslim Populations*, Cornell University Library, April 2017. https://guides.library.cornell.edu/IslamAsiaExhibit/MuslimPopulations
44 Ibid.
45 Mark Sedgwick, 'Sects in the Islamic world', *Nova Religio: The Journal of Alternative and Emergent Religions*, 3(2), 2000, pp. 195–240.
46 Ibid.
47 Abdullah Saeed, *Islam in Australia*, Allen & Unwin, Crows Nest, NSW, 2003; Humphrey.
48 Saeed, p. 1.

49 Hassan, p. 19.
50 The *hijrah* or withdrawal was the emigration of the Prophet Mohammed and his followers from Makkah to the city of Medina (formerly known as Yathrib) in 622 CE. The Prophet undertook the *hijrah* to Medina and made a new place for Islam— the *dar al-Islam* (home of Islam). Hence, Muslims who emigrate to the West are in a sense undertaking *hijrah* and will both find and help produce, in the new environment, a suitable place in which to engage in the practice of Islam.
51 Dale Eickelman & James Piscatori, 'Social theory in the study of Muslim societies', in Dale Eickelman & James Piscatori (eds), *Muslim Travellers: Pilgrimage, Migration, and the Religious Imagination*, University of California, Berkeley, 1990, p. 16.
52 Gary Bouma, Joan Daw & Riffat Munawar, 'Muslims managing religious diversity', in Saeed & Akbarzadeh (eds), p. 58.
53 By such travelling I do not mean just physical movement but spiritual as well.
54 Michael Humphrey, 'Racism and unemployment amongst Lebanese', in *Seminar Proceedings of the Arabic Community: Realities and Challenges*, Arabic Welfare Inter-Agency, Sydney, 1986, pp. 29–41.
55 Cleland.
56 Michael Humphrey, 'Australian Islam, the new global terrorism and the limits of citizenship', in Shahram Akbarzadeh & Samina Yasmeen (eds), *Islam and the West: Reflections from Australia*, UNSW Press, Sydney, 2005, pp. 132–48.
57 Jocelyne Cesari, 'Islam in France: The shaping of a religious minority', in Yvonne Haddad (ed.), *Muslims in the West: Sojourners to Citizens*, Oxford University Press, Oxford, 2002, pp. 36–51.
58 Steven Vertovec, 'Islamophobia and Muslim recognition in Britain', in Haddad (ed.), pp. 19–35.
59 Barbara Stowasser, 'The Turks in Germany: From sojourners to citizens', in Haddad (ed.), pp. 52–71.
60 Humphrey, 2005, p. 138.
61 Ibid.
62 Ibid.
63 Bouma, Daw & Munawar.
64 Ibid., p. 69.
65 Ibid., pp. 69–70.
66 Michael Humphrey, 'Globalisation and Arab diasporic identities: The Australian Arab case', *Bulletin of the Royal Institute for Inter-Faith Studies*, 2(1), 2000, pp. 1–18.
67 Tariq Ramadan, 'Islam and Muslims in Europe: A silent revolution toward rediscovery', in Haddad (ed.), pp. 158–66.
68 Ibid., p. 162.
69 Ibid., p. 159.
70 Ibid., p. 160.
71 Humphrey, 2005.
72 Samina Yasmeen, 'Muslim women as citizens in Australia: Perth as a case study', in Haddad & Smith (eds), pp. 217–32.
73 David Smith, Sanuki Jayarajah, Taya Fabjianic & Janice Wykes, *Citizenship in Australia*, Department of Immigration and Citizenship, Australian Government, Canberra, 2011.
74 Joshua Roose, 'Contesting Islam through the 2012 Sydney protests: An analysis of post-protest political discourse amongst Australian Muslims', *Journal of Islam and Christian–Muslim Relations*, 24(4), 2013, p. 482.
75 Shahram Akbarzadeh, 'The Muslim question in Australia: Islamophobia and Muslim alienation', *Journal of Muslim Minority Affairs*, 36(3), 2016, p. 329.

76 Greg Noble, 'Respect and respectability amongst second-generation Arab and Muslim Australian men', *Journal of Intercultural Studies*, 28(3), 2007, pp. 331–44.
77 Shahram Akbarzadeh, 'Investing in mentoring and educational initiatives: The limits of de-radicalisation programmes in Australia', *Journal of Muslim Minority Affairs*, 33(4), 2013, p. 452.
78 Scott Poynting & Greg Noble, *Living with Racism: The Experience and Reporting by Arab and Muslim Australians of Discrimination, Abuse and Violence since 11 September 2001*, Centre for Cultural Research, University of Western Sydney, Sydney, 2004.
79 Lars Pedersen, *Newer Islamic Movements in Western Europe*, Ashgate, London, 1999.
80 Jan Ali, *Islamic Revivalism Encounters the Modern World: A Study of the Tabligh Jama'at*, Sterling Publishers, New Delhi, 2012.

Chapter 2: Immigration, multiculturalism and Muslim migrants

1 Mary Jones, 'The years of decline: Australian Muslims 1900–40', in Mary Jones (ed.), *An Australian Pilgrimage: Muslims in Australia from the Seventeenth Century to the Present*, Victoria Press, Melbourne, 1993, pp. 63–86.
2 Ibid.
3 Michael Humphrey, *Islam, Multiculturalism and Transnationalism: From the Lebanese Diaspora*, IB Tauris Publishers, London, 1998; Nahid Kabir, *Muslims in Australia: Immigration, Race Relations and Cultural History*, Routledge, New York, 2010; Joshua Roose, *Contesting the Future: Muslim Men as Political Actors in the Context of Australian Multiculturalism*, PhD thesis, Arts—Asia Institute, University of Melbourne, 2012.
4 Bilal Cleland, *The Muslims in Australia: A Brief History*, Islamic Council of Victoria, Melbourne, 2002.
5 Humphrey, 1998.
6 In 2016 parts of Auburn City Council, Parramatta City Council and Holroyd City Council merged to form Cumberland Council as a new local government area. Thus, in the current top twenty LGAs in terms of number of Muslim residents, according to 2016 census data Auburn has been replaced by Cumberland.
7 Commonwealth of Australia, *2016 Census of Population and Housing: Reflecting Australia: Stories from the 2016 Census*, Catalogue No. 2071.0, Australian Bureau of Statistics, Canberra, 2017.
8 Gary Bouma, *Mosques and Muslim Settlement in Australia*, Commonwealth of Australia, Canberra, 1994.
9 Commonwealth of Australia, 2011, *Census of Population and Housing: Reflecting a Nation: Stories from the 2011 Census*, Catalogue No. 2071.0, Australian Bureau of Statistics, Canberra, 2012–13; Commonwealth of Australia, 2017.
10 Michael Humphrey, *Family, Work, and Unemployment: A Study of Lebanese Settlement in Sydney*, Australian Government Publishing Service, Canberra, 1984.
11 Humphrey, 1998, p. 21.
12 Ibid.
13 James Jupp (ed.), *The Australian People: An Encyclopedia of the Nation, Its People and Their Origins*, Cambridge University Press, Cambridge, 2001.
14 Michael Humphrey, 'Australian Islam, the new global terrorism and the limits of citizenship', in Shahram Akbarzadeh & Samina Yasmeen (eds), *Islam and the West: Reflections from Australia*, UNSW Press, Sydney, 2005, p. 136.
15 Selective immigration means permitting only those immigrants to settle in Australia who were deemed white and thus easily assimilable.
16 Douglas Cole, 'The crimson thread of kinship', *Journal of Historical Studies*, 14(56), 1971, p. 514.
17 Humphrey, 1984.

18 For more detailed discussion refer to James Jupp (ed.), *The Encyclopedia of Religion in Australia*, Cambridge University Press, Melbourne, 2009.
19 Kabir, 2010, p. 143.
20 Immigration: Government Policy. Ministerial Statement, 2 August 1945, *1944–45: The Parliament of the Commonwealth of Australia*, Vol. IV, Papers Presented to Parliament (and ordered to be printed), 1218.
21 Immigration: Government Policy. Ministerial Statement, 22 November 1946, *1946–47–48: The Parliament of the Commonwealth of Australia*, Vol. II, Papers Presented to Parliament (and ordered to be printed), 1049.
22 Ibid., 1059.
23 Andrew Jakubowicz, 'The state and the welfare of immigrants in Australia', *Ethnic and Racial Studies*, 12(1), 1989, pp. 1–35.
24 Reginald Appleyard, 'The population', in Alan Davies & Sol Encel (eds), *Australian Society: A Sociological Introduction* (2nd edn), Cheshire Publishing, Melbourne, 1971, p. 15.
25 Catriona Elder, *Being Australian: Narratives of National Identity*, Allen & Unwin, Crows Nest, 2007, pp. 130–1.
26 Humphrey, 1984.
27 Department of Immigration, Local Government and Ethnic Affairs, *Australia and Immigration 1788 to 1988*, Australian Government Publishing Service, Canberra, 1988, p. 42.
28 Ibid., pp. 43, 48.
29 Andrew Markus, *Race: John Howard and the Remaking of Australia*, Allen & Unwin, Crows Nest, 2001, p. 22.
30 Kabir, 2010, p. 147.
31 Engin Isin & Bryan Turner, 'Investigating citizenship: An agenda for citizenship studies', *Citizenship Studies*, 11(1), 2007, p. 11.
32 Lisa Irving, 'Teaching and learning halal sex: Discussing contrasting values among Muslim youth adults in Australia', in Erich Kolig & Malcolm Voyce (eds), *Muslim Integration: Pluralism and Multiculturalism in New Zealand and Australia*, Lexington Books, New York, 2016.
33 Ibid., p. 130.
34 Kabir, 2010, p. 146.
35 Ibid., p. 131.
36 Fiona Nicoll, 'Pseudo-hyphens and barbaric/binaries: Anglo-Celticity and the cultural politics of tolerance', *Queensland Review*, 6(1), 1999, p. 77.
37 *The People of Australia: Australia's Multicultural Policy*, Commonwealth of Australia, n.d. https://www.runnymedetrust.org/uploads/events/people-of-australia-multicultural-policy-booklet.pdf
38 Brian Graetz & Ian McAllister, *Dimensions of Australian Society* (2nd edn), Macmillan, Melbourne, 1994.
39 The term equality means 'of equal value'. For instance, while a Chinese-Australian and a white Anglo-Saxon Australian are not thought by some people to be equal, they are 'of equal value'. Equality, at least theoretically, denotes that difference in religious or cultural background does not amount to a handicap for a person or community when it comes to exercising legal, political or social rights in society.
40 Michael Humphrey, 'Muslim communities in Australia', in Abdullah Said & Shahram Akbarzadeh (eds), *Muslim Communities in Australia*, UNSW Press, Sydney, 2001, p. 37.
41 Garry Trompf, *Early Christian Historiography: Narratives of Retributive Justice*, Continuum, London, 2000.
42 Humphrey, 2001.

43 Ibid.
44 Ibid., p. 35.
45 Regina Ganter, 'Muslim Australians: The deep histories of contact', *Journal of Australian Studies*, 32(4), 2008, p. 482.
46 Kevin Dunn, Natascha Klocker & Tanya Salabay, 'Contemporary racism and Islamophobia in Australia: Racializing religion', *Ethnicities*, 7(4), 2007, p. 571.
47 Nahid Kabir, 'The media is one-sided in Australia', *Journal of Children and Media*, 2(3), 2008, p. 274.
48 Nahid Kabir, 'Muslim in Australia: The double edge of terrorism', *Journal of Ethnic and Migration Studies*, 33(8), 2007, p. 1286.
49 Liza Hopkins, 'A contested identity: Resisting the category Muslim-Australian', *Immigrants and Minorities*, 29(1), 2011, p. 111.
50 Humphrey, 2001.
51 Nahid Kabir, 'Representation of Islam and Muslims in the Australian media, 2001–2005', *Journal of Muslim Minority Affairs*, 26(3), 2006, p. 313.
52 Hopkins.
53 Gary Bouma, 'The settlement of Islam in Australia', *Social Compass*, 44(1), 1997, p. 74.
54 Ghassan Hage, *White Nation: Fantasies of White Supremacy in a Multicultural Society*, Pluto Press, Sydney, 1998.
55 'Conservative' signifies a proclivity towards a traditional or customary lifestyle.
56 Michael Humphrey, 'Globalisation and Arab diasporic identities: The Australian Arab case', *Bulletin of the Royal Institute for Inter-Faith Studies*, 2(1), 2000, pp. 1–18.
57 Ibid.
58 Graetz & McAllister.
59 Wendy Lowenstein & Morag Loh, *The Immigrants*, Hyland House, Melbourne, 1977, p. 10.
60 Humphrey, 2001.
61 Ibid.
62 Mario Peucker, Joshua Roose & Shahram Akbarzadeh, 'Muslim active citizenship in Australia: Socioeconomic challenges and the emergence of a Muslim elite', *Australian Journal of Political Science*, 49(2), 2014, p. 298.
63 Humphrey, 1984.

Chapter 3: Muslim community and organisational development and the institutionalisation of Islam
1 Gary Bouma, *Mosques and Muslim Settlement in Australia*, Commonwealth of Australia, Canberra, 1994.
2 Ibid., p. 13.
3 Nahid Kabir, *Muslims in Australia: Immigration, Race Relations and Cultural History*, Routledge, London, 2010.
4 Ibid.
5 Ibid.
6 'Notes and Proceedings of Parliament, WA 1898', cited in Madeleine Brunato, *Hanji Mahomet Allum: Afghan Camel-Driver, Herbalist and Healer in Australia*, Investigator Press, Leabrook, SA, 1972, pp. 16–18.
7 Christine Stevens, 'Afghan camel drivers: Founders of Islam in Australia', in Mary Jones et al. (eds), *An Australian Pilgrimage: Muslims in Australia from the Seventeenth Century to the Present*, Victoria Press in Association with the Museum of Victoria, Melbourne, 1993, p. 49.
8 Michael Cigler, *The Afghans in Australia*, Australian Ethnic Heritage Series, AE Press,

Melbourne, 1986.
9   Qazi Ahmad, 'Islam and Muslims in Australia', in Hussin Mutalib & Taj ul-Islam Hashmi (eds), *Islam, Muslims and the Modern State: Case-Studies of Muslims in Thirteen Countries*, St Martins Press, New York, 1994, pp. 317–38.
10 Mary Jones, 'The years of decline: Australian Muslims 1900–40', in Jones at al. (eds), pp. 63–86.
11 Anthony Johns & Abdullah Saeed, 'Muslims in Australia: The building of a community', in Yvonne Haddad & Jane Smith (eds), *Muslim Minorities in the West: Visible and Invisible*, AltaMira Press, Walnut Creek, CA, 2002, p. 198.
12 Ibid.
13 For a more detailed discussion, see James Jupp (ed.), *The Encyclopedia of Religion in Australia*, Cambridge University Press, Melbourne, 2009.
14 Bouma.
15 Michael Humphrey, 'Islam: A test for multiculturalism', *Asian Migrant*, 2(2), 1989, pp. 48–56.
16 Ibid.
17 Bouma.
18 Ryan Edwards, *Muslim Community Organisations and Leadership in Australia*, PhD thesis, Asian Institute, University of Melbourne, 2018, p. 127.
19 Humphrey.
20 Bouma, p. 65.
21 Michael Humphrey, 'Is this a mosque-free zone? Islam and the state in Australia', *Migration Monitor*, 3(12), 1989, p. 13.
22 Ibid.
23 Bouma, p. 57.
24 Ibid., p. 66.
25 Nora Amath, *The Phenomenology of Community Activism: Muslim Civil Society Organisations in Australia*, Melbourne University Publishing, Carlton, 2015, p. 97.
26 Mario Peucker, 'Muslim community organisations as agents of social inclusion, cohesion and active citizenship? A cross-national overview', in Mario Peucker & Rauf Ceylan (eds), *Muslim Community Organizations in the West: History, Developments and Future Perspectives*, Springer, Berlin, 2017, p. 40.
27 Qari Asim, *Mosques and Youth Engagement: Guidelines and Toolkit*, MINAB, London, 2011.
28 Michael Humphrey, 'Islam, immigration and the state: Religion in Australia', in Alan Black (ed.), *Religion in Australia: Sociological Perspectives*, Allen & Unwin, Sydney, 1991, pp. 185–6.
29 Bouma.
30 Husnia Underabi, *Mosques of Sydney and New South Wales: Research Report 2014*, Charles Sturt University, Islamic Sciences & Research Academy Australia & University of Western Sydney, 2014. In this report, all Islamic places of worship are considered to be mosques.
31 Underabi.
32 Edwards, p. 129.
33 Bouma.
34 Edwards, p. 129.
35 Michael Humphrey, 'Community, mosque, and ethnic politics', *Australian and New Zealand Journal of Sociology*, 23(2), 1987, pp. 233–45.
36 Amath, p. 103.
37 Humphrey, 1989.
38 Jones.

39 Edwards.
40 Bilal Cleland, *The Muslims in Australia: A Brief History*, Islamic Council of Victoria, Melbourne, 2002.
41 Peter Jones, 'Islamic schools in Australia', *La Trobe Journal*, 89, 2012, pp. 36–47.
42 Cleland, p. 28.
43 Alison Branley, '"One man show": Concerns Islamic Council may not have held annual meeting in 8 years', *AM*, 27 June 2015. https://www.abc.net.au/radio/programs/am/one-man-show-concerns-islamic-council-may-not-have/6577582
44 Edwards, p. 68.
45 Jan Ali, 'Muslim schools in Australia: Development and transition', in Mohamad Abdalla, Dylan Chow & Muhammad Abdullah (eds), *Islamic Schooling in the West: Pathways to Renewal*, Palgrave Macmillan, New York, 2018, pp. 35–62.
46 Amath.
47 Peucker.

Chapter 4: Muslim experience of social exclusion in Australia
1 Hilary Silver & Seymour Miller, 'A social exclusion: The European approach to social disadvantage', *Indicators*, 2(2), 2003, pp. 1–17; Dirk-Jan Omtzigt, *Survey on Social inclusion: Theory and Policy*, Working Paper, Oxford Institute for Global Economic Development, Oxford University, 2009.
2 Omtzigt.
3 Jane Mathieson et al., *Social Exclusion: Meaning, Measurement and Experience and Links to Health Inequalities: A Review of Literature*, World Health Organization Social Exclusion Knowledge Network Background Paper 1, Institute for Health Research, Lancaster, UK, 2008.
4 Eric Robinson, *Ancient Greek Democracy: Readings and Sources*, Blackwell, Oxford, 2004, p. 5.
5 Jules Klanfer, *L'Exclusion sociale: Étude de la marginalité dans les sociétés occidentales* [*Social Exclusion: The Study of Marginality in Western Societies*], Bureau de Recherches Sociales, Paris, 1995.
6 Dan Allman, 'The sociology of social inclusion', *SAGE Open*, 3(1), 2012, p. 8.
7 Nabin Rawal, 'Social inclusion and exclusion: A review', *Dhaulagiri Journal of Sociology and Anthropology*, 2, 2008, p. 162.
8 Allman, p. 8.
9 Rawal, p. 163.
10 Christine Cousins, 'Social exclusion in Europe: Paradigms of social disadvantage in Germany, Spain, Sweden and the United Kingdom', *Policy and Politics*, 26(2), 1998, pp. 127–46.
11 Alan Hayes, Matthew Gray & Ben Edwards, 'Social inclusion: Origin, concepts and key themes', Social Inclusion Unit, Australian Institute of Family Studies, Department of the Prime Minister and Cabinet, Canberra, 2008.
12 Ruth Lister, 'Strategies for social inclusion: Promoting social cohesion or social justice?', in Peter Askonas & Angus Stewart (eds), *Social Inclusion: Possibilities and Tensions*, Macmillan, London, 2000, pp. 37–54.
13 Brenden O'Flaherty, *Making Room: The Economics of Homelessness*, Harvard University Press, Cambridge, MA, 1996; Dragana Avramov, *People, Democracy, and Social Exclusion*, Population Studies Series no. 37, Council of European Publishing, Strasbourg, 2002, pp. 26–7.
14 Tamiru Berafe, 'Assessing the causes and effects of social exclusion: The case of "pot makers" in Yem Special Woreda in Southern Nation, Nationalities and Peoples Regional State in Ethiopia', *African Journal of Political Science and International*

Relations, 11(4), 2017, p. 75.
15 Gary Lafree, Losing Legitimacy, Westview, Boulder, CO, 1998.
16 Robert Oxoby, 'Cognitive dissonance, status, and growth of the underclass', Economic Journal, 114, 2004, pp. 729–49.
17 Anthony Atkinson, 'Social exclusion, poverty and unemployment', in Anthony Atkinson & John Hill (eds), Exclusion, Opportunity and Employment, Centre for Analysis of Social Exclusion, London, 1998, pp. 1–20.
18 Robert Putman, Bowling Alone: The Collapse and Revival of American Community, Simon & Schuster, New York, 2000.
19 Rawal, p. 165.
20 Avramov, pp. 26–7.
21 Graham Room, 'Poverty and social exclusion: The new European agenda for policy and research', in Graham Room (ed.), Beyond the Threshold, Policy Press, Bristol, 1995, pp. 1–9.
22 Hayes, Gray & Edwards; Tony Vinson, The Origins, Meaning, Definition and Economic Implications of the Concept of Social Inclusion/Exclusion, Department of Education, Employment and Workplace Relations, Commonwealth of Australia, Canberra, 2009.
23 Myfanwy McDonald, Social Exclusion and Social Inclusion: Resources for Child and Family Services, Australian Institute of Family Studies, Melbourne, 2011.
24 Amanda Wise & Jan Ali, Muslim-Australians and Local Government: Grassroots Strategies to Improve Relations Between Muslim and Non-Muslim Australians, Final Research Report, Department of Immigration and Citizenship and the Centre for Research on Social Inclusion, Macquarie University, Sydney, 2008.
25 Maharim (singular: mihram) are close male kin before whom one can appear without observing hijab (veil), and whom one cannot marry.
26 Muḥammad ibn Ismāʿīl Bukhārī, translated by Muḥammad Muḥsin Khān, Ṣaḥīḥ al-Bukhārī: The Translation of the Meanings of Ṣaḥīḥ al-Bukhārī (Arabic–English), Taleem-ul-Quran Trust, Gujranwala, Pakistan, 1971, p. 459.
27 Wise & Ali, p. 74.
28 Saba Mahmood, Politics of Piety: The Islamic Revival and the Feminist Subject, Princeton University Press, 2005, p. 158.
29 Economic Development Committee, Inquiry into the Incidence of Youth Unemployment in Victoria, Parliament of Victoria, Melbourne, 2002, p. 108.
30 Wise & Ali, p. 76.
31 Brotherhood of St Laurence, 'Seeking asylum: Living with fear, uncertainty and exclusion', Changing Pressures, 11, 2002, p. 7.
32 Mario Peucker, Joshua Roose & Shahram Akbarzadeh, 'Muslim active citizenship in Australia: Socioeconomic challenges and the emergence of a Muslim elite', Australian Journal of Political Science, 49(2), 2014, p. 294.
33 Brotherhood of St Laurence, p. 77.
34 Ibid.
35 Scott Poynting, Living with Racism: The Experience and Reporting by Arab and Muslim Australians of Discrimination, Abuse and Violence since 11 September 2001, Report to the Human Rights and Equal Opportunity Commission, Centre for Cultural Research, University of Western Sydney, 2004.
36 Derya Iner (ed.), Islamophobia in Australia, II (2016–2017), Charles Sturt University & ISRA, Sydney, 2019, p. 168.
37 Martin Barker, The New Racism: Conservatives and the Ideology of the Tribe, Junction Books, London, 1981; Jeffrey Cole, The New Racism in Europe, Cambridge University Press, 1997; Laksiri Jayasuriya, 'Understanding Australian racism', Australian

Universities Review, 45(1), 2002, pp. 40–4.
38 Kevin Dunn, Natascha Klocker & Tanya Salabay, 'Contemporary racism and Islamophobia in Australia: Racializing religion', Ethnicities, 7(4), 2007, pp. 564–89.
39 Phil Hubbard, 'Accommodating otherness: Anti-asylum centre protest and the maintenance of white privilege', Transactions of the Institute of British Geographers, 30, 2005, pp. 52–65.
40 Robert Park, 'Assimilation, social', in Edwin Seligman & Alvin Johnson (eds), The Encyclopaedia of the Social Sciences, Macmillan, New York, 1930, pp. 281–83.
41 Ellie Vasta, 'Dialectics of domination: Racism and multiculturalism', in Stephen Castles & Ellie Vasta (eds), The Teeth Are Smiling, Allen & Unwin, Sydney, 1996, pp. 46–72.
42 Stephen Castles et al., Mistaken Identity: Multiculturalism and the Demise of Nationalism in Australia, Pluto Press, Sydney, 1992.
43 Christian Joppke, 'The retreat of multiculturalism in the liberal states: Theory and policy', British Journal of Sociology, 55(2), 2004, pp. 237–57.
44 Riaz Hassan & Bill Martin, Islamophobia, Social Distance and Fear of Terrorism in Australia: A Preliminary Report, International Centre for Muslim and Non-Muslim Understanding, University of South Australia, Adelaide, 2015, p. 5.
45 Peucker, Roose & Akbarzadeh, pp. 289–90.
46 Hadi Sohrabi & Karen Farquharson, 'Discursive integration and Muslims in Australia', in Fathi Mansouri & Vince Marotta (eds), Muslims in the West and the Challenge of Belonging, Melbourne University Publishing, 2011, pp. 134–54.
47 Irene Bloemraad, 'Unity in diversity? Bridging models of multiculturalism and immigrant integration', Du Bois Review, 2(2), 2007, pp. 317–36.
48 John Gray, 'Inclusion: A radical critique', in Askonas & Stewart (eds), p. 24.
49 Vinson.
50 Peucker, Roose & Akbarzadeh, p. 295.
51 Iris Young, Inclusion and Democracy, Oxford University Press, 2000, pp. 13–14.

Chapter 5: The need for Muslim social inclusion
1   By this I mean the social structure—family, religion, law, economy and class—which in sociology generally refers to the patterned social arrangements in society that both emerge from and determine the actions of individuals.
2   Christa Freiler, What Needs to Change? Towards a Vision of Social Inclusion for Children, Families and Communities, Draft Concept Paper, Laidlaw Foundation, Toronto, 2001, p. 12.
3   Julia Gillard, 'The economics of social inclusion', Sydney Paper, 19(3), 2007, p. 103.
4   Eric Marlier et al., The EU and Social Inclusion: Facing the Challenges, Policy Press, Bristol, 2007.
5   Hugh Frazer & Eric Marlier, Assessment of Progress towards the Europe 2020 Social Inclusion Objectives: Main Findings and Suggestions on the Way Forward: A Study of National Policies, European Commission, Brussels, 2013.
6   Irene Bloemraad, Anna Korteweg & Gökçe Yurdakul, 'Citizenship and immigration: Multiculturalism, assimilation, and challenges to the nation-state', Annual Review of Sociology, 34(1), 2008, pp. 153–79.
7   Esuna Dugarova, Social Inclusion, Poverty Eradication and the 2030 Agenda for Sustainable Development, Working Paper no. 2015-15, United Nations Research Institute for Social Development (UNRISD), Geneva, 2015, p. 2.
8   Ibid.
9   Ibid., p. 1.
10 Frazer & Marlier.

11 Otto Hospes & Joy Clancy, 'Unpacking the discourse of social inclusion in value chains', in Bert Helmsing & Sietze Vellema (eds), *Value Chains, Inclusion and Endogenous Development: Contrasting Theories and Realities*, Routledge, London, 2011, pp. 23–41.
12 Jocelyne Cesari, 'Islam in France: The shaping of a religious minority', in Yvonne Haddad (ed.), *Muslims in the West: From Sojourners to Citizens*, Oxford University Press, 2002; Ake Sander, 'The status of Muslim communities in Sweden', in Gerd Nonneman, Tim Niblock & Bogdan Szajkowski (eds), *Muslim Communities in the New Europe*, Ithaca, London, 1996; Michael Humphrey, 'Muslim communities in Australia', in Abdullah Saeed & Shahram Akbarzadeh (eds), *Muslim Communities in Australia*, UNSW Press, Sydney, 2001.
13 Ryan Edwards, *Muslim Community Organisations and Leadership in Australia*, PhD dissertation, Asia Institute, Faculty of Arts, University of Melbourne, 2018, p. 47.
14 Shahram Akbarzadeh, 'Investing in mentoring and educational initiatives: The limits of deradicalisation programmes in Australia', *Journal of Muslim Minority Affairs*, 33(4), 2014, pp. 451–63; Semiha Sözeri, Hülya Kosar Altinyelken & Monique Volman, 'Training imams in the Netherlands: The failure of a post-secular endeavour', 41(4), 2018, pp. 435–45.
15 Jørgen Nielsen, *Muslims in Western Europe*, Edinburgh University Press, 1992.
16 Ibid.
17 Ibid.
18 Ibid.
19 Olivier Roy, 'EuroIslam: The jihad within?', *National Interest*, 71, 2003, pp. 63–73.
20 Nielsen, p. 153.
21 Yvonne Haddad & Jane Smith, 'Introduction', in Yvonne Haddad & Jane Smith (eds), *Muslim Minorities in the West: Visible and Invisible*, AltaMira Press, Walnut Creek, CA, 2002, pp. v–xviii.
22 Gary David & Kenneth Ayouby, 'Being Arab and becoming Americanized: Forms of mediated assimilation in metropolitan Detroit', in Haddad & Smith (eds), pp. 125–42.
23 Pierre Van Den Berghe, *The Ethnic Phenomenon*, Elsevier, Westport, CT, 1981, p. 215.
24 Sander.
25 Ibid., p. 272.
26 Ibid., p. 273.
27 Ibid., p. 274.
28 Muhammad Anwar, 'Religious identity in plural societies: The case of Britain', *Journal of the Institute of Muslim Minority Affairs*, 2(2–3), 1987, pp. 23–32.
29 Muhammad Anwar, *Pakistanis in Britain: A Sociological Study*, New Canterbury, London, 1985, p. 110.
30 Ibid., p. 9.
31 Rosalie Atie, Kevin Dunn & Mehmet Ozalp, 'Religiosity, attitudes on diversity and belonging among ordinary Australian Muslims', *Australian Journal of Islamic Studies*, 2(1), 2017, p. 12.
32 Mario Peucker, Joshua Roose & Shahram Akbarzadeh, 'Muslim active citizenship in Australia: Socioeconomic challenges and the emergence of a Muslim elite', *Australian Journal of Political Science*, 49(2), 2014, p. 283.
33 Esuna Dugarova & Tom Lavers, *Social Inclusion and the Post-2015 Sustainable Development Agenda*, Paper Prepared for UNITAR's Briefing for UN Delegates on Post-2015 Development Agenda: Social Inclusion, UNRISD, Geneva, 2014.
34 United Nations Research Institute for Social Development, *Transformative Social Policy: Lessons from UNRISD Research*, Research and Policy Brief no. 5, UNRISD,

Geneva, 2006.
35 Andrew Pearse & Matthias Stiefel, *Inquiry into Participation: A Research Approach*, UNRISD, Geneva, 1979, pp. 7–8.
36 Atie, Dunn & Ozalp, p. 10.
37 Michael Humphrey, 'Securitisation and domestication of diaspora Muslims and Islam: Turkish immigrants in Germany and Australia', *International Journal on Multicultural Societies*, 11(2), 2009, pp. 136–54.
38 Peucker, Roose & Akbarzadeh, p. 288.
39 Ibid.

Chapter 6: The formal accommodation of sharia in Australia

1 In Arabic, 's.w.t.' means *subhanahu wa ta'ala* ('the most glorified, the most high'). It is often said or written alongside 'Allah'.
2 Abdul Ansari, 'Preface', in Abdul Ansari (ed.), *Contemporary Issues in Islamic Law*, Serials Publications, New Delhi, 2011, p. vii.
3 Jan Ali, *Islamic Revivalism Encounters the Modern World: A Study of the Tabligh Jama'at*, Sterling, New Delhi, 2012.
4 Jacquelyn Hole, 'Muslim group wants sharia law in Australia', ABC News, 17 May 2011. https://www.abc.net.au/news/2011-05-17/muslim-group-wants-sharia-law-in-australia/2717096
5 'Call for parts of sharia law in Australia', ABC News, 8 March 2010. https://www.abc.net.au/news/2010-03-08/call-for-parts-of-sharia-law-in-australia/354906
6 Sami Zubaida, *Law and Power in the Islamic World*, IB Tauris, London, 2010, p. 2
7 Suha Taji-Farouki, *A Fundamental Quest: Hizb al-Tahrir and the Search for the Islamic Caliphate*, Grey Seal, London, 1996.
8 Jan Ali & Elisa Orofino, 'Islamic revivalist movements in the modern world: An analysis of Al-Ikhwan al-Muslimun, Tabligh Jama'at, and Hizb ut-Tahrir', *Journal for the Academic Study of Religion*, 31(1), 2018, pp. 27–54.
9 Jan Ali, 'Social construction of jihad and human dignity in the language of ISIS', in Fethi Mansouri & Zuleyha Keskin (eds), *Contesting the Theological Foundations of Islamism and Violent Extremism*, Palgrave Macmillan, New York, 2018, pp. 53–72.
10 Joseph Schacht, *An Introduction to Islamic Law*, Clarendon Press, Oxford, 1964; Noel Coulson, *A History of Islamic Law*, Edinburgh University Press, 1964.
11 Baber Johansen, *The Islamic Law on Land Tax and Rent: The Peasants' Loss of Property Rights as Interpreted in the Hanafite Legal Literature of the Mamluk and Ottoman Periods*, Croom Helm, London, 1988.
12 Adis Duderija, 'Critical-progressive Muslim thought: Reflections on its political ramifications', *Review of Faith & International Affairs*, 11(3), 2013, pp. 69–79.
13 Ziauddin Sardar, 'Rethinking Islam', *Journal of Futures Studies*, 6(4), 2002, pp. 117–24; Mohammad Arkoun, *The Unthought in Contemporary Islamic Thought*, al-Saqi Books, London, 2002.
14 Mohammad Hashim Kamali, *Shari'ah Law: An Introduction*, Oneworld, Oxford, 2008.
15 Qur'an, Chapter 45, Verse 18.
16 Mohammad Hashim Kamali, *An Introduction to Shari'ah*, Ilmiah, Kuala Lumpur, 2006.
17 Coulson.
18 Asifa Quraishi, 'What if sharia weren't the enemy: Rethinking international women's rights advocacy on Islamic law', *Columbia Journal of Gender and Law*, 22(1), 2011, p. 203.
19 Qur'an, Chapter 45, Verse 18.
20 Kamali, 2008.
21 Jan Otto, *Sharia and National Law in Muslim Countries: Tensions and Opportunities for*

Dutch and EU Foreign Policy, Amsterdam University Press, 2008.
22 Ebrahim Moosa, 'Allegory of the rule (hukm): Law as simulacrum in Islam?', *History of Religions*, 38(1), 1998, pp. 1–24.
23 Ism'ail Raji al Faruqi, *The Cultural Atlas of Islam*, Al-Saadawi, London, 1986, p. 246.
24 Wael Hallaq, *The Origins and Evolution of Islamic Law*, Cambridge University Press, 2005, p. 21.
25 Amanullah Fahad, *Sources and Principles of Islamic Law: A Study of Islamic Fiqh*, Jnanada Prakashan, New Delhi, 2009, p. 25.
26 Qur'an, Chapter 6, Verse 57.
27 Qur'an, Chapter 5, Verse 44.
28 Abdul Ansari & Saad Elgasim, 'Command theory of legal positivism and Hukum Shar'i: A comparison', in Ansari (ed.), p. 85.
29 Dominic McGoldrick, 'Accommodating Muslims in Europe: From adopting sharia law to religiously based opt outs from generally applicable law', *Human Rights Law Review*, 9(4), 2009, p. 605.
30 Zubaida, p. 4.
31 Max Weber, *Economy and Society* (Guenther Roth & Claus Wittich, eds), Bedminister, New York, 1968.
32 Qur'an, Chapter 4, Verse 59.
33 Fahad.
34 Sunan Ibn Majah, Vol. 1, Book 1, Hadith 10.
35 Fahad, p. v.
36 Khaled Abou El Fadl, *The Great Theft: Wrestling Islam from the Extremists*, HarperOne, San Francisco, 2007, p. 150.
37 Ghena Krayem, *Islamic Family Law in Australia: To Recognise or Not to Recognise*, Melbourne University Publishing, 2014.
38 Joint Standing Committee on Foreign Affairs, Defence and Trade, 'Federal protection of freedom of religion or belief', in *Interim Report: Legal Foundations of Religious Freedom in Australia*, Parliament of the Commonwealth of Australia, Canberra, 2017, pp. 31–50. https://www.aph.gov.au/Parliamentary_Business/Committees/Joint/Foreign_Affairs_Defence_and_Trade/Freedomofreligion/Interim_Report
39 Ann Black & Kerrie Sadiq, 'Good and bad sharia: Australia's mixed response to Islamic law', *UNSW Law Journal*, 34(1), 2011, p. 399.
40 *Mahr* is an Islamic legal requirement of payment from the husband or his family to the wife at the time of Islamic marriage.
41 Julie Posetti, 'Jihad sheilas or media martyrs: Muslim women and the media', in Halim Rane, Jacqui Ewart & Mohamad Abdalla (eds.), *Islam and the Australian News Media*, Melbourne University Publishing, 2010, pp. 69–70.
42 In July 2011, the New South Wales premier, Barry O'Farrell, declared that his cabinet was in the process of drafting new laws that would empower police to be able to force people to remove full face coverings. It was named the Identification Legislation amendment Act 2011 (NSW) and was passed on 15 September 2011.
43 Cory Bernardi, 'Burka bandits justify a burka ban', ABC News, 6 May 2010. http://www.abc.net.au/unleashed/33978.html
44 Fred Nile, 'An open society has no place for the burqa', *Sydney Morning Herald*, 20 May 2010. http://www.smh.com.au/opinion/politics/an-open-society-has-no-place-for-the-burqa-20100519-vezj.html
45 Helen McCue & Ghena Krayem, '*Shari'a* and Muslim women's agency in a multicultural context: Recent changes in sports culture', in Adam Possamai, James Richardson & Bryan Turner (eds), *The Sociology of Shari'a: Case Studies from Around the World*, Springer, London, 2015, pp. 103–18.

46   Qur'an, Chapter 24, Verses 30–31.
47   Katherine Bullock, *Rethinking Muslim Women and the Veil: Challenging Historical and Modern Stereotypes*, International Institute of Islamic Thought, London, 2002, p. 39.
48   Ghena Krayem, *Freedom of Religion, Belief and Gender: A Muslim Perspective*, Supplementary Paper Attached to: Freedom of Religion and Belief in the 21st Century, Report for Australian Human Rights Commission, Sydney, 2010.
49   Possamai, Richardson & Turner, 2017.
50   Ali.
51   Ibid.
52   Ibid.
53   Riaz Hassan, *Australian Muslims: A Demographic, Social and Economic Profile of Muslims in Australia*, International Centre for Muslim and Non-Muslim Understanding, University of South Australia, Adelaide, 2015.
54   Ann Black, 'In the shadow of our legal system: Shari'a in Australia', in Rex Ahdar & Nicholas Aroney (eds), *Sharia in the West*, Oxford University Press, 2010, pp. 239–54; Erich Kolig, 'To shari'aticize or not to shari'aticize: Islamic and secular law in liberal democratic society', in Ahdar & Aroney (eds), pp. 255–78.
55   Fahad.
56   Zubaida.
57   Ibid., pp. 159–60.
58   Bernard Botiveau, *Loi islamique et droit dans les societes arabes: Mutations des systemes juridiques du Moyen-Orient*, Karthala-IREMAM, Paris & Aix-en-Provence, 1993.
59   Jan Ali, 'Muslim schools in Australia: Development and transition', in Mohamad Abdalla, Dylan Chow & Muhammad Abdullah (eds), *Islamic Schooling in the West: Pathways to Renewal*, Palgrave Macmillan, New York, 2018, pp. 35–62.
60   Adam Possamai, Selda Dagistanli & Malcolm Voyce, 'Shari'a in everyday life in Sydney: An analysis of professionals and leaders dealing with Islamic law', *Journal for the Academic Study of Religion*, 30(2), 2017, pp. 109–28.
61   Wael Hallaq, *An Introduction to Islamic Law*, Cambridge University Press, 2009, p. 57.
62   Ann Black, 'Replicating "a model of mutual respect": Could Singapore's legal pluralism work in Australia?', *Journal of Legal Pluralism and Unofficial Law*, 44(65) 2012, p. 82.
63   Ann Black, 'Accommodating shariah law in Australia's legal system: Can we? Should we ?', *Alternative Law Journal*, 33, 2008, pp. 2–7.

Chapter 7: The role of Muslim clergy in Australia
1   In this book, Muslim clergy (religious experts or individuals knowledgeable in matters of Islamic theology) includes muftis (Muslim legal experts), sheikhs (Muslim scholars) and imams (prayer leaders and religious guides).
2   Hadi Sohrabi, 'Identity and Muslim leadership: The case of Australian Muslim leaders', *Contemporary Islam*, 10(1), 2015, p. 1.
3   Malise Ruthven, *Islam: A Very Short Introduction*, Oxford University Press, 1997.
4   Abdulkader Tayob, *Islam in South Africa: Mosques, Imams, and Sermons*, University Press of Florida, Gainesville, 1999.
5   Michael Humphrey, 'Community, mosque and ethnic politics', in Abe Ata (ed.), *Religion and Ethnic Identity: An Australian Study*, Spectrum, Melbourne, 1988, pp. 255–69.
6   Paul Tabar, Greg Noble & Scott Poynting, 'The rise and falter of the field of ethnic politics in Australia: The case of Lebanese community leadership', *Journal of Intercultural Studies*, 24(3), 2003, pp. 267–8.
7   Humphrey, 1988.

8   Michael Humphrey, 'Community, mosque and ethnic politics', *Australian and New Zealand Journal of Sociology*, 23(2), 1987, p. 236.
9   George Williams, 'The laws that erode who we are', *Sydney Morning Herald*, Sydney, 10–11 September 2011, p. 22.
10 Michael Humphrey, 'Securitisation, social inclusion and Muslims in Australia', in Samina Yasmeen (ed.), *Muslims in Australia: The Dynamics of Exclusion and Inclusion*, Melbourne University Publishing, 2010, pp. 56–78.
11 Sohrabi; Kevin Andrews, 'Australian government initiatives for social cohesion', in James Jupp, John Nieuwenhuysen & Emma Dawson (eds.), *Social Cohesion in Australia*, Cambridge University Press, New York, 2007, pp. 45–58.
12 Ibid.
13 Shafiur Rahman, Syed Tohel Ahmed & Shaynul Khan, *Voices from the Minaret: MCB Study of UK Imams and Mosques*, Muslim Council of Britain & C3ube Training and Consultancy, London, 2006.
14 Jean-François Husson, *Training Imams in Europe: The Current Status*, King Baudouin Foundation, Brussels, 2007.
15 'Unity declared only way to defeat terrorism', *Sydney Morning Herald*, 24 August 2005. https://www.smh.com.au/national/unity-declared-only-way-to-defeat-terrorism-20050824-gdlxor.html
16 Andrews.
17 Ameer Ali, *Building on Social Cohesion, Harmony and Security: An Action Plan by the Muslim Community Reference Group*, Muslim Community Reference Group, Canberra, 2006.
18 Sohrabi.
19 Commonwealth of Australia, *2016 Census of Population and Housing: Reflecting Australia: Stories from the 2016 Census*, Catalogue No.2071.0, Australian Bureau of Statistics, Canberra, 2017.
20 Riaz Hassan, *Australian Muslims: A Demographic, Social and Economic Profile of Muslims in Australia*, International Centre for Muslim and Non-Muslim Understanding, University of South Australia, Adelaide, 2015, p. 19.
21 Humphrey, 1988.
22 Fuad Khuri, *From Village to Suburb: Order and Change in Greater Beirut*, University of Chicago Press, 1976.
23 Mohamad Abdalla is a professor and the director of the Centre for Islamic Thought and Education in the School of Education at the University of South Australia.
24 Jørgen Nielsen, *Emerging Claims of Muslim Populations in Matters of Family Law in Europe*, Centre for the Study of Islam and Christian Muslim Relations, Birmingham, 1993; David Pearl, *Family Law and the Immigrant Communities*, Jordan & Sons, Bristol, 1986; Sebastian Poulter, *English Law and Ethnic Minority Customs*, Butterworth, London, 1986; Jan Rath, Kees Groenedijk & Rinos Penninx, 'The recognition and institutionalisation of Islam in Belgium, Great Britain and the Netherlands', *New Community*, 18(1), 1995, pp. 101–14.
25 Bustami Khir, 'Who applies Islamic law in non-Muslim countries? A study of the Sunni principle of the governance of the scholars (Wilyat al-'Ulama')', *Journal of Muslim Minority Affairs*, 27(1), 2007, pp. 78–91.
26 Kamal al-Dın Ibn al-Humam, *Sharh Fath al-Qadır* (The Bounty of the Mighty: A Commentary on Legal Issues), vol. 7, Dar al-Kutub al-'Ilmiyya, Beirut, 1995, p. 246.
27 Sophie Gilliat-Ray, *Muslims in Britain: An Introduction*, Cambridge University Press, 2010, p. 169.
28 Ryan Edwards, *Muslim Community Organisations and Leadership in Australia*, PhD dissertation, Asia Institute, Faculty of Arts, University of Melbourne, 2018, p. 116.

29 Hadi Sohrabi, 'Islam and community organisation in Australia', in Mario Peucker & Rauf Ceylan (eds), *Muslim Community Organisations in the West: History, Developments and Future Perspectives*, Springer, Wiesbaden, 2017, p. 212.
30 Australian National Imams Council, 'Find your local imam', n.d. https://www.anic.org.au/find-your-local-imam/
31 Brianna Roberts, 'Calls for registry to weed out "fake sheikhs"', SBS News, 14 January 2015. https://www.sbs.com.au/news/calls-for-registry-to-weed-out-fake-sheikhs
32 Ibid.
33 Mansur Ali, 'Muslim chaplaincy as a model for imamship', in Mohammed Hashas, Jan Jaap de Ruiter & Niels Valdemar Vinding (eds), *Imams in Western Europe: Developments, Transformations, and Institutional Challenges*, Amsterdam University Press, Leiden, 2018, pp. 295–314.
34 Sami Zubaida, *Law and Power in the Islamic World*, IB Tauris, London, 2003.
35 Ghena Krayem, *Islamic Family Law in Australia: To Recognise or Not to Recognise*, Melbourne University Publishing, 2014.
36 Riaz Hassan, *Australian Muslims: The Challenge of Islamophobia and Social Distance*, International Centre for Muslim and non-Muslim Understanding, University of South Australia, Adelaide, 2018. In his study Hassan found that 'About 83% of Australian Muslims report good or very good proficiency in the English language' (p. 11).
37 Nora Amath, '"We're serving the community, in whichever form it may be": Muslim community building in Australia', in Peucker & Ceylan (eds), p. 119.

Chapter 8: Origins and development of Muslim schools

1 Michael Humphrey, 'An Australian Islam? Religion in the multicultural city', in Abdullah Saeed & Shahram Akbarzadeh (eds), *Muslim Communities in Australia*, UNSW Press, Sydney, 2001, pp. 33–52.
2 Peter Jones, 'Islamic schools in Australia', *La Trobe Journal*, 89, 2012a, p. 38.
3 Aminah Mah, *Counselling and Wellbeing Support Services in Australian Muslim Schools*, doctoral dissertation, University of Western Australia, Perth, 2015.
4 Chris Hewer, 'Schools for Muslims', *Oxford Review of Education*, 27(4), 2001, p. 518.
5 Irene Donohoue Clyne, 'Educating Muslim children in Australia', in Saeed & Akbarzadeh (eds), pp. 116–37; Mahmoud Eid, *Public Schools or Islamic Colleges? Factors Impacting on Parental Choice of Schooling for Muslim Children*, doctoral dissertation, Edith Cowan University, Perth, 2008.
6 Sadaf Rizvi, 'How Muslim faith schools are teaching tolerance and respect through "Islamicised" curriculum', *The Conversation*, 15 October 2014. https://theconversation.com/how-muslim-faith-schools-are-teaching-tolerance-and-respect-through-islamicised-curriculum-32239
7 Irene Donohoue Clyne, 'Seeking education for Muslim children in Australia', *Muslim Education Quarterly*, 14(3), 1997, pp. 4–18.
8 Manar Chelebi, *The Australian Muslim Student*, David Barlow Publishing, Sydney, 2008.
9 Silma Ihram, Operations Manager at The Pharmacy Collective. https://au.linkedin.com/in/pharmacycollective
10 Ayda Succarie, Wayne Fallon & Gabriela Coronado, 'Towards a hybrid approach to the governance of Islamic schools in NSW', in Mohamad Abdalla, Dylan Chown & Muhammad Abdullah (eds), *Islamic Schooling in the West: Pathways to Renewal*, Palgrave, London, 2018, p. 66.
11 Jones, 2012a, p. 40.

12 Succarie, Fallon & Coronado, p. 66.
13 Eid.
14 Chelebi.
15 Jones, 2012a, p. 42.
16 Ibid.
17 Mah.
18 Jones, 2012a, p. 40.
19 Mah.
20 Jones, 2012a.
21 Mah.
22 Peter Jones, *Islamic Schools in Australia: Muslims in Australia or Australian Muslims?*, doctoral dissertation, University of New England, Sydney, 2012b.
23 Mah, p. 169.
24 Clyne, 2001, p. 117.
25 Linda Morris, 'Islam leads in rush to faith education', *Sydney Morning Herald*, 23 June 2003. https://www.smh.com.au/education/islam-leads-in-rush-to-faith-education-20030623-gdgz3g.html
26 Mark Sedgwick, *Making European Muslims: Religious Socialization Among Young Muslims in Scandinavia and Western Europe*, Routledge, UK, 2014, p. 241.
27 Ibrahima Diallo, *The Role and Importance of Islamic Studies and Faith in Community Islamic Schools in Australia: A Case Study of Adelaide (SA) and Darwin (NT), October 2016*, Research Centre for Languages and Cultures, University of South Australia, Adelaide, 2016, p. 13.
28 Rizvi.
29 Janet Phillips, 'Muslim Australians', E-Brief: Online Only issued 6 March 2007, Australian Government, 2007. https://www.aph.gov.au/About_Parliament/Parliamentary_Departments/Parliamentary_Library/Publications_Archive/archive/MuslimAustralians
30 Michael Merry & Geert Driessen, 'Islamic schools in three Western countries: Policy and procedure', *Comparative Education*, 41(4), 2005, p. 426.
31 Muhammad Musharraf & Fatima Nabeel, 'Schooling options for Muslim children living in Muslim-minority countries: A thematic literature review', *International Journal of Social Science and Humanities Research*, 3(4), 2015, p. 38.
32 Saied Ameli, Aliya Azam & Arzu Merali, *British Muslims' Expectations of the Government: Secular or Islamic? What Schools Do British Muslims Want for Their Children?*, Islamic Human Rights Commission, Wembley, 2005, p. 9.
33 Musharraf & Nabeel, p. 39.
34 Jones, 2012a, p. 36.
35 Ibid.
36 Michael Merry, *Culture, Identity, and Islamic Schooling: A Philosophical Approach*, Palgrave Macmillan, New York, 2007, p. 20.
37 Jones, 2012a, p. 36.
38 Mah, p. 88.
39 Ibid.; Clyne, 2001.
40 Asad Zaman, 'Developing an Islamic world view: An essential component of an Islamic education', *Lahore Journal of Policy Studies*, 1(1), 2007, p. 95.
41 Musharraf & Nabeel.
42 Saeeda Shah, 'Muslim schools in secular societies: Persistence or resistance!', *British Journal of Religious Education*, 34(1), 2012, p. 61.

Chapter 9: Islamic studies in Australia

1. Léon Buskens, 'Introduction: Dichotomies, transformations, and continuities in the study of Islam', in Léon Buskens & Annemarie van Sandwijk (eds), *Islamic Studies in the Twenty-first Century: Transformations and Continuities*, Amsterdam University Press, 2016, pp. 11–27.
2. Nidhal Guessoum, 'The Qur'an, science, and the (related) contemporary Muslim discourse', *Zygon: Journal of Religion and Science*, 43(2), 2008, p. 413.
3. Ira Lapidus, *A History of Islamic Societies*, Cambridge University Press, 2014.
4. Qur'an, Al-Mujadilah 58: 11.
5. Qur'an, Ta-Ha 20: 114.
6. Qur'an, Al-Baqarah 2: 282.
7. Qur'an, Al-Baqarah 2: 31.
8. Qur'an, Ya-Seen 39: 9.
9. Qur'an, Al-Alaq 96: 1–5.
10. Qur'an, Al-Baqarah 2:164.
11. Sunan Ibn Maajah, Vol. 1, Book 1, Hadith 224.
12. Robert Hefner & Muhammad Zaman, 'Introduction: The culture, politics, and future of Muslim education', in Robert Hefner & Muhammad Zaman (eds), *Schooling Islam: The Culture and Politics of Modern Muslim Education*, Princeton University Press, 2007, pp. 1–39.
13. Lapidus.
14. Jonathan Berkey, *The Transmission of Knowledge in Medieval Cairo: A Social History of Islamic Education*, Princeton University Press, 1992.
15. Dietrich Reetz, 'From madrasa to university: The challenges and formats of Islamic education', in Akbar Ahmed & Tamara Sonn (eds), *The Sage Handbook of Islamic Studies*, Sage, LA, 2010, pp. 106–39.
16. Ebrahim Moosa, *What is a Madrasa?*, University of North Carolina Press, Chapel Hill, 2015.
17. Ibid., p. 108.
18. Michael Chamberlain, *Knowledge and Social Practice in Medieval Damascus, 1190–1350*, Cambridge University Press, 1994.
19. Muhammad Zaman, 'Ulama', in Gerhard Bowering (ed.), *Islamic Political Thought: An Introduction*, Princeton University Press, 2015, pp. 252–62.
20. Carl Boyer, *A History of Mathematics*, Princeton University Press, 1985; John Esposito, *The Oxford History of Islam*, Oxford University Press, 1999.
21. Chamberlain.
22. George Makdisi, 'Madrasa and university in the Middle Ages', *Studia Islamica*, 32, 1970, pp. 255–64.
23. Reetz.
24. Gerhard Bowering, 'Introduction', in Bowering (ed.), p. 2.
25. Jan Ali, 'Australian Muslims as radicalized "Other" and their experiences of social exclusion', in Abe Ata & Jan Ali (eds), *Islam in the West: Perceptions and Reactions*, Oxford University Press, New Delhi, 2018, pp. 108–28.
26. Fethi Mansouri & Annelies Kamp, 'Structural deficiency or cultural racism: The educational and social experiences of Arab-Australian youth', *Australian Journal of Social Issues*, 42(1), 2007, pp. 87–102.
27. Shahram Akbarzadeh et al., *Australian-based Studies on Islam and Muslim Societies*, report sponsored by Australian Research Council Seed-funding, Monash University, Melbourne, 2004, p. 3.
28. Mohammad Kamali & Zarina Nalla, 'The teaching of Islam in Western universities: Reflections and impressions', in Paul Morris et al. (eds), *The Teaching and Study of*

Islam in Western Universities, Routledge, London, 2014, p. 67.
29 Akbarzadeh et al., p. 3.
30 Emily Daina Saras & Lara Perez-Felkner, 'Sociological perspectives on socialization', Oxford Bibliographies Online, 2018. DOI: 10.1093/OBO/9780199756384-0155 https://www.oxfordbibliographies.com/view/document/obo-9780199756384/obo-9780199756384-0155.xml
31 Morris et al.

Chapter 10: Radicalised Muslim 'Other' and countering violent extremism

1 Marieke Slootman & Jean Tillie, *Processes of Radicalisation: Why Some Amsterdam Muslims Become Radicals*, Institute for Migration and Ethnic Studies, Universiteit van Amsterdam, 2006; Mitchell Silber & Arvin Bhatt, *Radicalization in the West: The Homegrown Threat*, New York City Police Department, 2007.
2 Mitchel Dean, *Governmentality: Power and Rule in Modern Society*, Sage, London, 1999.
3 Nikolas Rose, *Powers of Freedom: Reframing Political Thought*, Cambridge University Press, 1999.
4 Ulrich Beck, *Risk Society: Towards a New Modernity* (trans. Mark Ritter), Sage, London, 1992; Ulrich Beck, *World Risk Society*, Blackwell, Cambridge, 1999.
5 Charlotte Heath-Kelly, 'Counter-terrorism and the counterfactual: Producing the "radicalisation" discourse and the UK PREVENT strategy', *British Journal of Politics and International Relations*, 15, 2013, pp. 394–415.
6 Claudia Aradau & Rens van Munster, 'Taming the future: The dispositif of risk in the war on terror', in Louise Amoore & Marieke De Goede (eds), *Risk and the War on Terror*, Routledge, Abingdon, 2008, pp. 23–40.
7 Gabe Mythen & Sandra Walklate, 'Criminology and terrorism: Which thesis? Risk society or governmentality?', *British Journal of Criminology*, 2005, 46(3), pp. 379–98.
8 Louise Amoore & Marieke De Goede, 'Introduction: Governing by risk in the war on terror', in Amoore & De Goede (eds), pp. 5–19.
9 Shahram Akbarzadeh, 'Investing in mentoring and educational initiatives: The limits of de-radicalisation programmes in Australia', *Journal of Muslim Minority Affairs*, 33(4), 2014, pp. 451–63.
10 Faisal Kutty, 'Issues in Islam: Islamists and the West: Co-existence or confrontation?', *Washington Report on Middle East Affairs*, 14(6), 1996, p. 34.
11 Ibid.
12 Abiodun Alao, 'Islamic radicalisation and violent extremism in Nigeria', *Conflict, Security & Development*, 13(2), 2013, pp. 127–47.
13 Rem Korteweg et al., 'Background contributing factors to terrorism: Radicalisation and recruitment', in Magnus Ranstorp (ed.), *Understanding Violent Radicalisation: Terrorist and Jihadist Movements in Europe*, Routledge, London, 2010, p. 31.
14 Tahir Abbas, 'Introduction: Islamic political radicalism in Western Europe', in Tahir Abbas (ed.), *Islamic Political Radicalism: A European Perspective*, Edinburgh University Press, 2007a, pp. 3–14.
15 Kutty, p. 34.
16 George Joffé, 'Introduction: Radicalisation and the Arab Spring', in George Joffé (ed.), *Islamist Radicalisation in Europe and the Middle East: Reassessing the Causes of Terrorism*, IB Tauris, London, 2013, pp. 2–3.
17 Tahir Abbas, 'A theory of Islamic political radicalism in Britain: Sociology, theology and international political economy', *Contemporary Islam*, 1(2), 2007b, p. 110.
18 Alao, p. 138.
19 I acknowledge that the West is not a homogeneous entity and that many Western countries differ from one another, particularly culturally and in terms of their

political system. When I refer to the West, my focus is particularly on countries' common secular democratic capitalist framework.
20 By functional Othering, I mean that the process of Othering assumes a function in the society that works at the coalface.
21 Sue Kenny, 'Risk society and the Islamic Other', in Shahram Akbarzadeh & Fethi Mansouri (eds), *Islam and Political Violence: Muslim Diaspora and Radicalism in the West*, IB Tauris, London, 2007, pp. 87–106.
22 Deborah Lupton, 'Dangerous places and the unpredictable stranger: Constructions of fear of crime', *Australian and New Zealand Journal of Criminology*, 32(1), 1999, pp. 1–15.
23 Mike Crang, *Cultural Geography*, Routledge, London, 1998, p. 61.
24 Lajos Brons, 'Othering: An analysis', *Transcience*, 6(1), 2015, p. 70.
25 Akbarzadeh, p. 452. The Battle of Broken Hill (1915) in New South Wales, where two Muslim men shot dead four Australians and wounded seven others on 1 January 1915, before the police and military officers killed them, is sometimes referred to as the first Muslim terrorist attack on Australian soil. It has been noted that the shooting was politically and religiously motivated, but the men were not members of any recognised religious or political movement and their acts were considered as criminal rather than terrorist. Shakira Hussein asserts that 'Investigations into these incidents are ongoing, as are heated debates as to whether they were motivated by religion, the fallout of distant wars, psychiatric illness, or the experience of racism' ('Battle of Broken Hill finds a resonance in terrorist incidents', *The Australian*, 24 January 2015). http://www.theaustralian.com.au/arts/review/battle-of-broken-hill-finds-a-resonance-in-terrorist-incidents/news-story/7a5da1b61d59032795cb37cb273dd037
26 George Williams, 'The legal legacy of the "war on terror"', *Macquarie Law Journal*, 12, 2013, pp. 6–7.
27 Ibid.
28 Kent Roach, *The 9/11 Effect: Comparative Counter-Terrorism*, Cambridge University Press, 2011, p. 309.
29 Nicola McGarrity, '"Let the punishment match the offence": Determining sentences for Australian terrorists', *International Journal for Crime, Justice and Social Democracy*, 2(1), 2013, p. 18.
30 Nada Roude, *Australian Muslim Leaders' Perspectives on Countering Violent Extremism: Towards Developing a Best Practice Model for Engaging the Muslim Community*, PhD dissertation, School of Theology, Faculty of Arts and Education, Charles Sturt University, Sydney, 2017, p. 77.
31 Lise Waldek & Julian Droogan, 'Partnering to build solutions: 2014 Countering Violent Extremism Symposium, Sydney', *Journal of Policing, Intelligence and Counter Terrorism*, 10(1), 2015, pp. 39–47.
32 Jonathan Matusitz, *Terrorism and Communication: A Critical Introduction*, Sage, LA, 2013, p. 21.
33 Australian Government, *Countering Violent Extremism*, Department of Home Affairs, Canberra, 2019. https://www.homeaffairs.gov.au/about-us/our-portfolios/national-security/countering-extremism-and-terrorism/countering-violent-extremism-(cve)
34 Akbarzadeh, p. 458. In 2017 some parts of the Attorney-General's Department were moved to the newly established Department of Home Affairs. The Countering Violent Extremism Taskforce/Unit no longer exists.
35 Department of the Prime Minister and Cabinet, *Review of Australia's Counter-Terrorism Machinery*, Commonwealth of Australia, Canberra, 2015, p. 2.
36 Ibid.

37 Ibid., p. 14.
38 Ibid., p. 16.
39 Ibid.
40 Ibid., p. 14.
41 Ibid., p. 14.
42 Ibid., pp. 13–14.
43 ABC Religion & Ethics, 'Australian Muslims denounce proposed "anti-terror" laws', 21 August 2014. https://www.abc.net.au/religion/australian-muslims-denounce-proposed-anti-terror-laws/10099066

Chapter 11: Securitised Muslims and Islam in Australia

1   Paddy Hillyard, 'The "war on terror": Lessons from Ireland', European Civil Liberties Network, Brussels, 2005; Paddy Hillyard & Janie Percy-Smith, *The Coercive State: The Decline of Democracy in Britain*, Fontana, London, 1988; Gabe Mythen, Sandra Walklate & Fatima Khan, '"I'm a Muslim, but not a terrorist":Victimization, risky identities and the performance of safety', *British Journal of Criminology*, 49(6), 2009, pp. 736–54.
2   Peter Mares, *Borderline: Australia's Treatment of Refugees and Asylum Seekers*, UNSW Press, Sydney, 2001.
3   Michael Humphrey, 'Securitisation and domestication of diaspora Muslims and Islam:Turkish immigrants in Germany and Australia', *International Journal on Multicultural Societies*, 11(2), 2009, pp. 136–54.
4   Ibid., p. 136.
5   Stanley Cohen, *Folk Devils and Moral Panics* (3rd edn), Routledge, Abingdon, 2002; Scott Poynting et al., *Bin Laden in the Suburbs: Criminalising the Arab Other*, Institute of Criminology, Sydney, 2004; Michael Welch, *Scapegoats of September 11th: Hate Crimes and State Crimes in the War on Terror*, New Rutgers University Press, New Brunswick, NJ, 2006.
6   Joanna Gilmore, 'Criminalizing dissent in the "war on terror": The British state's reaction to Gaza War protests of 2008–2009', in George Morgan & Scott Poynting (eds), *Global Islamophobia: Muslims and Moral Panic in the West*, Ashgate, Surrey, 2012, pp. 197–213.
7   Paul Silverstein, 'Immigrant racialization and the New Savage slot: Race, migration and immigration in the New Europe', *Annual Review of Anthropology*, 34, 2005, pp. 363–84.
8   Sue Kenny, 'Risk society and the Islamic Other', in Shahram Akbarzadeh & Fethi Mansouri (eds), *Islam and Political Violence: Muslim Diaspora and Radicalism in the West*, IB Tauris, London, 2007, pp. 87–106.
9   Joseph Wakim, 'The Gulf War within the Australian community and Arab Australians: Villains, victims or victors?', in Greta Bird (ed.), *Racial Harassment*, National Centre for Constitutional Studies in Law, Centre for Migrant and Intercultural Studies, Monash University, Clayton, 1992, p. 58.
10 Ayhan Kaya, *Islam, Migration and Integration: The Age of Securitization*, Palgrave, London, 2009.
11 Ibid., p. 8.
12 James Ferguson & Akhil Gupta, 'Spatializing states: Toward an ethnography of neoliberal governmentality', *American Ethnologist*, 29(4), 2002, pp. 981–1002.
13 Shahram Akbarzadeh & Gary Bouma, *Muslim Voices: Hopes and Aspirations of Muslim Australians*, Centre for Muslim Minorities and Islam Policy Studies, Monash University, Melbourne, 2009.
14 Michael Leach & Fethi Mansouri, *Lives in Limbo*, UNSW Press, Sydney, 2004, p. 124.

15 Mario Peucker, Joshua Roose & Shahram Akbarzadeh, 'Muslim active citizenship in Australia: Socioeconomic challenges and the emergence of a Muslim elite', *Australian Journal of Political Science*, 49(2), 2014, p. 288.
16 Riaz Hassan, *Australian Muslims: A Demographic, Social and Economic Profile of Muslims in Australia*, International Centre for Muslim and Non-Muslim Understanding, University of South Australia, Adelaide, 2015.
17 Australian Bureau of Statistics, *2011 Census of Housing and Population*, ABS, Canberra, 2011.
18 Hassan.
19 Ibid.
20 Tanja Dreher, *'Targeted': Experiences of Racism in NSW after September 11, 2001*, UTS Shopfront Series, University of Technology Sydney ePress, 2006, p. 1. DOI: https://doi.org/10.5130/978-1-86365-420-3
21 Greg Noble, 'The discomfort of strangers: Racism, incivility and ontological security in a comfortable and relaxed nation', *Journal of Intercultural Studies*, 26(1), 2005, p. 117.
22 Ibid.
23 Ferguson & Gupta.
24 Ibid.
25 Michel Foucault, 'Governmentality', in Graham Burchell, Colin Gordon & Peter Miller (eds), *The Foucault Effect: Studies in Governmentality*, University of Chicago Press, 1991, pp. 87–104.
26 Jef Huysmans, *The Politics of Insecurity: Fear, Migration and Asylum in the EU*, Routledge, London, 2006, p. xi.
27 Suzanne Risley, 'The sociology of security: Sociological approaches to contemporary and historical securitization', paper presented at Annual Meeting of American Sociological Association, Montreal, 2006. http://www.allacademic.com/meta/p105192_index.html
28 Kaya, 2009.
29 John Bowen, 'Two approaches to rights and religion in contemporary France', in Richard Wilson & John Mitchell (eds), *Human Rights in Global Perspective: Anthropological Studies of Rights, Claims and Entitlements*, Routledge, London, 2003, pp. 33–53.
30 Dragana Avramov, *People, Democracy, and Social Exclusion*, Population Studies Series no. 37, Council of European Publishing, Strasbourg, 2002, pp. 26–7.
31 Olivier Roy, 'Islamic terrorist radicalisation in Europe', in Samir Amghar, Amel Boubekeur & Michael Emerson (eds), *European Islam: Challenges for Public Policy and Society*, Centre for European Policy Studies, Brussels, 2007, p. 56.

Conclusion
1 Riaz Hassan, *Australian Muslims: The Challenge of Islamophobia and Social Distance*, International Centre for Muslim and non-Muslim Understanding, University of South Australia, Adelaide, 2018, p. 34.
2 Ibid., p. 94.

Glossary

ahkam	legal rulings
al-Qanun al-Islami	Islamic law
al-shari'at al-Islamiyya	Islamic law
alim	literally means 'the one who knows'; in a broader sense refers to an individual who has studied a wide range of Islamic disciplines for several years
'aql	intellect
burqa	full loose body covering
dar al-harb	abode of war; un-Islam
dar al-Islam	home or abode of Islam
dawah	preaching
fatwa	jurist's ruling; edict; legal opinion on specific point of law
fiqh	jurisprudence
fuqaha	Muslim jurists
ghusl	major canonical ablution; ritual bath
Hadith	the sayings and traditions of the Prophet Mohammed
halal	permissible
hawa	whimsical desire
hijab	veil, headscarf
hijrah	emigration of the Prophet Mohammed and his followers from Makkah to the city of Medina (formerly known as Yathrib) in 622 BCE
'ibadat	worship; private worship; ritual
ijaza	a licence to transmit a certain text or subject
ijma	scholarly or juristic consensus in which scholars and jurists rely on *'aql* to generate general principles based on the Qur'an and Sunna
ijtihad	independent reasoning

'ilm	knowledge
imam	the Prophet's chosen successor; Muslim prayer leader; religious guide
istinbat	inference
janaza	Islamic burial
jum'ah	Friday congregational prayer
kalam	Islamic scholastic theology
khatib	a figure who proclaims the *khutba* during the Friday congregational prayer and on other special occasions, such as during the month of Ramadan
khutba	sermon
madhab	jurisprudential school
madrasa	educational institution
maharim (singular: *mihram*)	close male kin before whom one can appear without observing hijab, and whom one cannot marry
mahr	dower; dowry
maktab	elementary school, often attached to a mosque
mu'amalat	social relations and human transactions
mufti	Islamic scholar with authority to issue fatwas; Muslim legal expert
mullah	a person who possesses religious knowledge or charisma
musalla	place for prayer
nikah	marriage
niqab	face covering
qadis	magistrate or judge of a sharia court
qari	reciter of the Qur'an
qira'at	Qur'anic recitation
qiyas	reasoning by analogy
ray	juristic opinion
sawm	fasting
sharia	Islamic law
sheikh	Muslim theologian or scholar; a learned person who plays an institutional role
shura	consultative committee
siraat al mustaqeem	the right path
Sunna	tradition; words, deeds and actions of the Prophet Mohammed, and his implicit approval or disapproval of others' actions around him
tafsir	Qur'anic exegesis
talaq	divorce
taqwa	piety

tawhid	unity of God
ulama/ulema (singular: *alim*)	Muslim scholars; religious scholars
ummah	community of believers; Muslim community
waqf	charitable endowment
zakat	alms

Bibliography

Abbas, Tahir, 'Introduction: Islamic political radicalism in Western Europe', in Tahir Abbas (ed.), *Islamic Political Radicalism: A European Perspective*, Edinburgh University Press, 2007, pp. 3–14.
—— 'A theory of Islamic political radicalism in Britain: Sociology, theology and international political economy', *Contemporary Islam*, 1(2), 2007, pp. 109–22.
ABC Religion & Ethics, 'Australian Muslims denounce proposed "anti-terror" laws', 21 August 2014. https://www.abc.net.au/religion/australian-muslims-denounce-proposed-anti-terror-laws/10099066
Abdalla, Mohamad, Chown, Dylan & Abdullah, Muhammad (eds), *Islamic Schooling in the West: Pathways to Renewal*, Palgrave, London, 2018.
Abou El Fadl, Khaled, *The Great Theft: Wrestling Islam from the Extremists*, HarperOne, San Francisco, 2007.
Ahmad, Qazi, 'Islam and Muslims in Australia', in Hussin Mutalib & Taj ul-Islam Hashmi (eds), *Islam, Muslims and the Modern State: Case-Studies of Muslims in Thirteen Countries*, St Martins Press, New York, 1994, pp. 317–38.
Akbarzadeh, Shahram, 'Investing in mentoring and educational initiatives: The limits of de-radicalisation programmes in Australia', *Journal of Muslim Minority Affairs*, 33(4), 2013, pp. 451–63.
—— 'The Muslim question in Australia: Islamophobia and Muslim alienation', *Journal of Muslim Minority Affairs*, 36(3), 2016, pp. 323–33
—— 'Unity or fragmentation?', in Abdullah Saeed & Shahram Akbarzadeh (eds), *Muslim Communities in Australia*, UNSW Press, Sydney, 2001, pp. 228–34.
Akbarzadeh, Shahram & Bouma, Gary, *Muslim Voices: Hopes and Aspirations of Muslim Australians*, Centre for Muslim Minorities and Islam Policy Studies, Monash University, Melbourne, 2009.
Akbarzadeh, Shahram, Boz, T, Baxter, K, McKay, J & Mogilevski, E, *Australian-based Studies on Islam and Muslim Societies*, report sponsored by Australian Research Council Seed-funding, Monash University, Melbourne, 2004.
Alao, Abiodun, 'Islamic radicalisation and violent extremism in Nigeria', *Conflict, Security & Development*, 13(2), 2013, pp. 127–47.
Ali, Ameer, *Building on Social Cohesion, Harmony and Security: An Action Plan by the Muslim Community Reference Group*, Muslim Community Reference Group, Canberra, 2006.
Ali, Jan, 'Australian Muslims as radicalized "Other" and their experiences of social exclusion', in Abe Ata & Jan Ali (eds), *Islam in the West: Perceptions and Reactions*, Oxford University Press, New Delhi, 2018, pp. 108–28.

—— 'A dual legal system in Australia: The formalization of *shari'a*', *Democracy and Security*, 7(4), 2011, pp. 354–73.
—— *Islamic Revivalism Encounters the Modern World: A Study of the Tabligh Jama'at*, Sterling Publishers, New Delhi, 2012.
—— 'Muslim schools in Australia: Development and transition', in Mohamad Abdalla, Dylan Chow & Muhammad Abdullah (eds), *Islamic Schooling in the West: Pathways to Renewal*, Palgrave Macmillan, New York, 2018, pp. 35–62.
Ali, Jan & Orofino, Elisa, 'Islamic revivalist movements in the modern world: An analysis of Al-Ikhwan al-Muslimun, Tabligh Jama'at, and Hizb ut-Tahrir', *Journal for the Academic Study of Religion*, 31(1), 2018, pp. 27–54.
Ali, Mansur, 'Muslim chaplaincy as a model for imamship', in Mohammed Hashas, Jan Jaap de Ruiter & Niels Valdemar Vinding (eds), *Imams in Western Europe: Developments, Transformations, and Institutional Challenges*, Amsterdam University Press, Leiden, 2018, pp. 295–314.
Allman, Dan, 'The sociology of social inclusion', *SAGE Open*, 3(1), 2012, pp. 1–16.
Amath, Nora, *The Phenomenology of Community Activism: Muslim Civil Society Organisations in Australia*, Melbourne University Publishing, Carlton, 2015.
—— '"We're serving the community, in whichever form it may be": Muslim community building in Australia', in Mario Peucker & Rauf Ceylan (eds), *Muslim Community Organizations in the West: History, Developments and Future Perspectives*, Springer, Berlin, 2017, pp. 93–124.
Ameli, Saied, Azam, Aliya & Merali, Arzu, *British Muslims' Expectations of the Government: Secular or Islamic?: What Schools Do British Muslims Want for Their Children?*, Islamic Human Rights Commission, Wembley, 2005.
Amoore, Louise & De Goede, Marieke, 'Introduction: Governing by risk in the war on terror', in Louise Amoore & Marieke De Goede (eds), *Risk and the War on Terror*, Routledge, Abingdon, 2008, pp. 5–19.
Andrews, Kevin, 'Australian government initiatives for social cohesion', in James Jupp, John Nieuwenhuysen & Emma Dawson (eds.), *Social Cohesion in Australia*, Cambridge University Press, New York, 2007, pp. 45–58.
Ansari, Abdul, 'Preface', in Abdul Ansari (ed.), *Contemporary Issues in Islamic Law*, Serials Publications, New Delhi, 2011, pp. vii–xiii.
Ansari, Abdul & Elgasim, Saad, 'Command theory of legal positivism and Hukum Shar'i: A comparison', in Abdul Ansari (ed.), *Contemporary Issues in Islamic Law*, Serials Publications, New Delhi, 2011, pp. 63–97.
Anwar, Muhammad, *Pakistanis in Britain: A Sociological Study*, New Canterbury, London, 1985.
—— 'Religious identity in plural societies: The case of Britain', *Journal of the Institute of Muslim Minority Affairs*, 2(2–3), 1987, pp. 23–32.
Appleyard, Reginald, 'The population', in Alan Davies & Sol Encel (eds), *Australian Society: A Sociological Introduction* (2nd edn), Cheshire Publishing, Melbourne, 1971, pp. 3–15.
Aradau, Claudia & van Munster, Rens, 'Taming the future: The dispositif of risk in the war on terror', in Louise Amoore & Marieke De Goede (eds), *Risk and the War on Terror*, Routledge, Abingdon, 2008, pp. 23–40.
Arkoun, Mohammad, *The Unthought in Contemporary Islamic Thought*, al-Saqi Books, London, 2002.
Asim, Qari, *Mosques and Youth Engagement: Guidelines and Toolkit*, MINAB, London, 2011.
Atie, Rosalie, Dunn, Kevin & Ozalp, Mehmet, 'Religiosity, attitudes on diversity and belonging among ordinary Australian Muslims, *Australian Journal of Islamic Studies*, 2(1), 2017, pp. 1–15.

Atkinson, Anthony, 'Social exclusion, poverty and unemployment', in Anthony Atkinson & John Hill (eds), *Exclusion, Opportunity and Employment*, Centre for Analysis of Social Exclusion, London, 1998, pp. 1–20.

Australian Bureau of Statistics, *2011 Census of Housing and Population*, ABS, Canberra, 2011.

Australian Government, *Countering Violent Extremism*, Department of Home Affairs, Canberra, 2019. https://www.homeaffairs.gov.au/about-us/our-portfolios/national-security/countering-extremism-and-terrorism/countering-violent-extremism-(cve)

Avramov, Dragana, *People, Democracy, and Social Exclusion*, Population Studies Series no. 37, Council of European Publishing, Strasbourg, 2002.

Barker, Martin, *The New Racism: Conservatives and the Ideology of the Tribe*, Junction Books, London, 1981.

Beck, Ulrich, *Risk Society: Towards a New Modernity* (trans. Mark Ritter), Sage, London, 1992.

—— *World Risk Society*, Blackwell, Cambridge, 1999.

Berafe, Tamiru, 'Assessing the causes and effects of social exclusion: The case of "pot makers" in Yem Special Woreda in Southern Nation, Nationalities and Peoples Regional State in Ethiopia', *African Journal of Political Science and International Relations*, 11(4), 2017, pp. 68–83.

Berkey, Jonathan, *The Transmission of Knowledge in Medieval Cairo: A Social History of Islamic Education*, Princeton University Press, Princeton, 1992.

Bernardi, Cory, 'Burka bandits justify a burka ban', ABC News, 6 May 2010. http://www.abc.net.au/unleashed/33978.html

Black, Ann, 'Accommodating shariah law in Australia's legal system: Can we? Should we?', *Alternative Law Journal*, 33, 2008, pp. 2–7.

—— 'In the shadow of our legal system: Shari'a in Australia', in Rex Ahdar & Nicholas Aroney (eds), *Sharia in the West*, Oxford University Press, 2010, pp. 239–54.

—— 'Replicating "a model of mutual respect": Could Singapore's legal pluralism work in Australia?', *Journal of Legal Pluralism and Unofficial Law*, 44(65), 2012, pp. 65–102.

Black, Ann & Sadiq, Kerrie, 'Good and bad sharia: Australia's mixed response to Islamic law', *UNSW Law Journal*, 34(1), 2011, pp. 383–412.

Bloemraad, Irene, 'Unity in diversity? Bridging models of multiculturalism and immigrant integration', *Du Bois Review*, 2(2), 2007, pp. 317–36.

Bloemraad, Irene, Korteweg, Anna, & Yurdakul, Gökçe, 'Citizenship and immigration: Multiculturalism, assimilation, and challenges to the nation-state', *Annual Review of Sociology*, 34(1), 2008, pp. 153–79.

Botiveau, Bernard, *Loi islamique et droit dans les sociétés arabes: Mutations des systèmes juridiques du Moyen-Orient*, Karthala-IREMAM, Paris and Aix-en-Provence, 1993.

Bouma, Gary, *Mosques and Muslim Settlement in Australia*, Bureau of Immigration and Population Research/Australian Government Publishing Service, Canberra, 1994.

—— 'The settlement of Islam in Australia', *Social Compass*, 44(1), 1997, pp. 71–82.

Bouma, Gary, Daw, Joan & Munawar, Riffat, 'Muslims managing religious diversity', in Abdullah Saeed & Shahram Akbarzadeh (eds), *Muslim Communities in Australia*, UNSW Press, Sydney, 2001, pp. 53–72.

Bowen, John, 'Two approaches to rights and religion in contemporary France', in Richard Wilson & John Mitchell (eds), *Human Rights in Global Perspective: Anthropological Studies of Rights, Claims and Entitlements*, Routledge, London, 2003, pp. 33–53.

Bowering, Gerhard, 'Introduction', in Gerhard Bowering (ed.), *Islamic Political Thought: An Introduction*, Princeton University Press, Princeton, 2015, pp. 1–24.

Boyer, Carl, *A History of Mathematics*, Princeton University Press, Princeton, 1985.

Branley, Alison, '"One man show": Concerns Islamic Council may not have held annual meeting in 8 years', *AM*, 27 June 2015. https://www.abc.net.au/radio/programs/am/one-man-show-concerns-islamic-council-may-not-have/6577582

Brons, Lajos, 'Othering: An analysis', *Transcience*, 6(1), 2015, pp. 69–90.

Brotherhood of St Laurence, 'Seeking asylum: Living with fear, uncertainty and exclusion', *Changing Pressures*, 11, 2002.

Brunato, Madeleine, *Hanji Mahomet Allum: Afghan Camel-Driver, Herbalist and Healer in Australia*, Investigator Press, Leabrook, SA, 1972.

Bukhārī, Muḥammad ibn Ismāʿīl, translated by Muḥammad Muḥsin Khān, *Ṣaḥīḥ al-Bukhārī : The Translation of the Meanings of Ṣaḥīḥ al-Bukhārī* (Arabic-English), Taleem-ul-Quran Trust, Gujranwala, Pakistan, 1971.

Bullock, Katherine, *Rethinking Muslim Women and the Veil: Challenging Historical and Modern Stereotypes*, International Institute of Islamic Thought, London, 2002.

Buskens, Léon, 'Introduction: Dichotomies, transformations, and continuities in the study of Islam', in Léon Buskens & Annemarie van Sandwijk (eds), *Islamic Studies in the Twenty-first Century: Transformations and Continuities*, Amsterdam University Press, 2016, pp. 11–27.

'Call for parts of sharia law in Australia', ABC News, 8 March 2010. https://www.abc.net.au/news/2010-03-08/call-for-parts-of-sharia-law-in-australia/354906

Castles, Stephen & Miller, Mark, *The Age of Migration: International Population Movements in the Modern World*, Guilford Books, New York, 1993.

Castles, Stephen, Cope, Bill, Kalantzis, Mary & Morrissey, Michael, *Mistaken Identity: Multiculturalism and the Demise of Nationalism in Australia*, Pluto Press, Sydney, 1992.

Cesari, Jocelyne, 'Islam in France: The shaping of a religious minority', in Yvonne Haddad (ed.), *Muslims in the West: Sojourners to Citizens*, Oxford University Press, Oxford, 2002, pp. 36–51.

Chamberlain, Michael, *Knowledge and Social Practice in Medieval Damascus, 1190–1350*, Cambridge University Press, Cambridge, 1994.

Chelebi, Manar, *The Australian Muslim Student*, David Barlow Publishing, Sydney, 2008.

Choudhury, Tufyal & Fenwick, Helen, 'The impact of counter-terrorism measures on Muslim communities', *International Review of Law, Computers & Technology*, 25 (3), 2011, pp.151–181.

Cigler, Michael, *The Afghans in Australia*, Australian Ethnic Heritage Series, AE Press, Melbourne, 1986.

Clarke, Anne, '"The Moormans Trowers": Aboriginal and Macassan interactions and the changing fabric of Indigenous social life', in Sue O'Connor & Peter Veth (eds), *East of Wallace's Line: Modern Quaternary Research in East Asia*, vol. 16, AA Balkema, Rotterdam, 2000, pp. 315–35.

Cleland, Bilal, 'The history of Muslims in Australia', in Abdullah Saeed & Shahram Akbarzadeh (eds), *Muslim Communities in Australia*, UNSW Press, Sydney, 2001, pp. 12–32.

—— *The Muslims in Australia: A Brief History*, Islamic Council of Victoria, Melbourne, 2002.

Clyne, Irene Donohoue, 'Educating Muslim children in Australia', in Abdullah Saeed & Shahram Akbarzadeh (eds), *Muslim Communities in Australia*, UNSW Press, Sydney, 2001, pp. 116–37.

—— 'Seeking education for Muslim children in Australia', *Muslim Education Quarterly*, 14(3), 1997, pp. 4–18.

Cohen, Stanley, *Folk Devils and Moral Panics* (3rd edn), Routledge, Abingdon, 2002.

Cole, Douglas, 'The crimson thread of kinship', *Journal of Historical Studies*, 14(56), 1971, pp. 511–25.

Cole, Jeffrey, *The New Racism in Europe*, Cambridge University Press, Cambridge, 1997.

Commonwealth of Australia, *1991 Census of Population and Housing*, Catalogue No. 2722.0, Australian Bureau of Statistics, Canberra, 1991.
—— *1996 Census of Population and Housing*, Catalogue No. 2901.0, Australian Bureau of Statistics, Canberra, 1997.
—— *2001 Census of Population and Housing*, Catalogue No. 2015.0, Australian Bureau of Statistics, Canberra, 2002.
—— *2006 Census of Population and Housing*, Catalogue No. 2068.0, Australian Bureau of Statistics, Canberra, 2007.
—— *2011 Census of Population and Housing: Reflecting a Nation: Stories from the 2011 Census*, Catalogue No. 2071.0, Australian Bureau of Statistics, Canberra, 2012–13.
—— *2016 Census of Population and Housing: Reflecting Australia: Stories from the 2016 Census*, Catalogue No. 2071.0, Australian Bureau of Statistics, Canberra, 2017.
Coulson, Noel, *A History of Islamic Law*, Edinburgh University Press, Edinburgh, 1984.
Cousins, Christine, 'Social exclusion in Europe: Paradigms of social disadvantage in Germany, Spain, Sweden and the United Kingdom', *Policy and Politics*, 26(2), 1998, pp. 127–46.
Crang, Mike, *Cultural Geography*, Routledge, London, 1998.
David, Gary & Ayouby, Kenneth, 'Being Arab and becoming Americanized: Forms of mediated assimilation in metropolitan Detroit', in Yvonne Haddad & Jane Smith (eds), *Muslim Minorities in the West: Visible and Invisible*, AltaMira Press, Walnut Creek, CA, 2002, pp. 125–42.
Dean, Mitchell, *Governmentality: Power and Rule in Modern Society*, Sage, London, 1999.
Department of Immigration, Local Government and Ethnic Affairs, *Australia and Immigration 1788 to 1988*, Australian Government Publishing Service, Canberra, 1988.
Department of the Prime Minister and Cabinet, *Review of Australia's Counter-Terrorism Machinery*, Commonwealth of Australia, Canberra, 2015.
Diallo, Ibrahima, *The Role and Importance of Islamic Studies and Faith in Community Islamic Schools in Australia: A Case Study of Adelaide (SA) and Darwin (NT) October 2016*, Research Centre for Languages and Cultures, University of South Australia, Adelaide, 2016.
Diamant, Jeff, *The Countries with the 10 Largest Christian Populations and the 10 Largest Muslim Populations*, Pew Research Centre, 1 April 2019. https://www.pewresearch.org/fact-tank/2019/04/01/the-countries-with-the-10-largest-christian-populations-and-the-10-largest-muslim-populations/
Dreher, Tanja, *'Targeted': Experiences of Racism in NSW after September 11, 2001*, UTS Shopfront Series, University of Technology Sydney ePress, 2006, p. 1. DOI: https://doi.org/10.5130/978-1-86365-420-3
Duderija, Adis, 'Critical-progressive Muslim thought: Reflections on its political ramifications', *Review of Faith & International Affairs*, 11(3), 2013, pp. 69–79.
Dugarova, Esuna, *Social Inclusion, Poverty Eradication and the 2030 Agenda for Sustainable Development*, UNRISD Working Paper no. 2015-15, United Nations Research Institute for Social Development (UNRISD), Geneva, 2015.
Dugarova, Esuna & Lavers, Tom, *Social Inclusion and the Post-2015 Sustainable Development Agenda*, Paper Prepared for the UNITAR's Briefing for UN Delegates on Post-2015 Development Agenda: Social Inclusion, UNRISD, Geneva, 2014.
Dunn, Kevin, Klocker, Natascha & Salabay, Tanya, 'Contemporary racism and Islamophobia in Australia: Racializing religion', *Ethnicities*, 7(4), 2007, pp. 564–89.
Dunn, Kevin, Atie, Rosalie Kennedy, Michael, Ali, Jan, O'Reilly, John & Rogerson, Lindsay, 'Can you use community policing for counter terrorism? Evidence from NSW, Australia', *Police Practice and Research: An International Journal*, 17(3), 2016, pp. 196–211.

Economic Development Committee, *Inquiry into the Incidence of Youth Unemployment in Victoria*, Parliament of Victoria, Melbourne, 2002.

Edwards, Ryan, *Muslim Community Organisations and Leadership in Australia*, PhD dissertation, Asia Institute, Faculty of Arts, University of Melbourne, Melbourne, 2018.

Eickelman, Dale & Piscatori, James, 'Social theory in the study of Muslim societies', in Dale Eickelman & James Piscatori (eds), *Muslim Travellers: Pilgrimage, Migration, and the Religious Imagination*, University of California, Berkeley, 1990, pp. 3–28.

Eid, Mahmoud, *Public Schools or Islamic Colleges? Factors Impacting on Parental Choice of Schooling for Muslim Children*, doctoral dissertation, Edith Cowan University, Perth, 2008.

Elder, Catriona, *Being Australian: Narratives of National Identity*, Allen & Unwin, Crows Nest, 2007.

Esposito, John, *The Oxford History of Islam*, Oxford University Press, Oxford, 1999.

Exhibition: Islam in Asia: Diversity in Past and Present: Muslim Populations, Cornell University Library, April 2017. https://guides.library.cornell.edu/IslamAsiaExhibit/MuslimPopulations

Fahad, Amanullah, *Sources and Principles of Islamic Law: A Study of Islamic Fiqh*, Jnanada Prakashan, New Delhi, 2009.

Ferguson, James & Gupta, Akhil, 'Spatializing states: Toward an ethnography of neoliberal governmentality', *American Ethnologist*, 29(4), 2002, pp. 981–1002.

Field, Harry, *Citizen or Resident? Australian Social Security Provision to Immigrants*, doctoral dissertation, University of New South Wales, Sydney, 2000.

Forrest, James, 'Suburbs "swamped" by Asians and Muslims? The data show a different story', *The Conversation*, 5 July 2017.

Foucault, Michel, 'Governmentality', in Graham Burchell, Colin Gordon & Peter Miller (eds), *The Foucault Effect: Studies in Governmentality*, University of Chicago Press, Chicago, 1991, pp. 87–104.

Frazer, Hugh & Marlier, Eric, *Assessment of Progress towards the Europe 2020 Social Inclusion Objectives: Main Findings and Suggestions on the Way Forward: A Study of National Policies*, European Commission, Brussels, 2013.

Freiler, Christa, *What Needs to Change? Towards a Vision of Social Inclusion for Children, Families and Communities*, Draft Concept Paper, Laidlaw Foundation, Toronto, 2001.

Ganter, Regina, 'Muslim Australians: The deep histories of contact', *Journal of Australian Studies*, 32(4), 2008, pp. 481–92.

Gillard, Julia, 'The economics of social inclusion', *Sydney Paper*, 19(3), 2007, pp. 102–12.

Gilliat-Ray, Sophie, *Muslims in Britain: An Introduction*, Cambridge University Press, Cambridge, 2010.

Gilmore, Joanna, 'Criminalizing dissent in the "war on terror": The British state's reaction to Gaza War protests of 2008–2009', in George Morgan & Scott Poynting (eds), *Global Islamophobia: Muslims and Moral Panic in the West*, Ashgate, Surrey, 2012, pp. 197–213.

Graetz, Brian & McAllister, Ian, *Dimensions of Australian Society* (2nd edn), Macmillan, Melbourne, 1994.

Gray, John, 'Inclusion: A radical critique', in Peter Askonas & Angus Stewart (eds), *Social Inclusion: Possibilities and Tensions*, Macmillan, London, 2000, pp. 19–36.

Guessoum, Nidhal, 'The Qur'an, science, and the (related) contemporary Muslim discourse', *Zygon: Journal of Religion and Science*, 43(2), 2008, pp. 411–31.

Haddad, Yvonne & Smith, Jane, 'Introduction', in Yvonne Haddad & Jane Smith (eds), *Muslim Minorities in the West: Visible and Invisible*, AltaMira Press, Walnut Creek, CA, 2002, pp. v–xviii.

Hage, Ghassan, *White Nation: Fantasies of White Supremacy in a Multicultural Society*, Pluto Press, Sydney, 1998.

Hallaq, Wael, *An Introduction to Islamic Law*, Cambridge University Press, Cambridge, 2009.

—— *The Origins and Evolution of Islamic Law*, Cambridge University Press, Cambridge, 2005.

Hassan, Riaz, *Australian Muslims: The Challenge of Islamophobia and Social Distance*, International Centre for Muslim and non-Muslim Understanding, University of South Australia, Adelaide, 2018.

—— *Australian Muslims: A Demographic, Social and Economic Profile of Muslims in Australia*, International Centre for Muslim and Non-Muslim Understanding, University of South Australia, Adelaide, 2015.

Hassan, Riaz & Martin, Bill, *Islamophobia, Social Distance and Fear of Terrorism in Australia: A Preliminary Report*, International Centre for Muslim and non-Muslim Understanding, University of South Australia, Adelaide, 2015.

Hayes, Alan, Gray, Matthew & Edwards, Ben, 'Social inclusion: Origin, concepts and key themes', Social Inclusion Unit, Australian Institute of Family Studies, Department of the Prime Minister and Cabinet, Canberra, 2008.

Heath-Kelly, Charlotte, 'Counter-terrorism and the counterfactual: Producing the "radicalisation" discourse and the UK PREVENT strategy', *British Journal of Politics and International Relations*, 15, 2013, pp. 394–415.

Hefner, Robert & Zaman, Muhammad, 'Introduction: The culture, politics, and future of Muslim education', in Robert Hefner & Muhammad Zaman (eds), *Schooling Islam: The Culture and Politics of Modern Muslim Education*, Princeton University Press, Princeton, 2007, pp. 1–39.

Hewer, Chris, 'Schools for Muslims', *Oxford Review of Education*, 27(4), 2001, pp. 515–27.

Hillyard, Paddy, 'The "war on terror": Lessons from Ireland', European Civil Liberties Network, Brussels, 2005.

Hillyard, Paddy & Percy-Smith, Janie, *The Coercive State: The Decline of Democracy in Britain*, Fontana, London, 1988.

Hole, Jacquelyn, 'Muslim group wants sharia law in Australia', ABC News, 17 May 2011. https://www.abc.net.au/news/2011-05-17/muslim-group-wants-sharia-law-in-australia/2717096

Hopkins, Liza, 'A contested identity: Resisting the category Muslim-Australian', *Immigrants and Minorities*, 29(1), 2011, pp. 110–31.

Hospes, Otto & Clancy, Joy, 'Unpacking the discourse of social inclusion in value chains', in Bert Helmsing & Sietze Vellema (eds), *Value Chains, Inclusion and Endogenous Development: Contrasting Theories and Realities*, Routledge, London, 2011, pp. 23–41.

Hubbard, Phil, 'Accommodating otherness: Anti-asylum centre protest and the maintenance of white privilege', *Transactions of the Institute of British Geographers*, 30, 2005, pp. 52–65.

Humphrey, Michael, 'Australian Islam, the new global terrorism and the limits of citizenship', in Shahram Akbarzadeh & Samina Yasmeen (eds), *Islam and the West: Reflections from Australia*, UNSW Press, Sydney, 2005, pp. 132–48.

—— 'An Australian Islam? Religion in the multicultural city', in Abdullah Saeed & Shahram Akbarzadeh (eds), *Muslim Communities in Australia*, UNSW Press, Sydney, 2001, pp. 33–52.

—— 'Community, mosque, and ethnic politics', *Australia and New Zealand Journal of Sociology*, 23(2), 1987, pp. 233–45.

—— 'Community, mosque and ethnic politics', in Abe Ata (ed.), *Religion and Ethnic Identity: An Australian Study*, Spectrum, Melbourne, 1988, pp. 255–69.

—— *Family, Work, and Unemployment: A Study of Lebanese Settlement in Sydney*, Australian Government Publishing Service, Canberra, 1984.

—— 'Globalisation and Arab diasporic identities: The Australian Arab case', *Bulletin of the Royal Institute for Inter-Faith Studies*, 2(1), 2000, pp. 1–18.

—— 'Is this a mosque-free zone? Islam and the state in Australia', *Migration Monitor*, 3(12), 1989, pp. 12–17.
—— 'Islam, immigration and the state: Religion in Australia', in Alan Black (ed.), *Religion in Australia: Sociological Perspectives*, Allen & Unwin, Sydney, 1991, pp. 176–93.
—— *Islam, Multiculturalism and Transnationalism: From the Lebanese Diaspora*, IB Tauris Publishers, London, 1998.
—— 'Islam: A test for multiculturalism', *Asian Migrant*, 2(2), 1989, pp. 48–56.
—— 'Muslim communities in Australia', in Abdullah Saeed & Shahram Akbarzadeh (eds), *Muslim Communities in Australia*, UNSW Press, Sydney, 2001, pp. 33–52.
—— 'Racism and unemployment amongst Lebanese', in *Seminar Proceedings of the Arabic Community: Realities and Challenges*, Arabic Welfare Inter-Agency, Sydney, 1986, pp. 29–41.
—— 'Securitisation and domestication of diaspora Muslims and Islam: Turkish immigrants in Germany and Australia', *International Journal on Multicultural Societies*, 11(2), 2009, pp. 136–54.
—— 'Securitisation, social inclusion and Muslims in Australia', in Samina Yasmeen (ed.), *Muslims in Australia: The Dynamics of Exclusion and Inclusion*, Melbourne University Publishing, 2010, pp. 56–78.
Husson, Jean-François, *Training Imams in Europe: The Current Status*, King Baudouin Foundation, Brussels, 2007.
Huysmans, Jef, *The Politics of Insecurity: Fear, Migration and Asylum in the EU*, Routledge, London, 2006.
Ibn al-Humam, Kamal al-Dın, *Sharh Fath al-Qadır (The Bounty of the Mighty: A Commentary on Legal Issues)*, vol. 7, Dar al-Kutub al-'Ilmiyya, Beirut, 1995.
Ihram, Silma, Operations Manager at The Pharmacy Collective. https://au.linkedin.com/in/pharmacycollective
Iner, Derya (ed.), *Islamophobia in Australia, II (2016–2017)*, Charles Sturt University & ISRA, Sydney, 2019.
Irving, Lisa, 'Teaching and learning halal sex: Discussing contrasting values among Muslim youth adults in Australia', in Erich Kolig & Malcolm Voyce (eds), *Muslim Integration: Pluralism and Multiculturalism in New Zealand and Australia*, Lexington Books, New York, 2016, pp. 191–209.
Isin, Engin & Turner, Bryan, 'Investigating citizenship: An agenda for citizenship studies', *Citizenship Studies*, 11(1), 2007, pp. 5–17.
Jakubowicz, Andrew, 'Political Islam and the future of Australian multiculturalism', *National Identities*, 9(3), 2007, pp. 265–80.
—— 'The state and the welfare of immigrants in Australia', *Ethnic and Racial Studies*, 12(1), 1989, pp. 1–35.
Jayasuriya, Laksiri, 'Understanding Australian racism', *Australian Universities Review*, 45(1), 2002, pp. 40–4.
Joffé, George, 'Introduction: Radicalisation and the Arab Spring', in George Joffé (ed.), *Islamist Radicalisation in Europe and the Middle East: Reassessing the Causes of Terrorism*, IB Tauris, London, 2013, pp. 1–16.
Johansen, Baber, *The Islamic Law on Land Tax and Rent: The Peasants' Loss of Property Rights as Interpreted in the Hanafite Legal Literature of the Mamluk and Ottoman Periods*, Croom Helm, London, 1988.
Johns, Anthony & Saeed, Abdullah, 'Muslims in Australia: The building of a community', in Yvonne Haddad & Jane Smith (eds), *Muslim Minorities in the West: Visible and Invisible*, AltaMira Press, Walnut Creek, CA, 2002, pp. 195–216.
Joint Standing Committee on Foreign Affairs, Defence and Trade, 'Federal protection of freedom of religion or belief', in *Interim Report: Legal Foundations of Religious Freedom in*

Australia, Parliament of the Commonwealth of Australia, Canberra, 2017, pp. 31–50. https://www.aph.gov.au/Parliamentary_Business/Committees/Joint/Foreign_Affairs_Defence_and_Trade/Freedomofreligion/Interim_Report

Jones, Mary, 'The years of decline: Australian Muslims 1900–40', in Mary Jones (ed.), *An Australian Pilgrimage: Muslims in Australia from the Seventeenth Century to the Present*, Victoria Press, Melbourne, 1993, pp. 63–86.

Jones, Peter, 'Islamic schools in Australia', *La Trobe Journal*, 89, 2012, pp. 36–47.

—— *Islamic Schools in Australia: Muslims in Australia or Australian Muslims?*, doctoral dissertation, University of New England, Sydney, 2012.

Joppke, Christian, 'The retreat of multiculturalism in the liberal states: Theory and policy', *British Journal of Sociology*, 55(2), 2004, pp. 237–57.

Jotia, Agreement Lathi, 'Globalization and the nation-state: Sovereignty and state welfare in jeopardy', *US-China Education Review*, B 2, 2011, pp. 243–50.

Jupp, James (ed.), *The Australian People: An Encyclopedia of the Nation, Its People and Their Origins*, Cambridge University Press, Cambridge, 2001.

—— *The Encyclopedia of Religion in Australia*, Cambridge University Press, Melbourne, 2009.

Kabir, Nahid, 'The media is one-sided in Australia', *Journal of Children and Media*, 2(3), 2008, pp. 267–81.

—— 'Muslim in Australia: The double edge of terrorism', *Journal of Ethnic and Migration Studies*, 33(8), 2007, pp. 1277–97.

—— *Muslims in Australia: Immigration, Race Relations and Cultural History*, Routledge, New York, 2010.

—— 'Representation of Islam and Muslims in the Australian media, 2001–2005', *Journal of Muslim Minority Affairs*, 26(3), 2006, pp. 313–28.

Kamali, Mohammad, *An Introduction to Shariah*, Ilhiah, Kuala Lumpur, 2006.

—— *Shari'ah Law: An Introduction*, Oneworld Publications, Oxford, 2008.

Kamali, Mohammad & Nalla, Zarina, 'The teaching of Islam in Western universities: Reflections and impressions', in Paul Morris et al. (eds), *The Teaching and Study of Islam in Western Universities*, Routledge, London, 2014, pp. 65–84.

Kaya, Ayhan, *Islam, Migration and Integration: The Age of Securitization*, Palgrave, London, 2009.

Kenny, Sue, 'Risk society and the Islamic Other', in Shahram Akbarzadeh & Fethi Mansouri (eds), *Islam and Political Violence: Muslim Diaspora and Radicalism in the West*, IB Tauris, London, 2007, pp. 87–106.

Khir, Bustami, 'Who applies Islamic law in non-Muslim countries? A study of the Sunni principle of the governance of the scholars (Wilyat al-'Ulama')', *Journal of Muslim Minority Affairs*, 27(1), 2007, pp. 78–91.

Khuri, Fuad, *From Village to Suburb: Order and Change in Greater Beirut*, University of Chicago Press, Chicago, 1976.

Klanfer, Jules, *L'Exclusion sociale: Étude de la marginalité dans les sociétés occidentales [Social Exclusion: The Study of Marginality in Western Societies]*, Bureau de Recherches Sociales, Paris, 1995.

Kolig, Erich, 'To shari'aticize or not to shari'aticize: Islamic and secular law in liberal democratic society', in Rex Ahdar & Nicholas Aroney (eds), *Sharia in the West*, Oxford University Press, Oxford, pp. 255–78.

Korteweg, Rem, Gohel, Sajjan, Heisbourg, François, Ranstorp, Magnus & De Wijk, Rob, 'Background contributing factors to terrorism: Radicalisation and recruitment', in Magnus Ranstorp (ed.), *Understanding Violent Radicalisation: Terrorist and Jihadist Movements in Europe*, Routledge, London, 2010, pp. 21–49.

Krayem, Ghena, *Freedom of Religion, Belief and Gender: A Muslim Perspective*, Supplementary Paper Attached to: Freedom of Religion and Belief in the 21st Century, Report for Australian Human Rights Commission, Sydney, 2010.
—— *Islamic Family Law in Australia: To Recognise or Not To Recognise*, Melbourne University Publishing, Melbourne, 2014.
Kutty, Faisal, 'Issues in Islam: Islamists and the West: Co-existence or confrontation?', *Washington Report on Middle East Affairs*, 14(6), 1996, pp. 34–6.
Lafree, Gary, *Losing Legitimacy*, Westview, Boulder, CO, 1998.
Lapidus, Ira, *A History of Islamic Societies*, Cambridge University Press, Cambridge, 2014.
Leach, Michael & Mansouri, Fethi, *Lives in Limbo*, UNSW Press, Sydney, 2004.
Lister, Ruth, 'Strategies for social inclusion: Promoting social cohesion or social justice?', in Peter Askonas & Angus Stewart (eds), *Social Inclusion: Possibilities and Tensions*, Macmillan, London, 2000, pp. 37–54.
Lowenstein, Wendy & Loh, Morag, *The Immigrants*, Hyland House, Melbourne, 1977.
Lupton, Deborah, 'Dangerous places and the unpredictable stranger: Constructions of fear of crime', *Australian and New Zealand Journal of Criminology*, 32(1), 1999, pp. 1–15.
Mah, Aminah, *Counselling and Wellbeing Support Services in Australian Muslim Schools*, doctoral dissertation, University of Western Australia, Perth, 2015.
Mahmood, Saba, *Politics of Piety: The Islamic Revival and the Feminist Subject*, Princeton University Press, Princeton, 2005.
Makdisi, George, 'Madrasa and university in the Middle Ages', *Studia Islamica*, 32, 1970, pp. 255–64.
Mansouri, Fethi & Kamp, Annelies, 'Structural deficiency or cultural racism: The educational and social experiences of Arab-Australian youth', *Australian Journal of Social Issues*, 42(1), 2007, pp. 87–102.
Mares, Peter, *Borderline: Australia's Treatment of Refugees and Asylum Seekers*, UNSW Press, Sydney, 2001.
Markus, Andrew, *Race: John Howard and the Remaking of Australia*, Allen & Unwin, Crows Nest, 2001.
Marlier, Eric, Atkinson, Tony, Cantillon, Bea & Nolan, Brian, *The EU and Social Inclusion: Facing the Challenges*, Policy Press, Bristol, 2007.
Marranci, Gabriele, *The Anthropology of Islam*, Berg, London & New York, 2008.
—— 'Sociology and anthropology of Islam: A critical debate', in Bryan Turner (ed.), *The New Blackwell Companion to the Sociology of Religion*, Blackwell, Malden, 2010, pp. 364–87.
—— *Understanding Muslim Identity: Rethinking Fundamentalism*, Palgrave Macmillan, London & New York, 2009.
Mathieson, Jane, Popay, Jennie, Enoch, Etheline, Escorel, Sarah, Hernandez, Mario, Johnston, Heidi & Rispel, Laetitia, *Social Exclusion: Meaning, Measurement and Experience and Links to Health Inequalities: A Review of Literature*, World Health Organization Social Exclusion Knowledge Network Background Paper 1, Institute for Health Research, Lancaster, UK, 2008.
Matusitz, Jonathan, *Terrorism and Communication: A Critical Introduction*, Sage, LA, 2013.
McCue, Helen & Krayem, Ghena, '*Shari'a* and Muslim women's agency in a multicultural context: Recent changes in sports culture', in Adam Possamai, James Richardson & Bryan Turner (eds), *The Sociology of Shari'a: Case Studies from Around the World*, Springer, London, 2015, pp. 103–18.
McDonald, Myfanwy, *Social Exclusion and Social Inclusion Resources for Child and Family Services*, Australian Institute of Family Studies, Melbourne, 2011.
McGarrity, Nicola, '"Let the punishment match the offence": Determining sentences for Australian terrorists', *International Journal for Crime, Justice and Social Democracy*, 2(1), 2013, pp. 18–34.

McGoldrick, Dominic, 'Accommodating Muslims in Europe: From adopting sharia law to religiously based opt outs from generally applicable law', *Human Rights Law Review*, 9(4), 2009, pp. 603–45.

McIntosh, Ian, 'Islam and Australia's Aborigines? Perspective from north-east Arnhem Land', *Journal of Religious History*, 20(1), 1996, pp. 53–77.

Merry, Michael, *Culture, Identity, and Islamic Schooling: A Philosophical Approach*, Palgrave Macmillan, New York, 2007.

Merry, Michael & Driessen, Geert, 'Islamic schools in three Western countries: Policy and procedure', *Comparative Education*, 41(4), 2005, pp. 411–32.

Mograby, Abdallah, 'Muslim migration and settlement: The Australian experience', *Islam in Australia*, Middle East Research and Information Section / NSW Anti-Discrimination Board, Sydney, 1985, pp. 25–35.

Moosa, Ebrahim, 'Allegory of the rule (hukm): Law as simulacrum in Islam?', *History of Religions*, 38(1), 1998, pp. 1–24.

—— *What is a Madrasa?* University of North Carolina Press, Chapel Hill, 2015.

Morris, Linda, 'Islam leads in rush to faith education', *Sydney Morning Herald*, 23 June 2003. https://www.smh.com.au/education/islam-leads-in-rush-to-faith-education-20030623-gdgz3g.html

Morris, Paul, Shepard, William, Trebilco, Paul & Tidswell, Toni (eds), *The Teaching and Study of Islam in Western Universities*, Routledge, London, 2014.

Mulvaney, John & Kamminga, Johan, *Prehistory of Australia*, Smithsonian Institution Press, Washington, DC, 1999.

Musharraf, Muhammad & Nabeel, Fatima, 'Schooling options for Muslim children living in Muslim-minority countries: A thematic literature review', *International Journal of Social Science and Humanities Research*, 3(4), 2015, pp. 29–62.

Mythen, Gabe & Walklate, Sandra, 'Criminology and terrorism: Which thesis? Risk society or governmentality?', *British Journal of Criminology*, 2005, 46(3), pp. 379–98.

Mythen, Gabe, Walklate, Sandra & Khan, Fatima, '"I'm a Muslim, but not a terrorist": Victimization, risky identities and the performance of safety', *British Journal of Criminology*, 49(6,) 2009, pp. 736–54.

Nasr, Seyyed Hossein, *Islam: Religion, History, and Civilization*, HarperSanFrancisco, San Francisco, 2003.

Nebhan, Katy, 'Identifications: Between nationalistic "cells" and an Australian Muslim ummah', *Australian Journal of Social Issues*, 34(4), 1999, pp. 371–85.

Nicoll, Fiona, 'Pseudo-hyphens and barbaric/binaries: Anglo-Celticity and the cultural politics of tolerance', *Queensland Review*, 6(1), 1999, pp. 77–84.

Nielsen, Jørgen, *Emerging Claims of Muslim Populations in Matters of Family Law in Europe*, Centre for the Study of Islam and Christian Muslim Relations, Birmingham, 1993

—— *Muslims in Western Europe*, Edinburgh University Press, Edinburgh, 1992.

Nile, Fred, 'An open society has no place for the burqa', *Sydney Morning Herald*, 20 May 2010. http://www.smh.com.au/opinion/politics/an-open-society-has-no-place-for-the-burqa-20100519-vezj.html

Noble, Greg, 'The discomfort of strangers: Racism, incivility and ontological security in a comfortable and relaxed nation', *Journal of Intercultural Studies*, 26(1), 2005, pp. 107–20.

—— 'Respect and respectability amongst second-generation Arab and Muslim Australian men', *Journal of Intercultural Studies*, 28(3), 2007, pp. 331–44.

O'Flaherty, Brenden, *Making Room: The Economics of Homelessness*, Harvard University Press, Cambridge, MA, 1996.

Omar, Wafia & Allen, Kirsty, *The Muslims in Australia*, Australian Government Publishing Service, Canberra, 1997.

Omtzigt, Dirk-Jan, *Survey on Social inclusion: Theory and Policy*, Working Paper, Oxford Institute for Global Economic Development, Oxford University, 2009.
Otto, Jan, *Sharia and National Law in Muslim Countries: Tensions and Opportunities for Dutch and EU Foreign Policy*, Amsterdam University Press, Amsterdam, 2008.
Oxoby, Robert, 'Cognitive dissonance, status, and growth of the underclass', *Economic Journal*, 114, 2004, pp. 729–49.
Park, Robert, 'Assimilation, social', in Edwin Seligman & Alvin Johnson (eds), *The Encyclopaedia of the Social Sciences*, Macmillan, New York, 1930, pp. 281–83.
Pearl, David, *Family Law and the Immigrant Communities*, Jordan & Sons, Bristol, 1986.
Pearse, Andrew & Stiefel, Matthias, *Inquiry into Participation: A Research Approach*, UNRISD, Geneva, 1979.
Pedersen, Lars, *Newer Islamic Movements in Western Europe*, Ashgate, London, 1999.
The People of Australia: Australia's Multicultural Policy, Commonwealth of Australia, n.d. https://www.runnymedetrust.org/uploads/events/people-of-australia-multicultural-policy-booklet.pdf
Peucker, Mario, 'Muslim community organisations as agents of social inclusion, cohesion and active citizenship? A cross-national overview', in Mario Peucker & Rauf Ceylan (eds), *Muslim Community Organizations in the West: History, Developments and Future Perspectives*, Springer, Berlin, 2017, pp. 35–57.
Peucker, Mario, Roose, Joshua & Akbarzadeh, Shahram, 'Muslim active citizenship in Australia: Socioeconomic challenges and the emergence of a Muslim elite', *Australian Journal of Political Science*, 49(2), 2014, pp. 282–99.
Phillips, Janet, 'Muslim Australians', E-Brief: Online Only issued 6 March 2007, Australian Government, 2007. https://www.aph.gov.au/About_Parliament/Parliamentary_Departments/Parliamentary_Library/Publications_Archive/archive/MuslimAustralians
Posetti, Julie, 'Jihad sheilas or media martyrs: Muslim women and the media', in Halim Rane, Jacqui Ewart & Mohamad Abdalla (eds.), *Islam and the Australian News Media*, Melbourne University Publishing, 2010, pp. 69–103.
Possamai, Adam, Dagistanli, Selda & Voyce, Malcolm, 'Shari'a in everyday life in Sydney: An analysis of professionals and leaders dealing with Islamic law', *Journal for the Academic Study of Religion*, 30(2), 2017, pp. 109–28.
Poulter, Sebastian, *English Law and Ethnic Minority Customs*, Butterworth, London, 1986.
Poynting, Scott & Noble, Greg, *Living with Racism: The Experience and Reporting by Arab and Muslim Australians of Discrimination, Abuse and Violence Since 11 September 2001*, Report to the Human Rights and Equal Opportunity Commission, Centre for Cultural Research, University of Western Sydney, Sydney, 2004.
Poynting, Scott, Noble, Greg, Tabar, Paul & Collins, Jock, *Bin Laden in the Suburbs: Criminalising the Arab Other*, Institute of Criminology, Sydney, 2004.
Putnam, Robert, *Bowling Alone: The Collapse and Revival of American Community*, Simon & Schuster, New York, 2000.
Quraishi, Asifa, 'What if sharia weren't the enemy: Rethinking international women's rights advocacy on Islamic law', *Columbia Journal of Gender and Law*, 22(1), 2011, pp. 173–249.
Rahman, Shafiur, Ahmed, Syed Tohel & Khan, Shaynul, *Voices From the Minaret: MCB Study of UK Imams and Mosques*, The Muslim Council of Britain & C3ube Training and Consultancy, London, 2006.
Raji al Faruqi, Ism'ail, *The Cultural Atlas of Islam*, Al-Saadawi Publications, London, 1986.
Rajkowski, Pamela, *In the Tracks of the Camelmen*, Angus & Robertson, North Ryde, NSW, 1987.

Ramadan, Tariq, 'Islam and Muslims in Europe: A silent revolution toward rediscovery', in Yvonne Haddad (ed.), *Muslims in the West: Sojourners to Citizens*, Oxford University Press, Oxford, 2002, pp. 158–66.

Rath, Jan, Groenedijk, Kees & Penninx, Rinos, 'The recognition and institutionalisation of Islam in Belgium, Great Britain and the Netherlands', *New Community*, 18(1), 1995, pp. 101–14.

Rawal, Nabin, 'Social inclusion and exclusion: A review', *Dhaulagiri Journal of Sociology and Anthropology*, 2, 2008, pp. 161–80.

Reetz, Dietrich, 'From madrasa to university: The challenges and formats of Islamic education', in Akbar Ahmed & Tamara Sonn (eds), *The Sage Handbook of Islamic Studies*, Sage, LA, 2010, pp. 106–39.

Risley, Suzanne, 'The sociology of security: Sociological approaches to contemporary and historical securitization', paper presented at Annual Meeting of American Sociological Association, Montreal Convention Center, Montreal, 2006. http://www.allacademic.com/meta/p105192_index.html

Rizvi, Sadaf, 'How Muslim faith schools are teaching tolerance and respect through "Islamicised" curriculum', *The Conversation*, 15 October 2014. https://theconversation.com/how-muslim-faith-schools-are-teaching-tolerance-and-respect-through-islamicised-curriculum-32239

Roach, Kent, *The 9/11 Effect: Comparative Counter-Terrorism*, Cambridge University Press, Cambridge, 2011.

Roberts, Brianna, 'Calls for registry to weed out "fake sheikhs"', SBS News, 14 January 2015. https://www.sbs.com.au/news/calls-for-registry-to-weed-out-fake-sheikhs

Robinson, Eric, *Ancient Greek Democracy: Readings and Sources*, Blackwell, Oxford, 2004.

Room, Graham, 'Poverty and social exclusion: The new European agenda for policy and research', in Graham Room (ed.), *Beyond the Threshold*, Policy Press, Bristol, 1995, pp. 1–9.

Roose, Joshua, *Contesting the Future: Muslim Men as Political Actors in the Context of Australian Multiculturalism*, PhD thesis, Arts—Asia Institute, University of Melbourne, 2012.

—— 'Contesting Islam through the 2012 Sydney protests: An analysis of post-protest political discourse amongst Australian Muslims', *Journal of Islam and Christian–Muslim Relations*, 24(4), 2013, pp. 479–99.

Rose, Nikolas, *Powers of Freedom: Reframing Political Thought*, Cambridge University Press, Cambridge, 1999.

Roude, Nada, *Australian Muslim Leaders' Perspectives on Countering Violent Extremism: Towards Developing a Best Practice Model for Engaging the Muslim Community*, PhD dissertation, School of Theology, Faculty of Arts and Education, Charles Sturt University, Sydney, 2017.

Roy, Olivier, 'EuroIslam: The jihad within?', *National Interest*, 71, 2003, pp. 63–73.

—— 'Islamic terrorist radicalisation in Europe', in Samir Amghar, Amel Boubekeur & Michael Emerson (eds), *European Islam: Challenges for Public Policy and Society*, Centre for European Policy Studies, Brussels, 2007, pp. 52–60.

Ruthven, Malise, *Islam: A Very Short Introduction*, Oxford University Press, Oxford, 1997.

Saeed, Abdullah, *Islam in Australia*, Allen and Unwin, Crows Nest, NSW, 2003.

Sander, Ake, 'The status of Muslim communities in Sweden', in Gerd Nonneman, Tim Niblock & Bogdan Szajkowski (eds), *Muslim Communities in the New Europe*, Ithaca, London, 1996, pp. 269–89.

Saras, Emily Daina & Perez-Felkner, Lara, 'Sociological perspectives on socialization', Oxford Bibliographies Online, 2018. DOI: 10.1093/OBO/9780199756384-0155

https://www.oxfordbibliographies.com/view/document/obo-9780199756384/obo-9780199756384-0155.xml
Sardar, Ziauddin, 'Rethinking Islam', *Journal of Futures Studies*, 6(4), 2002, pp. 117–24.
Schacht, Joseph, *An Introduction to Islamic Law*, Clarendon Press, Oxford, 1964.
Sedgwick, Mark, *Making European Muslims: Religious Socialization Among Young Muslims in Scandinavia and Western Europe*, Routledge, UK, 2014.
—— 'Sects in the Islamic world', *Nova Religio: The Journal of Alternative and Emergent Religions*, 3(2), 2000, pp. 195–240.
Shah, Saeeda, 'Muslim schools in secular societies: Persistence or resistance!', *British Journal of Religious Education*, 34(1), 2012, pp. 51–65.
Sikorski, Christian von, Schmuck, Desiree, Matthes, Jorg & Blinder, Alice, '"Muslims are not terrorists": Islamic State coverage, journalistic differentiation between terrorism and Islam, fear reactions, and attitudes toward Muslims', *Journal of Mass Communication and Society*, 20(6), 2017, pp. 825–48.
Silber, Mitchell & Bhatt, Arvin, *Radicalization in the West: The Homegrown Threat*, New York City Police Department, New York, 2007.
Silver, Hilary & Miller, Seymour, 'A social exclusion: The European approach to social disadvantage', *Indicators*, 2(2), 2003, pp. 1–17.
Silverstein, Paul, 'Immigrant racialization and the New Savage slot: Race, migration and immigration in the New Europe', *Annual Review of Anthropology*, 34, 2005, pp. 363–84.
Slootman, Marieke & Tillie, Jean, *Processes of Radicalisation: Why Some Amsterdam Muslims Become Radicals*, Institute for Migration and Ethnic Studies, Universiteit van Amsterdam, Amsterdam, 2006.
Smith, David, Jayarajah, Sanuki, Fabjianic, Taya & Wykes, Janice, *Citizenship in Australia*, Department of Immigration and Citizenship, Australian Government, Canberra, 2011.
Sohrabi, Hadi, 'Identity and Muslim leadership: The case of Australian Muslim leaders', *Contemporary Islam*, 10(1), 2015, pp. 1–16.
—— 'Islam and community organisation in Australia', Mario Peucker & Rauf Ceylan (eds), *Muslim Community Organizations in the West: History, Developments and Future Perspectives*, Springer, Berlin, 2017, pp. 205–18.
Sohrabi, Hadi & Farquharson, Karen, 'Discursive integration and Muslims in Australia', in Fathi Mansouri & Vince Marotta (eds), *Muslims in the West and the Challenge of Belonging*, Melbourne University Publishing, 2011, pp. 134–54.
Sonn, Tamara, *A Brief History of Islam*, Polity Press, London, 2004.
Sözeri, Semiha, Altinyelken, Hülya Kosar & Volman, Monique, 'Training imams in the Netherlands: The failure of a post-secular endeavour', *British Journal of Religious Education*, 41(4), 2018, pp. 435–45.
Stephenson, Peta, *Islam Dreaming: Indigenous Muslims in Australia*, UNSW Press, Sydney, 2010.
Stevens, Christine, 'Afghan camel drivers: Founders of Islam in Australia', in Mary Jones et al. (eds), *An Australian Pilgrimage: Muslims in Australia from the Seventeenth Century to the Present*, Melbourne Victoria Press in Association with the Museum of Victoria, 1993.
—— *Tin Mosques & Ghantowns: A History of Afghan Cameldrivers in Australia*, Oxford University Press, Melbourne, 1989.
Stowasser, Barbara, 'The Turks in Germany: From sojourners to citizens', in Yvonne Haddad (ed.), *Muslims in the West: Sojourners to Citizens*, Oxford University Press, Oxford, 2002, pp. 52–71.
Succarie, Ayda, Fallon, Wayne & Coronado, Gabriela, 'Towards a hybrid approach to the governance of Islamic schools in NSW', in Mohamad Abdalla, Dylan Chown & Muhammad Abdullah (eds), *Islamic Schooling in the West: Pathways to Renewal*, Palgrave, London, 2018, pp. 63–96.

Sunan Ibn Majah, Volume 1, Book 1, Hadith 10.

Tabar, Paul, Noble, Greg & Poynting, Scott, 'The rise and falter of the field of ethnic politics in Australia: The case of Lebanese community leadership', *Journal of Intercultural Studies*, 24(3), 2003, pp. 267–87.

Taji-Farouki, Suha, *A Fundamental Quest: Hizb al-Tahrir and the Search for the Islamic Caliphate*, Grey Seal, London, 1996.

Tayob, Abdulkader, *Islam in South Africa: Mosques, Imams, and Sermons*, University Press of Florida, Gainesville, 1999.

Trompf, Garry (ed.), *Cargo Cults and Millenarian Movements: Transoceanic Comparisons of New Religious Movements*, Mouton de Gruyter, Berlin & New York, 1990.

—— *Early Christian Historiography: Narratives of Retributive Justice*, Continuum, London, 2000.

Turner, Bryan & Nasir, Kamaludeen (eds), *The Sociology of Islam: Collected Essays of Bryan S Turner* (Contemporary Thought in the Islamic World), Routledge, London & New York, 2016.

Underabi, Husnia, *Mosques of Sydney and New South Wales: Research Report 2014*, Islamic Sciences & Research Academy Australia, Charles Sturt University/University of Western Sydney, 2014.

United Nations Research Institute for Social Development, *Transformative Social Policy: Lessons from UNRISD Research*, Research and Policy Brief no. 5, UNRISD, Geneva, 2006.

'Unity declared only way to defeat terrorism', *Sydney Morning Herald*, 24 August 2005. https://www.smh.com.au/national/unity-declared-only-way-to-defeat-terrorism-20050824-gdlxor.html

Van Den Berghe, Pierre, *The Ethnic Phenomenon*, Elsevier, Westport, CT, 1981.

Vasta, Ellie, 'Dialectics of domination: Racism and multiculturalism', in Stephen Castles & Ellie Vasta (eds), *The Teeth Are Smiling*, Allen & Unwin, Sydney, 1996, pp. 46–72.

Vertovec, Steven, 'Islamophobia and Muslim recognition in Britain', in Yvonne Haddad (ed.), *Muslims in the West: Sojourners to Citizens*, Oxford University Press, Oxford, 2002, pp. 19–35.

Vinson, Tony, *The Origins, Meaning, Definition and Economic Implications of the Concept of Social Inclusion/Exclusion*, Department of Education, Employment and Workplace Relations, Commonwealth of Australia, Canberra, 2009.

Waines, David, *An Introduction to Islam*, Cambridge University Press, Cambridge, 1995.

Wakim, Joseph, 'The Gulf War within the Australian community and Arab Australians: Villains, victims or victors?', in Greta Bird (ed.), *Racial Harassment*, National Centre for Constitutional Studies in Law, Centre for Migrant and Intercultural Studies, Monash University, Clayton, 1992, pp. 41–61.

Waldek, Lise & Droogan, Julian Drogan, 'Partnering to build solutions: 2014 Countering Violent Extremism Symposium, Sydney', *Journal of Policing, Intelligence and Counter Terrorism*, 10(1), 2015, pp. 39–47.

Weber, Max, *Economy and Society* (Guenther Roth & Claus Wittich, eds), Bedminister, New York, 1968.

Welch, Michael, *Scapegoats of September 11th: Hate Crimes and State Crimes in the War on Terror*, New Rutgers University Press, New Brunswick, NJ, 2006

Williams, George, 'The laws that erode who we are', *Sydney Morning Herald*, Sydney, 10–11 September 2011.

—— 'The legal legacy of the "war on terror"', *Macquarie Law Journal*, 12, 2013, pp. 1–16.

Wise, Amanda & Ali, Jan, *Muslim-Australians and Local Government: Grassroots Strategies to Improve Relations Between Muslim and Non-Muslim Australians*, Final Research Report

Department of Immigration and Citizenship and the Centre for Research on Social Inclusion, Macquarie University, Sydney, 2008.
Yasmeen, Samina, 'Muslim women as citizens in Australia: Perth as a case study', in Yvonne Haddad & Jane Smith (eds), *Muslim Minorities in the West: Visible and Invisible*, AltaMira Press, Walnut Creek, CA, 2002, pp. 217–32.
Young, Iris, *Inclusion and Democracy*, Oxford University Press, Oxford, 2000.
Zaman, Asad, 'Developing an Islamic world view: An essential component of an Islamic education', *Lahore Journal of Policy Studies,* 1(1), 2007, pp. 95–105.
Zaman, Muhammad, 'Ulama', in Gerhard Bowering (ed.), *Islamic Political Thought: An Introduction*, Princeton University Press, 2015, pp. 252–62.
Zubaida, Sami, *Law and Power in the Islamic World*, IB Tauris, London, 2010.

Index

'Aql 101
Aboriginal population 28
Afghans 2, 13–14, 46–47
Ahkam 101
Ahl al–Bayt 20
Ahmadiyya 21
Alawis 22
Alevis 22
Alienation 10, 26, 30, 37, 60, 65, 75, 79, 176–177, 181
Alim 116, 148
Allah 2–3, 13, 72, 95, 98–101, 135, 147, 150
Anglo-Celtic 29, 32, 35–36, 38, 43, 48, 75–77, 80, 178–179
Antisocial behaviour 70
Aqeedah 154
Arab Spring 82
Asharites 185
Assimilation 1, 5, 23, 31–35, 39, 41, 48, 78, 86–88, 122, 139, 187
Aussie-Islam 146, 153
Australian Constitution 44, 103
Australian Department of Immigration and Multicultural and Indigenous Affairs (DIMIA) 74
Australian Federation of Islamic Councils (AFIC) 24, 56–59, 96, 114
Australian immigration 5, 31
Australian legal system 103–104, 107–108, 112, 120, 124
Australian National Imams Council (ANIC) 125–127, 129–130, 136
Ayat 100

burqa 104–105

Cameleers 2, 13–14, 44, 46–48
Catholicism 116
Chain migration 31
Christian 8, 11, 35, 37–38, 45, 119, 123, 134, 138, 186
Christianity 20, 121, 159
Civic Society Organisations (CSOs) 43, 48, 55–61, 129, 151, 153
Colonialism 145
Colonialists 47
Community 1–3, 5–8, 12–15, 20, 23–25, 27, 29, 31–32, 37–38, 41–62, 70–71, 73–75, 82, 84, 86, 90, 92, 104–106, 108–126, 128–130, 133–137, 139, 141–144, 146, 152–155, 157, 159, 166, 170–172, 174–178, 180–181, 183, 185–186, 188–192
Conflict theory 163–164
Constitutionalisation 103
Counter Terrorism 172–174
Cultural alienation 37
Cultural Assimilation 1, 23, 122

Dar al–harb 25
Dar al–Islam 25, 150
Dawah 50, 60
De–ethnicisation 27
Demonisation 180
Deprivation 36–37, 58, 65–66, 68–70, 79, 184
Deradicalisation 165, 171, 176
Discrimination 6, 24, 26–27, 29, 33–36, 38, 61, 71, 75, 77, 84, 91, 143, 164, 167, 180, 188–189, 191
Druze 21

Egalitarian 2, 39, 42, 66, 78, 82, 90–91, 112
Eid al–Adha 50
Eid al–Fitr 50
Enclavement 42, 121
Equality 6, 24, 36–38, 42, 84–85, 88, 90, 105, 142
Essentialisation 38, 183
Ethnic culture 38, 40
Ethnic identity 35, 59, 87
Ethnic minorities 39
Ethnic politics 58–59, 119
Ethnic segregation 24
Ethnocultural 5, 34, 61, 184
European Muslims 29
European settlers 28
Extremism 8, 44, 55, 115, 118, 151, 163–164, 168, 171–174, 176, 178, 180, 191–192

Fasting 36, 104
Fatwa 102, 115, 117, 125, 129
Fiqh 101–103, 109, 126, 148–149, 154, 157–158
Fuqaha 101

Gender segregation 72–73, 134, 137
Ghans 2, 13–14, 46
Ghusl 124
Global Terrorism 6
Globalisation 8, 27, 97–98, 115, 151

Hadith 100–101, 116, 147–149, 151, 154, 156, 158–159, 189
Halal 6, 12, 50, 57, 95, 134, 188
Hijab 36, 52, 65, 104, 136
Hijrah 23
Hizb ut–Tahrir 26–27, 96–97, 107, 114
Homogeneity 27, 29, 32
Hukm 100

Ibadat 72, 95, 110
Ijaza 148
Ijma 100–101, 103
Ijtihad 87, 100–101, 103
Ilm 101
Imams 23, 45, 52–53, 86, 109, 111, 114, 116–118, 121, 124–125, 127–128, 148, 164
Immigrant culture 12, 48, 58
Immigration policy 29, 41, 44
Immigration Restriction Act 5, 28, 32–33

Indigenous Communities 13
Inequality 68–69, 81, 89, 180
Institutionalisation 2, 43–44, 55, 61
Integration 1, 4–5, 8, 31, 34–36, 43, 55, 66–67, 78–79, 82, 84, 86–88, 91–92, 115, 122, 135, 140, 142, 180, 182, 188, 192
Islamic civilisation 151, 156
Islamic education 6, 10, 50, 60, 110, 137, 140–141, 143, 146–147, 149–150, 153–154, 190–191
Islamic finance 107
Islamic identity 3, 24–25, 37, 39, 48, 87, 107, 150
Islamic institutions 49, 119
Islamic knowledge 107, 109, 116, 141, 146, 150, 154, 191
Islamic law 4, 10, 25, 71, 96, 98, 110–112, 126, 128, 151, 154, 156–158
Islamic revivalism 71, 96, 108, 152, 156
Islamic sciences 127, 134–135, 157
Islamic state 82, 167
Islamic Studies 8, 45, 53, 110, 123, 134, 136, 138, 140, 145–147, 150–159, 190
Islamic theology 146, 151, 154, 156–158
Islamic tradition 51, 146, 150
Islamic values 24, 41, 55, 107, 119, 134, 137–138, 140–143, 159
Islamisation 3, 107–108, 110, 133, 190
Islamophobia 27, 76–77, 181–182
Isolation 5, 66, 69, 77, 84, 152–153, 164, 175, 184
Istinbat 101

Janaza 104
Judaism 20, 159
Judeo-Christian 11, 38, 134, 138, 186
Jum'ah 50, 52

Kalam 146
Kharijites 185
Khatib 116–117
Khutba 117
Kurds 23

Macassan fishers 12–13
Madhabs 20, 102
Maharim 71
Mahr 104, 128
Maktabs 148
Marginalisation 25–26, 29–30, 37, 40–42, 65, 70, 78–79, 81–82, 91, 121, 142–143, 164–165, 181–182, 188, 191

Martyr 166
Masjid al-Aqsa 51
Masjid al-Nabawi 51
Mass migration 14, 32, 61, 187,
Modernisation 97–98
Modernity 37, 45, 79, 95–97, 152, 156,
    165, 167, 181, 186
Monocultural 5, 32, 36, 41, 118, 179
Mosque 2, 6–7, 12, 14, 23, 45–61, 77,
    95–96, 107, 109, 114, 117–119, 122, 124,
    126, 128, 136, 148–149, 154, 188
Mu'amalat 95
Muftis 114, 116, 148
Multiculturalism 1, 5, 8, 24–25, 28, 31,
    33–39, 41,–44, 78, 80–82, 86, 88–89, 97,
    107, 112–113, 115, 118–119, 140, 182,
    184, 187–188, 192
Murjites 2, 185
Musalla 118
Muslim clergy 114, 115–118, 120–130,
    190
Muslim communities 7–8, 12, 14, 25,
    30–31, 39, 43, 48–50, 52–53, 55, 57,
    59–61, 65, 97, 108, 112, 114–115,
    117–118, 121–127, 129–130, 135, 141,
    148, 150, 171, 175, 177, 180, 183, 190
Muslim community 2, 6–8, 15, 20, 31, 37,
    41–49, 51, 53, 57–58, 61, 92, 104,
    108–110, 112, 114–116, 118–120, 122,
    126, 128–129, 134, 141, 144, 146, 153,
    155, 159, 175–177, 185, 188, 190–191
Muslim identity 3, 7, 24, 26, 114, 134–137,
    140, 143, 156
Muslim ideologists 97
Muslim immigrants 15, 23–25, 29–31, 37,
    39–41, 45, 49–50, 54, 56, 59–61, 87,
    120–122, 180, 184, 188
Muslim immigration 6, 14, 23, 26, 45, 49,
    59, 95
Muslim migrants 22, 28, 30, 48–49, 60–61,
    82, 188
Muslim migration 14, 29, 82, 121, 187
Muslim radicalism 118, 159, 165–169, 171,
    178, 184, 192
Muslim schools in Australia 110, 133–136,
    141, 144
Muslim settlement 11–12, 14, 27, 43, 49,
    123, 188
Muslim societies 4, 7, 117, 145, 151, 156,
    158–159
Muslim terrorism 44, 170, 184, 191–192

Muslim women 6, 36, 95, 104–107, 114

National mass immigration program 12
Nikah 104
Niqab 104

Oppression 30, 106
Ostracism 67

Prayer 13, 36, 45, 48, 50–53, 107, 117–118,
    122–123, 134, 148
Prejudice 6, 25–26, 30, 35, 42, 44, 82, 104,
    167, 180, 188
Prophet Mohammed 2, 20, 51, 71, 96, 99,
    102, 116, 127, 147–148, 157–158, 185,
Prophetic tradition 71–72, 118, 127, 147,
    156–158
Proselytisation 27, 107

Qadis 110, 116, 148
Qira'at 148
Qiyas 100–101, 103
Qur'an 45, 96, 100–101, 103, 106, 116,
    118, 127, 134, 146–149, 151, 153–154,
    156, 159, 189
Qur'anic 7, 97–100, 136, 139, 148–149,
    151, 157–158

Racial Discrimination 27, 29, 33
Racial discrimination Act 33
Racial intolerance 170
Racialisation 29
Racism 7, 23–26, 44, 71, 75–79, 105, 139,
    180
Radicalisation 120–121, 163–165,
    167–168, 171–177, 191
Radicalism 118, 159, 163, 165–169, 171,
    175–176, 178, 184, 192
Reconciliation 40
Religious identity 1, 46, 48, 50, 55, 106,
    133, 144, 180
Religious pluralism 107
Religious segregation 23

Sawm 104
Secular 1, 6, 8, 37–39, 44–45, 58, 73, 82,
    86–87, 95, 97, 102, 105, 110, 112, 115,
    117, 122, 124, 126, 128, 133–135,
    137–144, 146, 150, 152, 166–167, 178,
    191–192
Secularisation 37, 86

Secularism 37, 82, 115, 126, 141, 167
Secularists 45, 97
Securitisation 118, 120, 178–184, 192
Seerah 154
Self-alienation 37
Sharia 1, 4–6, 8, 71, 95–104, 106–113, 116, 118, 123–124, 126–128, 148–149, 154, 166–167, 189–190
Sheikhs 45, 107, 109, 111, 114, 116–118, 125, 127–128, 164
Shi'ah 20–21
Shi'ism 20, 22
Shi'ite 2, 56
Shura 123
Siraat al mustaqeem 98
Social categorisation theory 163
Social cohesion 71, 79, 82, 84, 112–113, 121, 140
Social exclusion 5, 7, 44, 65–71, 73, 75, 77, 79–80, 82, 85, 91, 95, 164, 181, 184, 192
Social identity 163–164, 169
Social identity theory 163–164
Social inclusion 34, 70–71, 77–79, 81–86, 89–92, 171
Social integration 67, 78–79, 82, 84, 115, 135, 142
Social microcosms 31
Social polarisation 67, 143
Socialisation 51, 71–74, 120, 141, 152, 163, 168
Socialisation theory 163
Sociocultural 3, 8, 27–28, 30, 36, 41–43, 66, 74, 90, 121, 144–145, 149, 151–152, 159, 175, 177, 185–186, 189
Socioeconomic 8, 18, 25, 36–27, 40, 66, 78, 80–82, 89–90, 122, 181–182, 192
Sociological 4, 7, 22, 73, 119, 129, 134, 151, 165, 175, 186
Sociologically 4, 43, 73
Socio–religious 37, 41, 182
Stigmatisation 69

Submissiveness 105
Sufism 22–23
Sunna 96, 98–99, 101, 103, 148
Sunnis 2, 20–22, 185
Suppression 44

Tabligh Jama'at 26–27
Tafsir 148–149, 154, 157–158
Tahfiz 154
Tajweed 154
Talaq 104
Taqwa 72
Tarbiyah 154
*Tariqah*s 21
Tawhid 150
Terrorism 1, 4–8, 44, 55, 120, 150, 159, 164–166, 168–175, 177, 180, 184, 191–192
Terrorist 30, 81, 89, 120, 168–175, 177–180, 184, 191
Torah 99
Trepang 1
Turks 23, 25

Ulama 102, 116, 148–150
Ummah 7, 27, 56, 87, 99, 101, 116, 123, 144, 150
Unassimilable 29

Victimisation 176
Vilification 26, 38, 76, 150

Waqf 149
War on Terror 145, 159, 163, 165, 168–169, 176, 183–184, 191
Westernisation 96–97
Westernism 167
White Australia policy 5, 14, 28–29, 32–33, 41, 46–48, 187

Xenophobia 7, 180, 188–189